Slow Boat

ON

Rum Row

Slow Boat

ON

Rum Row

FRASER MILES

HARBOUR PUBLISHING

Harbour Publishing
Box 219
Madeira Park, BC V0N 2H0

Cover painting by John Waldin
Page design by Eye Design Inc.
Printed and bound in Canada
Published with the assistance of the Canada Council and
the British Columbia Cultural Fund.

Vancouver Public Library photographs: p. 34 (#3837),
p. 92 (#10532), p. 134 (#10538), p.151 (#24529).

Canadian Cataloguing in Publication Data
Miles, Fraser
    Slow Boat on Rum Row
    ISBN 1-55017-069-4
    1. Miles, Fraser.
2. Smuggling—British Columbia—Pacific Coast—History.
3. Smugglers—British Columbia—Biography.
4. Mission (B.C .)—History.
I. Title. HV5091.C2M54 1992 364.1'33 C92-091511-6

*I would like to dedicate this book
to the memory of three Mission boys,
my friends of long ago.*

*Captain Ernie Catherwood – killed in Italy
Pilot Officer Dick Weatherhead – shot down Bay of Biscay
Flying Officer Billy White – disappeared off Malta*

*Five of us went to war
in 1940 – 1945, but only
Gordon Vosburgh and I came back.*

Contents

Acknowledgements

I WOULD LIKE TO ACKNOWLEDGE THE ASSISTANCE OF THE United States National Archives in Washington, DC, who provided me with many hundreds of pages of copies of Pacific Coast US Coastguard Cutter cruise reports for several years in the rum running period. In addition, they provided copies of trial documents in legal cases arising from the seizure of Canadian rum running ships, and were overall most helpful.

In Vancouver, I would like to thank the librarian of the Maritime Museum, for access to their many volumes of Canadian shipping records, which made possible the complete charting of Canadian ship rum running voyages, both ships and crews, from 1922 to 1933.

The Archivist of the City of Vancouver also deserves thanks for making available to me the log books of famous rum running ships, which would have been invaluable, except that the rum running skippers kept two separate log books—one official and one unofficial—and wrote nothing whatever in the official ones which ended up in the Archives.

My thanks to Jack Wolf for several photos and his comments on the *SS Chasina* disappearances, and to Jack Adams for photos and interviews on his own rum running experiences.

And thanks to the late Jack Hacking, former marine editor of the Vancouver *Province*, for copies of letters, and a great deal of encouragement.

Finally, thanks to my son, Jim Miles, for his many hours of keyboarding, which transformed my pages of handwriting into a legible typed manuscript.

Fraser Miles

Preface

S*LOW BOAT ON RUM ROW* IS THE ACCOUNT OF MY STRANGE
life and what I saw and did in two years at sea on Pacific
Coast rum running boats operating out of Vancouver, Canada in
the early 1930s. There was a great deal going on, of course, that
I did not see and did not hear about. Rum runners, as a group,
made the Sphinx sound like a chatterbox.

The silence of Captain Charles Hudson, the man who was
allegedly in charge of the whole west coast operations and who
surely knew more than anyone, was my biggest frustration. I visited him several times after it was all over, after the war. On my
last talk with him—I did all the talking—shortly before he died,
he would only mumble over and over as before: "And nobody
ever talked."

And that in spite of my earnest appeals, reminding him of
his duty to history, the assurance of world fame as the master-
mind of Canadian rum ships, and so on. All in vain.

Nobody ever wrote anything either, that I could find. That
is, nobody but me. I kept a diary.

Ruth Green, in her book *Personality Ships of British Columbia,* quotes Charlie Hudson at some length. I have trouble recon-
ciling Ruth Greene's Charlie Hudson with the extremely close-
mouthed man I knew. Charlie, was that the real you chattering
away like that to Ruth?

He mentions fabulous sums of money earned in rum running. While I was at sea, the two boats I was on handled fifteen
thousand cases of firewater and brand name whiskeys. My total
pay was about twenty-four hundred dollars.

Sixteen whole cents a case. Fabulous.

I

Coming
of Age

Fraser Miles, Mission City Boat Club, circa 1925.

1

ORIGINALLY, THIS WAS TO BE THE DEFINITIVE BOOK ON west coast rum running and nothing more. Then someone asked me a question.

"How did a high type fella like you get into rum running?"

"Money," I said.

"That's no answer," he said. "Everybody, or nearly everybody, does what they are doing, legal or illegal, for money. You should tell about your early life, before you took to crime. You went to rum running school, maybe?"

Quite funny, that guy, but he hit it closer than he knew.

He got me thinking about my earlier life—I was all of twenty-one years old in 1933—and I thought I remembered quite a few experiences that most kids never know, and some they are lucky not to.

However, I never got around to writing it all down until I was over seventy-five. Big gaps in my memory make my early story disconnected. But not vague. What I do remember is crystal clear. Maybe it was as I've written, but whole truth or not, this is what I remember.

We were living somewhere in New Westminster after Dad went away to the war. One day, when I went into the house, I heard lot of noise in Mom's bedroom. She was hunched on the edge of her bed, a piece of paper in her hand, crying and sobbing like I had never seen anyone do before.

She looked up and said, "Oh Fraser, your Uncle Cecil's been killed in France," and kept on crying for most of the day. I didn't know what to do, so I just left and sat outside until she called me in for supper.

Uncle Cecil was Mom's younger brother and it seemed a long time before she did any smiling. That was 1918. I was six years old, and did not really understand it all, but I sure didn't like it.

Mom was a great mother who spent a lot of time with my younger brother Lloyd and me. One of our favourite walks in New Westminster was out to Burnaby Lake, a small lake surrounded by a swamp full of cat-tails. One day we were walking along the wood plank walkway from land to the water, where we could throw bread crusts to the ducks, when two brown bears, a big one and a small one, stepped out of the cat-tails onto the wooden planks, turned and looked at us, and sniffed the air.

We stopped and looked too, but I wasn't even breathing, and Mom was holding my hand pretty hard. Soon the bears walked off into the cat-tails.

"Bears are nice, they won't hurt you," Mom said, heading off toward the lake again. But neither Lloyd nor I would move. We went home, but still walked out to the lake quite often after that.

In the summer of 1919, we went back to my Uncle Bob's farm in Ontario, to meet my dad coming back from the war. This is my first memory of him, a rather tall, not very healthy looking man, hoeing weeds in a field.

What dimmed this memory was the stupendous summer thunderstorms, which we didn't get on the west coast. One day one of these was rattling the windows and Mom was playing the piano real loud, to drown the noise because Lloyd and I were darned good and scared.

Then there was a terrifying flash and blast and the next thing I knew we were looking at three dead cows beside the barn, killed by an immense strike that had hit the barn. So lightning was what killed things, I thought.

"Did lightning kill Uncle Cecil?" I asked Mom.

"No, Fraser, the Germans killed him," she said. So I got the impression early that Germans must be very bad people, to kill Uncle Cecil and make my mother cry so much.

We came back to Mission City, where I had been born. Dad intended to raise chickens, but just as he got the chicken house built—it was a lot bigger than the two-room shack we lived in— he got a job as a night watchman with the Canadian Pacific Railway, looking after a steam locomotive that was stationed at the

Mission rail yard between daily runs south across the Fraser River. He had been a fireman on the CPR before he went away in the army.

Dad took me down with him several times. Down, because almost everybody in Mission lived north of the railway tracks on the high ground—the "flats" south of the railway flooded every summer when the snow melted in the mountains.

The engine cab was pretty scary—hot and stuffy, loud clanking noises every few minutes, and steam hissing out the top all the time.

Of the next three or four years—1920 to 1923—I recall only that our shack went from two rooms to five rooms, still no indoor plumbing except the cold water tap in the kitchen sink, and still only the kitchen stove for heat. We lived in the kitchen in winter, except when we were in bed.

Going to bed in a bedroom at outside temperatures was not as painful as it sounds—Lloyd and I each had two hot bricks from the oven wrapped in cloth, one for our feet and one for our backs, to help us thaw the icy sheets.

In winter, when the cold northern outflow winds came down the river and lake valleys off the interior plateau, that little kitchen range was dull red day and night. For our Saturday night bath, we used a big galvanized tub on the kitchen floor, as close to the stove as we could get, surrounded by a folding screen to hold the heat. Not very convenient, but we got clean and stayed warm.

We were happy, but suddenly it all went bad.

Dad got really sick. I remember him in bed, in Lloyd's old bedroom, with the blinds down and the light out, coughing and coughing, and spitting into a square cup with a spring lid. I sneaked a look into the cup one day when Mom was out and Dad was asleep. There was an awful lot of blood in it.

He was finally taken away in an ambulance, a long way away to Tranquille, a tuberculosis sanatorium near Kamloops. We visited him once there, but I never saw him after that until he was transferred to the Shaughnessy hospital in Vancouver several years later.

I asked my mother when Dad would be back.

"Oh, Fraser, not for a long, long time. He got poison gas in his lungs when the Germans used it in France and the doctors didn't check him for any trouble when he left the army."

From the way she said it, I sensed that the answer was "never," and "a long, long time" was just the way it came out.

So Lloyd and I became fatherless, not that things really changed much, since Dad had been away all night anyway looking after the steam engine, and would sleep all day.

I have often wondered how I would have gotten along with my father if he had been home. Quite all right I think; after all, I have never had any trouble getting along with anybody, as long as I had my own way in everything.

As for the world around me, there were doubts. Every once in a while one kid or another would show up, when we were swimming, with black and blue welts all over his back. And we had a neighbour, I can't remember his name, who would pick up any dishes his wife cooked that he didn't like and throw them out into the back yard, plates and all, yelling like crazy. He sure scared me and I was glad when they moved.

2

WHILE I DIDN'T KNOW IT THEN, THE FIRST YEAR AFTER Dad went into the hospital—in 1924, when I was twelve—was probably the worst one in Mom's whole life—no money at all, two little kids to feed and keep in school, and a husband she knew was never going to work again.

How we made it I don't know for sure, aside from the unlimited credit given us by the DesBrisay's department store. Two things I remember. Once when I was in DesBrisay's with my mother, she was talking to a man who worked there. I didn't hear what she was saying, but the man said, "Don't worry about it. I've got lots of accounts I worry about a lot more than yours."

And I'm sure the neighbours, particularly the Solloways and

the Osbornes, helped out. I think it was "Uncle" Fred Solloway who paid for our milk, just a guess, because he had a regular job in the jam factory down by the railway bridge.

In those hard years, a fair number of families in Mission would now be classified as having "no visible means of support." And from what I knew of them, whatever invisible means kept them going was small, real small.

I never really knew at the time how tough Mom had it. But I did notice that we ate an awful lot of fried parsnips. A parsnip is like a large white carrot, but tougher. Fried parsnip is not at all bad, especially when it is the only thing on your plate. We ate bread pudding too, stale bread soaked in hot milk.

We were on rock bottom, so things could only get better.

I remember quite a lot of Dad's second year away. Early in the spring Mom got me going, digging a garden in the part of our yard that didn't have raspberry bushes. Our fried parsnip diet sure never hurt me, and all the digging and planting got me well started on muscle building. Mom grew up on a farm, and knew all about canning, so she canned a lot of the garden vegetables, as well as lots of cherries, plums, pears, applesauce, raspberries and strawberries.

My guess is that, without money to pay, most of this was given to us. We did the picking. Maybe that year the eggs were supplied too, dozens and dozens put away in big earthenware crocks full of a preserving solution called water-glass, which looked like water but wasn't. The eggs kept for months and months in the basement.

As well as developing some muscles by digging, I got a good workout splitting and piling wood. Mom ordered a couple of truckloads of slabwood from a local mill—Osborne's—and Ted Osborne hauled it for us on his truck, most certainly all for free.

Slabwood is the outer part trimmed off a log to make it square for sawing boards. Green fir slabs, with the bark on, are easy to split, being about half water, and I split countless slabs into firewood-size pieces and piled them in the basement to dry out before winter.

The basement was full: piles of drying wood, shelves and shelves of canned fruit, vegetables and eggs and a bin full of coal—that came from Christies, maybe not for free, but surely on some very long-term pay-later plan.

When I think about it now, the conclusion is there were some pretty high type people in Mission, small town or not.

Though I never had an allowance, I was never completely without money for long. But it took effort. Beer bottles from roadside ditches and scraps of copper from electric poles sold readily at Lawrence's Second Hand (and junk) Store, fifteen cents a dozen for bottles. Luckily there were still enough men in Mission with extra money to buy beer, to provide a continuous supply of bottles. In Mission, the beer drinkers looked on anyone who saved his empties and sold them as a cheapo, not fit to associate with real men, who threw their empties into the ditch.

Another irregular but unreliable source of money was Mission's main street sidewalk, made of planks with wide cracks between. The sidewalk was built between the south side of the street, held up by wooden cribbing, and the store basement walls. A lot of the change dropped by Saturday night shoppers fell through the cracks, making Sunday morning the best hunting time. You could only get under the sidewalk at either end. The headroom was three or four feet, so it was a rough hands-and-knees crawl in the dim light filtering through the cracks. If it was raining the search was off—besides the water and ordinary dirt underneath the sidewalk, there were enough horses around to enrich the drainage water considerably.

Failing anything else, we could always get a bag of candy from the Chinese men living in the old wooden buildings on the flats. The men had been brought to Canada to work on the CPR line in the 1880s and had never gone back to China. No women, no young men, just these two or three groups of old men. We did barter deals—one bag of candy for a big lard pail full of river suckers. The candy tasted a little funny, but we soon got used to that.

1925 was the second and last tough year for my mother, for towards the end of the year she started getting a war pension. A rather modest one, I think, as it was quite a time before I heard her say with relief, "All our bills are paid at last."

We then got a cow, which we kept in a small shed in the back, and I built up still more muscle shovelling manure. Year-round muscle too—the garden got dug in the spring, and the wood split in the summer, but the manure went on and on—that cow never took a day off.

3

I N MY EARLY TEENS, I BEGAN SHOWING AN INTEREST IN TECH-nical experiments. There was a minor misadventure with a plug of tobacco, a particularly near thing with a cap pistol and a barrel of gasoline, and the short, painful story of my first venture into crime (a later venture, as a rum runner, was an unqualified success, but that's a long way ahead).

I had read that if a cat fell from a height, it would always land on its feet. Both the cat—our big black tomcat "Nigger," and the height—the roof of our house—were handy. I decided to see if it was true.

Niggy was a easy-going old cat, and didn't make any trouble when I stood on the back porch railing and tossed him up on the roof. From the railing I could reach the wooden eavestrough on the porch roof, and was strong enough, then, to chin myself up over the trough and lever myself onto the roof.

Niggy was sitting up there, placidly watching me. I picked him up and carried him up to the peak. It looked high enough for a good test, if I tossed him up a bit when I threw him over. Just as I wound back my arm, Niggy realized that something very bad was going to happen to him. Four black feet with five big sharp claws on each went into lightning action and in a flash I earned a dozen medals for dishonourable wounds. I lost all interest in finding out how cats landed—if indeed they ever fell.

"Whatever happened to you?" Mom asked when I came

into the kitchen later, covered in clawmarks and dried blood.

"I fell on Niggy and he scratched me," I lied. It didn't appear that telling the truth would serve any useful purpose.

Not many sportsmen and loggers around Mission smoked cigarettes. Most of them chewed snoose or tobacco and any would-be he-man had to do the same. Of all the kids I knew, only Billy White chewed tobacco. His prestige was so great that smoking the occasional rolled cigarette wasn't held against him, even though he would roll it like a Chinaman, a bulge of tobacco in the middle and only paper at each end. Nobody ever picked up a Chinaman's butts; they were nothing but paper.

Tobacco chewing looked real easy, so I asked Billy about it one day, while we were sitting on the river bank under the steamboat wharf fishing for suckers.

Arthur Cade fording Suicide Creek.

"Here Fraser, have a chaw," he said, handing over his plug, "and remember, you shouldn't swallow any."

I bit off a big corner, like I was biting into a chocolate bar, and started munching away. In no time at all, I began to feel that something was wrong—the light under the wharf was going a funny green colour. Then it went light green, and finally nearly white, and I don't remember anything more, how I got home, or anything except that the next day I was too sick even to eat—which is pretty sick for a growing boy. So I never made he-man status by the tobacco chewing route, not even close.

Arthur Cade lived on the river bank, so he played there. I was the only other kid in all of Mission lucky enough to be allowed to play there as well. We had a lot of fun getting small empty tins from the garbage dump in front of the jam factory, punching a small hole to let in some water, plugging the hole with wood, and heating the can till it exploded. Real good fun, but the explosions weren't very big.

One day we found a forty-gallon hot water tank on the dump—usually anything not wanted in Mission was thrown into the river, along with all the mouldy fruit, bad jam and garbage from the factory.

"Hey, look at this!" Arthur said, pointing at the tank name-plate. "A hundred pounds working pressure, two hundred pounds test pressure. Oh boy! Let's blow it up!"

We plugged the pipe holes in the tank and floated it upstream to Arthur's place, got a fire going, poured water into the tank, pounded the wooden plugs back in with a rock, propped the tank up in the fire with the plugs up in the air so they wouldn't burn off, and watched, not quite as close to the fire as when we exploded the tin cans.

It took a while, but eventually steam hissed out around the plugs, watery at first, then a blue-white as the hissing got louder and finally, a great *whoosh*. as the plugs blew out in an immense cloud of flashed steam. Pretty good, but it wasn't the big bang we expected. We tried several times more, but the wooden plugs always blew out before the tank exploded.

"We need real pipe plugs," Arthur said. "Let's go up to Windebank's and find some."

Windebank was the local plumber. We went and looked all through the junk out back of his store. We were lucky. We didn't find any the right size. This was probably the first, but certainly not last time that luck helped to prolong or advance my career. A galvanized tank testing at a couple of hundred pounds pressure would blow at goodness knows how much more. Had the tank exploded, Arthur and I would have enjoyed, however briefly, the biggest bang anyone could hope to achieve in a short, short life.

My luck held. Another guy and I, John Windebank, were playing cowboys and Indians with long pieces of half-inch pipe for spears. We raced around chasing each other, and came together unexpectedly at the corner of our house, running hard in opposite directions. John's spear got me in the head, deflecting sideways off my cheekbone and up towards my right eye. A dramatic amount of blood, but no eye damage.

Still more luck. Victor Osborne was three or four years older than me, maybe sixteen or seventeen, and drove a small truck delivering wheat, oats, hay and other stuff for his family's feed store. They bought gasoline in barrels. One day I was watching Vic filling the two-gallon can he used to pour gas into the truck's tank. I had my loaded cap gun. It made smoke and sparks when it fired.

Vic had finished filling the two-gallon can, when he suddenly reached over, took my cap gun and fired it into the open bung of the gas barrel. The barrel erupted like a volcano, and the blast knocked us both over. Vic ran for his house holding his face, and I ran for mine. Neither one of us was on fire. I was enough off to the side to avoid the blast, and Vic had on his "tin" coat and "tin" pants, standard logger's and truck driver's gear made out of double thickness of waterproof khaki canvas. They were somewhat less flexible than a suit of armour, but fortunately, just as fireproof.

"What happened? What happened?" Mom kept asking when I ran in our front door, scared speechless, but plenty mobile. All

I could do was point over to Osborne's and say "Vic, Vic, Vic," so she ran over to Osborne's. Here again, luck. Vic lost his hair and eyebrows and the skin peeled off his face like a terrible sunburn, but there were no flesh burns.

"Victor said you had a cap gun. Why did you shoot it?" Mom asked, when she came back later. What Vic said was true, but not the whole truth, which sure wouldn't do Vic any good. If Vic's dad ever found out he fired the cap gun, he would certainly yank Vic off the truck and put him back to sweeping floors. I really liked riding in that truck with Vic, who treated me real good all the time, including free ice cream in the Osborne's ice cream parlor on Saturdays.

With nobody hurt too badly, I figured I could take the blame and not suffer all that much.

So I avoided Mom's eye and mumbled, "It was an accident." Vic went back to driving truck as soon as the skin grew back on his face, and I still rode with him, and still got free ice cream on Saturdays.

Mom confiscated the cap gun. I was tired of it anyway.

One night near dark another guy and I were down at Mandale's dyke—we had been swimming off the deep water side—and almost without thought, pried open a pumphouse door and went inside. All we found loose was a shiny five-cell flashlight.

"We can have fun with that," the other kid said, whoever he was. So we took it with us, and I hid it under our chicken house. The next day we took it out to play with, and realized right away that a couple of dirt poor kids could never explain, in a town as small as Mission, how they got such an expensive item. Bought it? What store? No way, only one store sold big flashlights like this—Alanson's Hardware.

Borrowed it? Who from? Mandale, in a way, though he didn't know he'd loaned it yet.

Take it back? We were too scared. Sell it? No way, only Lawrence's Second Hand Store bought old stuff, and he knew I had no money to buy flashlights with. Keep it and play with it? No fun in daylight, and risky anyway. Fun at night, but too dangerous.

"Give me a dime, and you can have my half," the other kid finally said. He took the dime and left. An expensive solution but I could now dispose of the dangerous thing without a witness. Even if the kid blabbed later, it would be his word against mine that we had taken it, and I had it. It disappeared forever, into a hole I dug in the raspberry bushes. So far, so bad. My other burglary attempt had a more fitting conclusion.

Several times, when I was dead broke, no beer bottles or scrap copper to be found and I didn't want Chinese candy, I had taken small amounts of money from Mom's purse: twenty-five cents, maybe even fifty cents, sums I could claim as fairly earned, with a good chance Mom would believe me, for lack of evidence otherwise.

The trouble was caused by my addiction to one certain brand of chocolate bar, a semi-sweet dark chocolate. They cost ten cents each, so two dozen beer bottles only bought three, and I had such a taste that one bar a day was hardly enough.

My system was blown when my younger brother Lloyd also got into Mom's purse and took the enormous sum of two dollars, which Mom missed immediately. Maybe she already suspected me, as the only store in Mission that sold dark chocolate was Lightbody's Drug Store. Everybody talked to or knew everybody else in Mission, so it is quite possible old blabbermouth Lightbody could have mentioned to Mom how much I liked dark chocolate.

I knew it was all over when Mom came out of her bedroom with a hefty leather belt in her hand, her face madder than I ever saw, either before or after.

"You sneak, you." was all she said before she laid into me with the belt, not holding back at all. It was the only beating I ever got, and it was a dandy.

She had been having a rough time getting by and the petty thievery pushed her briefly over the edge. I got a beating I remember clearly sixty-five years later. I don't think Lloyd got hit as hard. I hope not, since I don't think he even understood how bad it all was. He acted really young for his age, and had problems getting through school.

4

W E DIDN'T HAVE MANY TOYS. I HAD A MECCANO SET, LOTS
of little steel plates, wheels and pulleys fastened together
with nuts and bolts, with which I could make an endless variety
of cranes, bridges, ships and trucks. Lloyd—always called Lloydyboy—had a Tinker Toy set, a box of round wood wheels with
holes all over, and lots of wooden rods of assorted lengths that
fitted the holes, from which he built things on our kitchen table
unlike anything in the world.

We used the kitchen table because the kitchen was the only
heated room in the house. For playing outside we had a four-
wheeled wooden wagon, which we shared equally; that is, Lloydyboy could always play with it whenever I didn't want it.

Or whenever it wasn't broken. It was broken fairly often. In
spite of its sturdy construction, it had one weak point, the axles,
small iron rods with holes drilled through just inside each wheel,
for screws to hold the axles to the wagon frame. For some reason, the builders never seemed to have considered that it would
be used for high speed downhill running.

On our east-west street, the block west of our corner went
up a good grade to Windebank's and Pierce's and on the north
side there was a wooden sidewalk made up of three parallel two-
by-twelve inch planks, quite smooth running compared to our
local gravel roads. The wagon wheels had roller bearings, and
after I learned to oil these, a run down on the sidewalk, from
over half-way up by Windebank's, built up to a splendid speed by
the time I reached the end of the plank sidewalk and leaped out
into space to cross Osborne's gravel and sand driveway. The drop
was several inches and increasing, as each heavy landing gouged
dirt away.

Lloydyboy watched, and laughed and laughed, but would
never ride passenger. He was slow, but not slow enough to drive
at high speed into a pile of sand.

Before we had the wagon, and even after when it was broken, we played in the sand pit in the vacant lot behind our place, with toy trains made up of several short blocks of wood, with nails in each end, linked together with short loops of string. More fun, though, was playing in the sand downstream of a small spring that bubbled up just outside our fence and ran down between the road and the fence until it disappeared into the sand by our chicken house.

We were into hydraulic construction in a big way—dams, bridges, canals, waterfalls—we had to make these out of wood—culverts, we made them all. Then one day a couple of men came along in a truck, dug down into the spring, and plugged the leaking wooden water-main that was the source of our water. Lloydyboy and I watched all this going on.

For a time we had neither wagon nor water, only the sand pit. I remembered though, that the water-main was not very far down in the sand, less than a couple of feet, so after a springless week or two I got the garden shovel out and started digging. I uncovered the pipe plug and a couple of sideways swipes at it with a piece of two-by-four started it squirting water, and we had our spring back, hardly any trouble at all. I think this is called private enterprise.

Several times I have said Lloydyboy was slow, and he sure was in school at least, but I don't think it was all his fault. Mr. Eckhardt taught Grade Eight and Mr. Stafford taught Grade Seven; we liked them, and what's more, they seemed to like us, something kids can tell pretty easy.

Grades one to six were taught by ladies, or girls, or women. Most of them surely classified as ladies, but there were one or two who were real bitches. I don't remember any of them by name, or anything that ever happened to me personally in their classes, but Lloydyboy had it pretty rough from one or two of them. He was an obliging and easy-going kid, a bit simple-minded, sure, but I couldn't find out what the trouble was—I don't think he even knew himself most of the time.

Anyway, every once in a while he would come home from school after being kept in, and show me his hands and arms—he had been strapped so hard by his teacher his arms were black and blue, really black and blue, nearly up to his elbows. The strap was regular punishment for kids, but you were supposed to be hit only on the hand, with the flat of a ruler or something light, not have your whole arm beaten black and blue with a heavy piece of horse harness, by a mad bitch who must have been around the bend, or very near it, to do that to a little kid, no matter how slow.

So maybe he was a bit slow in school, but nobody is likely to learn any better sitting in class all day terrified he would be beaten again at the end of it. The strappings sure didn't help Lloydy-boy learn any more, if that was the intention.

Sometimes in good weather when I was sitting around and Mom wanted to go out for a while she would say, "You go up to Mrs. B's and play with Wesley. I'll call you to come home." Mrs. B. was a close friend of Mom's, and they had this funny way of talking to each other. Mom was Mrs. M. and Mrs. Bidnall was Mrs. B.—no first names, and not Auntie May or whatever like all Mom's other friends.

Wesley's father was a carpenter, a good one, and worked nearly all the time. Wesley had a tricycle, and when I came to play he would haul it out, and ride endlessly around little roads he had made in his yard, while I sat on a stump. He never offered to let me ride, and I was always so mad at him I couldn't bring myself to ask for a turn, much as I wanted to ride a tricycle.

So I sat on the big fir stump in Mrs. B.'s yard and watched the little creep ride his trike. Wesley B. was a nice kid I guess, and we were neighbours for years, but we never got close.

Maybe Wesley was the cause, maybe only the revelation of the fact that I am a complete non-watcher of anything. Or maybe it was the discovery, a little after this, that doing things, or especially making things or learning something, is a lot more interesting than watching somebody else do something, with some exceptions.

I like watching deer, bears, eagles, ospreys, whales, beavers and muskrats, and people, as people, but not people doing something, when I could be doing something myself.

In the late summer and fall millions of salmon run up the Fraser River to spawn hundreds of miles from the ocean. Some hundreds of these diverge into Silver Creek, a small stream running into the river a mile west of Mission. They were humpies—humpbacked salmon—that no one ate then except Indians. Nowadays they are called pinks, and fishermen call them slimeballs.

Spawning humpies are bright red, except the few jacks, which are dark, like a big trout without a bump. I liked fishing but spawning humpy jacks won't bite. The only way to catch them was by spear or gaff. A gaff was the surest, made up of a large needle-sharp fish hook tied on the end of a flexible four-foot hazelnut pole.

It was wet work. The best place for jacks was in the deep run below the falls—not a real falls, but a short steep rapid the spawners could struggle up when the creek was running high.

To get to the falls I had to wade up the creek in places where salmonberry swamp lined both banks, so I hardly noticed the wet moss on the cedar log where I lay out over the deep run, gaff hook on the bottom, and waited. The run was full of red humpies slowly drifting around, resting for another leap at the falls.

There were hardly any jacks, and if I had to wait a long time for the first one, I would leave right away, my blue hands shaking with cold. My feet never bothered me. They didn't have any feeling at all.

If I gaffed one right away, I waited for another, but only got two once in a while. One three-pound jack was a good meal, but two was two meals. Mom canned the second one for the winter.

Back then, we didn't have a radio of our own. Up the street, Pearce's had one of the few radios in town, a two-tube set with two pairs of earphones, and it was a rare treat when Jim Pearce invited me up. There were usually four boys there, with one half a pair of earphones each. On a good reception night, the thin tinny sounds saying we were listening to KNX in Los Angeles, a thousand miles away, was incredible. As a matter of fact I didn't really believe what I heard—it was against all common sense, music and words travelling through wires, okay, but through the air? No way. It was faked I was sure.

And when someone told us they—whoever "they" were—would soon be able to send pictures through the air as well, we laughed ourselves silly.

During the school lunch hour we played football and basketball. After school there were never enough players to make up a game. Kids outside Mission had to leave when the school bus left, the Japanese kids had to leave for Japanese school, and others had strict orders to come straight home, when class was dismissed.

Except for the school lunch hour games, we made most of our outdoor playthings ourselves. In the horse chestnut season we strung the biggest chestnut we could find on the end of a string. One kid held his up, while a second one whaled away at it with his chestnut. Whichever chestnut broke first was the loser. Pretty tame stuff, as the green chestnuts broke easily. There was always marbles, but on the dirt school grounds, play had to wait for dry weather.

"Gyp" was a two-boy game we played a lot. The equipment was two sticks of equal length, about thirty inches long, and thick, an inch in diameter, and one short stick six inches long and just as thick, and a small hole in the ground.

The short stick straddled the hole, and the first player used his long stick to flip the short stick as far as he could. The second player then threw the short stick back as close as he could to the hole, while the first player tried to bat it away while it was still in the air. The first player's score was the number of long stick lengths from the hole to where the short stick finally landed.

A real good game, playable in any weather anywhere you could cut a couple of sticks and make a hole. While I'm talking about ball games, I'd like to tell you about Roy Patton, who lived near us. Roy had something real bad wrong with him, he was just bones and skin, and undressed he would have looked like a Tinker Toy creation, knobs for joints and the thin sticks for arms and legs.

Most of anything in the world, he wanted to play baseball with everyone else, and when he was well enough to be outside we—the neighbourhood gang, Chuck Christie, Jim Pearce, Jack Alanson, John Windebank and a couple more I've forgotten, and me—made a little baseball diamond on Roy's front lawn, outside his fence, and played a "scrub" baseball game, where every player rotated through every position in turn, but only batted once whether he struck out or not, then went out to start at the bottom of the list as combined outfielder, baseman and shortstop. We were usually limited in our fielding ability.

We gave Roy a place in our batting lineup, but wouldn't let him play any field position as he was so weak-muscled and uncoordinated he could hardly pick up a dead ball, let alone catch anything moving, even if he saw it.

The pure pleasure on that poor sick kid's face when he got up to bat paid us for all our trouble. He insisted he had to run his own bases, no substitute runners, and with our special rules he always got to run. By our rules, the batter always ran on the fourth pitch, whether he hit it or not. If it was just a ball out of any batter's reach, he ran anyway.

Roy was just able to hold the bat up, but had no chance whatsoever of hitting a pitched ball, no matter how easy it was. On the fourth pitch, whether Roy tried to hit it or not we all yelled, "Run Roy! Run!" and away he went head down, legs and arms jerking like a puppet on a string. The catcher dropped the ball or fumbled around until Roy had passed first base—the baseline was twenty feet or so, then threw the ball high over the second baseman's head.

Roy was always assured of a home run, as the road went downhill for half a block past second base and the second baseman took it as easy as necessary to get Roy a home run. The first couple of times Roy jerked his way around all four bases, gasping for breath, eyes bulging, he looked so near total collapse he scared the hell out of us.

"Gee, Roy, are you sure your mother likes you to run like that?"

Roy could only nod until he got some breath back. "Sure,

she wants me to play ball when I'm outside."

We didn't totally believe him, but as we were right in his own front yard, and his mother never stopped him, he must have been right.

So that is the story of Roy Patton, a fantastically gutsy kid whose name does not appear in baseball's Hall of Fame—though he is probably the only baseball player ever known to make a home run every time at bat, though he never hit the ball.

Sports for kids on their own were rather simple—fishing, walking on stilts, rolling a hoop, or shooting with a slingshot. Rolling a hoop was fun and splendid training for long distance running. Equipment was free, a necessary condition for most anything we did. All that was needed was a short stick nailed at right angles on the end of a longer stick, and a wheel—baby carriage wheels were best. You just ran and ran, rolling the wheel along ahead of you with the stick.

Slingshots were the most fun though and both ammunition and targets came easy—the ammunition from Mission's gravel roads, and targets from the nearest pile of discarded cans, and any unsaleable beer bottles with broken necks. There was no garbage collection in Mission, so almost everybody threw empty cans onto a pile somewhere on their property. Ours was in the vacant lot behind the cowshed.

The best slingshots were home-made—a fork cut from a vine maple tree, rubber bands sliced from old inner tubes any garage would give you, and a leather pouch for the rocks. Most of the time we shot at cans or bottles perched on a fence post, but not always. Once in a while we disgraced ourselves—without being caught—by shooting at street lights and telephone pole insulators. Electric pole insulators were too big and tough for our small rocks.

Always out for improvement, Arthur Cade and I made huge slings and could throw bigger rocks a lot further than our slingshots would throw little rocks, but there was a problem.

We could never be sure which direction the rocks would take when they left our slings. So we would practise only along the river bank, with wide empty flats behind us and the even wider river in front. After a lot of effort we could manage to land over half our rocks somewhere in the river, until one day I hit Arthur in the head, luckily with rather a small rock. Since he was standing safely behind me at the time, I decided we didn't know enough about the dynamics of slings and again, I was just plain lucky. We went back to the smaller, but safer, slingshots.

A few hundred feet west of Mission City's railway station, the City had built a couple of shacks we called "the hobo shacks." Mission City, with a population of only twelve hundred, never thought it was a city; the name was just to separate it from the Indian Mission on a bench a couple of hundred feet above the river, run by some priests and nuns.

Quite a few of the men in the hobo shacks weren't real hoboes. They were mostly young fellows who were riding the freights looking for work; regular decent fellows down on their luck, and hungry, real hungry. They often knocked at our door and asked, quiet like, almost expecting to be told no, "Got any work I can do for a bite to eat?"

We didn't have any work, but I never saw Mom send anyone away—she even took the man right into the house and sat him at our kitchen table to eat whatever she put out—the man never spoke, just ate and ate, and said lots of thanks when he left. They never asked for money, just for work.

Stealing rides on passenger trains was something Art and I did when we wanted a change from playing by the river. All the CPR stations were on the north side of the tracks, above the summer high water. On the south side the passenger car end platforms were never raised by the conductor.

Art and I would wait on the south side until the train stopped, crawl up on the steps and ride all the way to Haney hunched up under the car platform. We had to leave the westbound train at Haney to catch the eastbound train back to Mission, which stopped at Haney just a few minutes after the westbound train pulled out for Vancouver. It was different, but not real fun like we had at the river.

The silk train was the only train that didn't stop at Mission.

The silk came from Japan on the big Empress passenger liners coming to Vancouver. We knew from the station master's kid, Vic Ogle, when a silk train was coming, a dozen or more baggage cars and a big engine going all out to someplace called New York. We wondered why silk was so important to New York, needing a whole train going so fast. Mission, itself, wasn't real big on silk.

In the fall of 1925 at the age of thirteen I came into money, every month, guaranteed. In Vancouver there were two daily newspapers, the *Province* and the *Sun*. I got the *Province* route for Mission, a sixty-paper route straggling all over town.

Subscriptions were thirty-five cents a month, which I collected, and paid out twenty cents for the papers, leaving me fifteen cents clear, nine whole dollars a month.

The papers came out from Vancouver on the electric train to Abbotsford south of the river, and a car took them north to the ferry slip, around four in the afternoon, six days a week. Paper boys rode the ferry free. We picked up our papers and reached the Mission wharf around four-thirty, no problem most of the year, but dark in midwinter, when the sun sets before four-thirty.

Joe Gardner, an Indian boy whose family lived in a house in town like the white men—Joe's father was a pilot on the Yukon River sternwheelers—had the *Sun* route. He rode horseback, but for the first month all I had for transportation was our little wagon, which only carried the papers. The papers rode well, but I walked, and took until well after six to finish the route.

At the end of the month, with my first nine dollars heavy in my pocket, I headed into the local bicycle store and bought a fifty dollar bike—five dollars down, and five dollars a month for another nine months. I was really pleased that the store was so trusting, but no doubt it was Mom's credit that swung the deal.

The bike took the drudgery out of delivering papers. From across the river, Mission looks like it is all hills, but it is actually a series of four more or less flat benches. Main Street, just above the railway tracks, was the first and smallest, then up a couple of blocks to where I lived, and the public school, high school, a couple of tennis courts and a football field. Above that, three blocks back, the third bench had the fair grounds and a bigger football field, and a lot of raspberry farms. The fourth bench was the biggest and farthest above the river, but not many people lived back there, and luckily, none of them were on my paper route.

So my route had a lot of level in it, if you went west on the Main Street bench, up at the end, and east on the second bench, then up and west again, then home, level or downhill all the way.

That was the good part. The bad part came in winter, when the river froze hard enough to stop the ferry, but not hard enough to stand on. Then we walked across the eleven-span steel railway bridge, on the ties between the rails. Joe Gardner borrowed somebody's bike to cross the bridge as his horse wouldn't walk ties, with only air between them.

Coming back with our papers, we also walked. A couple of times we tried riding our bikes, between the rails, bumping along on the ties, which was probably safe enough, even without any hand-rails on the bridge. We saved a few minutes crossing, but it was scary. I chickened out after a couple of tries, and went back to walking. I think Joe did too.

After paying for my bike each month, I had four dollars left, or would have had, but for my ongoing addiction to dark chocolate. Lightbody's Drug Store regularly raked in ten cents a day from me for a chocolate bar, plus most of the rest of my money as well, as about then I also became a confirmed pulp magazine reader—*Sea Stories*, *Bluebook*, and *Ranch Romances* were a must each month.

Then once in a while, fifteen cents for the Friday night movie when it was a real good show, like Victor McLaglan or a cowboy movie. Easy come, easy go.

5

THE FRASER RIVER IS ONE THOUSAND FEET WIDE AT MISSION, and in freshet can flow at over four hundred thousand cubic feet per second, filling its banks to the top of the railway bridge piers with dirty grey water, melted out of a snowfield or glacier up north only two or three days previous. When the river was rising in late spring, it carried floating logs and debris that had accumulated on its banks since the last high water, or had been washed down by flooding tributaries. Arthur Cade and I often caught logs for firewood.

Uncle George—Arthur's father—had a bag boom hung inside the river pilings upstream of the steamboat wharf. The wharf builders had sunk these piles, with a string of boomsticks along their outside edge, to divert debris from the wharf. Uncle George's boom was on the inside, with a side gap at the upstream end, parallel to a gap in the outside boomsticks, where

Arthur Cade (left) and Fraser Miles, with dog Nailer on foredeck, Mission City Boat Club.

they opened into the slack water at the downstream end of Copp's Eddy.

We caught logs with rowboats. I borrowed Felix Copp's boat and Arthur used his dad's, built out of one-inch cedar planks, somewhat more streamlined than a coffin, but little easier to row.

Felix Capp was an Indian living in a one-room shack on the river bank just upstream from Cade's, with his daughter and fat wife. Felix's boat was a dream to row. "I build him like the fish," he would say whenever I asked to borrow it.

He kept the boat in a small back eddy between Cade's boom and a log jam a hundred yards further upstream, trees and river debris hung up on the remains of an old scow or flat-bottomed boat sticking out into the river. Copp's Eddy was the key to log catching.

Most of the logs seemed to float past Mission from daylight—a little after four in summer—to about nine in the morning, or maybe we just quit then for breakfast at Arthur's place. Opposite Arthur's, they were near midstream, too far to row out, dog the log or timber and row in; if you were carried below the steamer's wharf, you had to let your prize go. There was no way you could tow it upstream, and if you were carried below the railway bridge, you couldn't even row the boat back against the freshet.

At Hatzic, a mile or so above Mission, the river flow changed from northwest to west, the bend throwing the fastest current and most logs and debris towards the north bank, where it ran a half mile or so to Indian Mission Point, a solid bar of rocks jutting into the fast current, deflecting current and debris back to the river at a long angle.

We started upriver from Copp's Eddy, rowing easily in the slack water behind the log jam, then speeding up to run the faster water outside the jam, until we reached the easy water in the half mile or so to Indian Mission Point. This was as far upstream as we could go, as above the Point you could neither row nor track a boat along the bank.

We would sit in complete silence, resting on our oars in

slack water, watching upstream towards the bend at Hatzic. The river slid past, grey with silt, in utter silence, no wind, no wave noise, not even a ripple on the surface, a somewhat spooky silence in the early morning light. A low mist hung over the cold water, so that the river seemed actually heaped up several feet in the middle, a ghostly illusion that only disappeared after the sun came up.

When the river was rising fast, we seldom had to wait long for action. Which of us went first depended on the size of a desirable saw log and how far it was from the bank.

"OK, I see one for me," Arthur would say, as usually he had first choice to start, with his scow-shaped rowboat. He would wait until he figured he would reach the log with the least lost distance, then pull out. I could follow his progress without taking my eyes off the river upstream. The *chunk-chunk-chunk* of his oarlocks carried a long way over the great silent river. The chunks stopped, only briefly, giving way to the *chink-chink-chink* as Arthur drove in the iron dog, then more chunks, at a slower pace as he headed for Copp's Eddy.

If he saw he wasn't going to make the Eddy, he would knock out the dog, and run back into slack water to return upstream for another try.

With my better boat, I could in theory get bigger logs close in, or smaller logs farther out—but Arthur was a year or so older than me, a right solid kid and I never averaged more or bigger logs. We also caught shingle bolts, pieces of split cedar a bit over four feet long, and about ten inches a side, light enough to lift into the rowboat.

We had to reach Copp's Eddy to secure our log—an all out pull that didn't last long. We were little more than half a mile above the Eddy, and a six-mph current flows that distance in five minutes. So out of every half hour or so, we rowed like galley slaves for less than five minutes, even counting the short strenuous pull around the jam above the Eddy.

The log-catching season was short, lasting only as long as the river kept rising and floating debris off the banks. Once the river crested, logs and debris stopped coming downstream almost overnight.

Rowing, particularly rowing on empty stomachs before sunrise, makes for a fantastic appetite. After we had our logs safely transferred from Copp's Eddy into Uncle George's boom, we headed for Arthur's house.

In the warm summer weather, the house doors were always open. Arthur would walk in first, shoo the chickens outside, pick a couple of dirty plates out of the sink, wipe them off with water and some newspaper, and set them on a couple of chairs, as the kitchen table was full up with more dirty dishes, an uncovered jug of milk with dead flies in it, an open tin of jam and a loaf of bread, and in the air, a great cloud of flies circling slowly.

Arthur would saw off a couple of enormous slices of bread, smear them with butter, with a generous layer of strawberry jam on top, and pour out two mugs of milk. The chicken shit on the floor didn't bother me at all, and the way he washed dishes only a bit, but the milk I managed to avoid. Mom was real strong on not drinking milk with dead flies in it.

Mrs. Cade—Aunt Somebody I suppose, but I don't remember her name—was never around in summer. She worked in the jam factory down by the railway bridge, the local sweatshop where a sixteen-hour day was normal. Anyway, the bread and jam got me home for a second, larger breakfast and a little more sleep.

What did we do with all the logs? They ended up as firewood. Uncle George—at least I assumed it was him—hauled the logs onto level land with a horse as soon as the river started to drop, cut them into cordwood lengths with a Wee MacGregor gasoline cross-cut saw, and Arthur and I split and piled the forty-eight-inch lengths to dry.

The shingle bolts likely ended up at the shingle mill at Ruskin, where the Stave River entered the Fraser. That was all shingle bolts were good for, except making model sailboats, and shingle bolt running.

6

OUR FIRST SUMMER CATCHING LOGS WAS, FROM OUR POINT of view, by far the most rewarding, not from the number of logs we caught, but from our luck in catching drifting boats. Arthur caught an Indian dugout canoe that didn't really leak very much, and I caught a flat-bottomed duck punt, complete with oars and oarlocks.

Arthur decked his canoe with boards acquired from the nearby lumber yard, covered with some old canvas, as new deckboards were a bit conspicuous. The man who ran the lumber yard also looked after the steamboat wharf and knew all about our log catching and other activities, so we didn't want any unpleasant questions about where the new deckboards came from. We rigged masts from poles and baling wire, but never thought about sails.

The boats were a real find, for now we could row anywhere, anytime, except when the river froze in midwinter. Rowing was a much more pleasant occupation than our other diversions, "running" logs or shingle bolts. There was no thrill in running logs. You simply started from Cade's outer boomstick, a big solid log, and ran straight across to shore, at right angles to the logs. This wasn't a real challenge. It was almost impossible to fall into the river, as the logs were close together and were comparatively large.

Shingle bolts are much smaller and much lighter, and never arranged themselves in regular order. The game was the same as log running, to run from one side of the boomed shingle bolts to the other, stepping real fast, like you were running across a burning sand beach barefoot. We resorted to this sport only on hot days. When we got the breaks, we could make three or four runs across before we landed in the river, but the average was closer to one success before ending up in the silty grey river, grabbing a shingle bolt for support as we went down.

At most we were only ten feet or so from the nearest boom

log, no distance at all to swim, but the bolts held close together by the current. Anyway Arthur couldn't swim. So we hung onto a bolt with one arm, while we pushed and hauled with the other, slowly moving towards the boom, all the while up to our necks in muddy water that had been snow or ice a few days before. We didn't do much bolt running after we found our boats.

After the salmon spawn in late summer, they die in the millions. As the river level drops in the fall, numbers of dead salmon are left on the banks.

In the water, the dead flesh just seemed to disintegrate, but in the warm air on the banks, they rotted and smelled. Felix Copp, and all river Indians, netted spawners for food, splitting the fish lengthwise and hanging the red slabs in a lean-to with a smoky fire going to reduce the flesh to a half-dried, half-smoked condition for winter storage.

We generally avoided Felix Copp's place when he was curing salmon. The hordes of blue-green flies laid white patches of eggs everywhere—which the smoke apparently killed, as we never saw

Shingle bolts in the Pitt River, with CPR bridge in background, 1923.

any moving larvae or grubs in the fish. Not that Arthur or I ever looked very closely in that over-ripe atmosphere. The ultimate in gut pinching smells was a tub of salmon roe, salted maybe, but with an incredibly strong vapour rising from it. Felix acted as though this roe mixture was a very special treat only Indians could appreciate.

All this is the very likely explanation of why I've never been able to eat fresh salmon since those young, carefree days. We found still another boat, not drifting but partly buried in sand, just at the upstream edge of the log jam above Copp's Eddy. We seldom walked on the river bank, boats being our thing, but this day we were walking upstream with our slingshots, pockets full of small rocks to fire at the crows and seagulls feeding on dead salmon.

"Hooboy!" Arthur said. "Look at this dandy big boat. We can dig her out and have something we can really ride on." The boat didn't look all that dandy to me, just a hull, half full of sand, no deck or cabin or insides, that had once been a river gillnet boat. Small gillnetters were around twenty-four feet long, double-ended, strongly built, and powered by a single cylinder gas engine.

Arthur ran back to his house for a shovel, as though after removing a few spadefuls of sand, our new find would somehow slide gracefully into the water, and let us have an afternoon afloat. The river bank was hard fine sand that stood vertical when you dug a hole, no mud and no gravel or rocks. We dug away steadily until I had to leave to deliver my papers, and we dug again the next day, and made some progress, enough to encourage us to keep digging.

During the next week I had school and papers to deliver, but Arthur dug some on his own—he was supposed to be in school too, but went only when he didn't have anything better to do. I think he found lots of everything better, as I don't remember seeing him around school very much.

Finally, a weekend or so later, our boat was dug out. We stuffed rags into the open seams we could see, and plugged the propeller shaft hole. We were set to launch, and took a heavy lift together on one end. The boat wiggled a bit, but didn't move sideways even a quarter inch.

"We gotta get some skids under her," Arthur said, so we dug some more, and finally had three skids under the keel, one near each end, one in the middle, and dug out more sand so the hull settled down on the skids.

We heaved again, and again nothing happened, so we cut a couple of short poles, both prying at the same end, and it moved maybe a tenth of an inch, while we heaved until we were gasping for breath.

"That's it, we just need more power," Arthur said, breathing hard. The additional power was Arthur's older brother Amos, whom we talked into helping us launch our treasure. We floated the derelict at last, stuffing more rags into leaking seams, until we hardly had to bail at all, only five minutes or so out of every quarter hour.

When we had our new ship safely beached inside Cade's boom, we first realized that the pleasure to be had using it was limited to sitting in it quietly on the beach, or setting it afloat and bailing it out. We had rigged wooden pins on the sides so we could use Arthur's oars, one each, and we barely moved the hulk upstream in the slack water of the boom, by heaving away like galley slaves, though galley slaves no doubt had a better boat. Outside the boom, in faster current, we could only drift slowly downstream, pull as we might. When we stopped rowing to bail, we drifted faster.

We needed a crew of three for rowing, two to row and one to bail, and Amos had declined our suggestion that he join us in having such fun. Arthur was equal to the occasion.

"If we had a sail we could really go places without Amos. Let's rig a square sail," he said. A most useful idea, since even with Amos we weren't ever going very far, especially upstream.

Rigging the mast was easy, with a twenty-foot pole guyed every way with some heavy iron fence wire, with a fifteen-foot yard to support the sail hauled up by a rope through a big pulley, and two short poles at gunwale level to hold out the foot of the sail. That was the total of our running and standing rigging, the fast easy part. The slow easy part was the sail.

Arthur came out of Uncle George's barn—it was really a large storage shed used occasionally by the steamboat people—with an armful of gunny sacks, a sack needle and a ball of coarse string, like binder twine. We laid the yard out on level grass, slitted the sacks down the sides and laid them out flat, as many as the yard would take, twelve or fourteen feet deep.

Sewing the sacks together took a lot of twine and a lot of time, but finally the sail was done, bundled along the boom, and carried to our ship. We made a steering oar, a board nailed to a pole, and could have sailed our great ship away, but there were problems.

At Mission in summer the west wind gets up in the late morning, blows steadily most of the afternoon, and dies off around supper-time. In winter, an east wind blows harder, but not with any regularity. In the fall and spring, the wind blows hardly at all, from either direction.

We tried our rig in a couple of half-hearted breezes from the west, which gave us just enough speed to stem the slow fall current, but little more. I think we did make it above Copp's Eddy once. Our loggy craft needed a big wind.

Finally we got our big wind, a strong warm easterly, and after sitting a good while watching the small grey waves race downstream, we gave in to temptation.

"We gotta use this wind, Fraser," Arthur said. "Let's sail her down to Mandale's slough. We can tie her there until we can sail back up."

So we bailed out, edged our way out of Cade's boom, squared away downstream before the wind and hoisted sail. Man, it was beautiful. This was what it was all about. Through the water, we probably were only making about four miles an hour, over the land, about double that. Arthur settled in to steer as we flashed by the steamboat wharf. I kept bailing slowly, to keep us high out of the water, for maximum possible speed.

All of a sudden Arthur yelled something, and took a heave on his steering oar to head for shore. The oar broke, but it didn't matter, because at almost the same moment we stopped dead, rammed hard up on the inshore pier of the railway bridge. Our noble mast went by the board, collapsing our sail, and the old rotten hull just split open, like you would open a book on the table, but it didn't sink.

We sat in ice water up to our waists as the wreck slowly swung inside the huge concrete pier and drifted gently in towards the boomsticks keeping debris clear of the ferry wharf. We got within ten feet or so of the boomsticks, and were starting to move away, when we jumped into the water. Arthur had his dad's oars—our auxiliary power—clamped under his left arm, and with his other arm and legs churning like a demented three-legged water skeeter, he made the booms as soon as I did.

"Well, we don't have to sail her back, anyway," Arthur said as we sat shivering on the bank, letting our clothes drain. Quite a philosopher, that Arthur, but as a steersman, just so-so.

Arthur wasn't much on hiking either, though I talked him into it once in a while. Clothes were his problem mostly. Neither of us wore more than a shirt, pants and tennis shoes—wearing anything more only took us longer to dry out, and we weren't any warmer.

While my shirt and pants, though patched, were nearly whole, Arthur's shirt looked like a third time hand-down from his older brothers, which I'm sure it was. His pants, held up by one half of a pair of suspenders, were even more ragged.

Mission's gravel roads made hiking troublesome. With Arthur's nearly sole-less tennis shoes, he was in fact nearly barefoot, about as painful a way of personal transportation as can be found on a gravel road, and definitely not fun.

So, mostly Arthur rowed far and wide, but seldom went any place where he had to walk. As you can see, I played with Arthur most of the time. We got along fine, and liked the same things, but I liked other boys who liked the same things just about as much. Arthur and I were different from the other kids—boys that is, as no boy in Mission ever played with girls, who were kept inside at home all the time anyway.

Except for me going to school regularly, and Arthur once in a while, we both could otherwise do anything, any time we felt like it. We sure felt sorry for all the other kids, kept at home day and night; they could never do anything, and we were sure they weren't having any fun at all.

7

IN THE EARLY SPRING OF 1926, "UNCLE" CLIVE TYLER BOARD-ed with us for a while. He was "Grandpa" Tyler's son, and lived in Seattle until his doctor ordered him to work outdoors for a year, for his health. Grandpa Tyler had a ranch on a bench beyond Silver Creek, but it was really just a stump farm, too poor a place for real farming. Uncle Clive went to work for Osborne's, who were then building a small sawmill north of Mission. The Osbornes lived just across the road and drove to the mill site every day. Grandpa Tyler's place was miles away in the bush, so Uncle Clive stayed with us.

At first I thought he was a bit off his head. He was a great fan of Bernard MacFadden, who ran *Physical Culture Magazine*. Uncle Clive soon converted Mom to physical culture stuff. Barbells, deep breathing and sit-ups looked all right to me, as long as I didn't have to do them, but this Bernard MacFadden was also real strong on juice diets. Orange juice, carrot juice, cabbage juice, spinach juice; if you could squeeze juice out of it, you had another diet.

They worried me at first: just drinking juice for two or three days, not eating anything else. No boy in his right mind ever missed a chance to eat all he could hold. Juice diets were fine on top of meals, but as a substitute, nothing doing. The only Mac-Fadden bit I liked was sleeping outdoors all year round—I started that and kept on for years, winter and summer.

Uncle Clive also got me into woodworking. He cleared out the upper storey of our never-used chicken house, built a workbench all along the south side under the chicken wire screens, dug out Dad's tool chest from the basement, cleaned the rust off the tools, added a bench vise to the bench; and I was in business, saw, plane, hammer, chisels, draw knife, wood brace and bits, and spoke shave, all clean and sharp.

All I knew about was boats—sailboats, from my diligent reading of *Sea Stories* magazine. So I carved models out of solid cedar shingle bolts. The first one, a two-masted schooner, looked rather odd, but I sold it to "Aunt" Millie Cade for a dollar for a present to her nephew. The second attempt was better—it floated upright anyway, but wouldn't sail by itself. Mom was my rather unwilling sailmaker. Then Vic Osborne gave me a model magazine telling how to make a sailing model of the King's yacht *Britannica,* a good three feet long. It was a time-consuming job, but the boat sailed beautifully, with sails Mom made from some thin cloth, all the way across the river, with me following in my duck punt to turn it around on the other side. That was a really big day for me, something I made myself, working so well.

Then I got ambitious and built a full-rigged ship model: masts, spars and rigging, with a hull four feet long. It never sailed, as Mom declined to make the twenty-five sails it needed.

Uncle Clive was a great violin player. He soon organized a band that played for local dances—Mom on piano, Uncle Clive with his violin, Vic Osborne playing saxophone, and Cecil Morehouse with a trumpet. They practised at our house, where the piano was, and sounded pretty good to me. It was the first live music I ever heard, if you didn't count the sound-effects piano that Old Bannister pounded away at during the local movies. He was good and loud, but not very musical.

The dance music our band practised was okay, though I thought it all sounded the same. What I really liked was when Uncle Clive practised classical music by himself. He said he had taken lessons from a person called Fritz Kreisler, and you knew from the way he said it that it was important to him.

Just before Osborne's mill started up in the spring, Uncle Clive went to Seattle and brought his car back, a two-door Overland Coupe. He moved out to live at the mill, but came in on weekends for band practice and to practise himself. He taught me to drive on the football field at the fair grounds, where there was lots of room and no other cars. He taught Mom to drive too, or said he had. Going for a Sunday drive was a big adventure in 1926, especially on our gravel roads.

One Sunday afternoon we started out, not as usual with Uncle Clive driving, but with Mom driving, Uncle Clive in the middle giving directions, and me on the other side with a firm grip on the door handle, picking out soft spots along the road to jump into.

We headed off west towards Silverdale, I thought to visit Mom's friends the Manzers, but we kept right on past Gagliardi's store towards Ruskin, heading around Ruskin Prairie to cross the Stave River on the Red Bridge, at the upper end of Ruskin Canyon.

The single-lane road climbs north up over the east side of the canyon, drops down the east side canyon wall, makes a sharp turn onto the bridge, then another sharp left turn at the west wall, and south to the Fraser River again. Most people with cars took another but longer road out of Mission to cross the Stave River at the power dam three miles upstream, rather than drive that canyon road, which was a real he-man road, no guard-rails at all.

It was quickly obvious that Mom wasn't really sure what was going to happen when she tried to change gears, and she hit the wrong one rather often. When we started up the hill on the west side, I was all set to bail out fast, which was possible since I was on the cliff side of the car.

Near the highest point on the up-grade, just before the road turned downhill to the Red Bridge, Uncle Clive said, "Now shift down to low gear, until we cross the bridge."

Mom shifted, but landed in reverse instead of low, trod hard on the throttle when the car bucked, and backed off the road on the canyon side, all in one horrifying second. I didn't need a second thought. I was out and tumbling on the road in a tenth that time. I scrambled to my feet and looked over the edge, scared witless, but there was the car, some ten feet down, jammed right back against a solid fir stump, just where the cliff dropped a hundred feet or so straight into deep water in the canyon. There were no other stumps in either direction for sixty or seventy feet.

Uncle Clive got out, white faced, and using the running board and front fender to pull himself up, got around to the front bumper, where he tied the short tow rope he brought with him. Getting Mom out was safe enough with the rope, I guess, but with the car door opening downhill, and the loose gravel sloping right to the edge of the canyon, it looked pretty dicey to me. I don't know what happened after that, probably they just sat and waited for a car to come along. But I'd had enough car riding for one day, and walked home. In one day you can only have so much good luck, and I was sure I'd used up mine for several days ahead.

Queen Victoria's birthday, the twenty-fourth of May, was a big celebration in Mission. The public school girls danced around maypoles with coloured paper streamers, and the boys, from about grade five up, called Cadets, were decked out in khaki wool army-style uniforms, and marched, we weren't sure what for. We hated polishing brass buttons, we hated marching and drilling, and most of all we hated wrapping our legs in wool put-tees. But our teachers, Mr. Stafford and Mr. Eckhardt, were officers in the local militia, so we were Cadets for a few weeks every spring, puttees, brass buttons, and all.

Seventh and eighth graders were also allowed to use the small bore rifle range under the drill hall; free guns, targets and ammunition. Only a few of us liked shooting, and as the ammu-nition ration was apparently based on more shooters than ever appeared, three or four of us regulars blazed away to our heart's content. Dick Weatherhead, Jim Pearce and I all received gold or silver medals after a couple of years' unlimited practice, given out by the Dominion Cadet Rifle Association, which we guessed was run by the government like the militia. Anyway, they had lots of money for ammunition.

8

AFTER MAY DAY, UNCLE CLIVE DROVE ME AND HIS SON ROY back to Seattle in the Overland. That is, he made me and Roy take turns driving for practice on the cement roads south of the border. Man, that car really flew—once when I was driving on a slight downgrade, we hit forty-two miles an hour! I couldn't decide whether my knuckles were whiter when Roy was driving, or when I had both hands clenched on the steering wheel myself.

While we were riding I never relaxed enough to even see any scenery, let alone enjoy it. All I remember of Seattle was a wax museum we visited, part of some sort of physical culture show.

"I just want you boys to know what terrible diseases you can catch from bad women," Uncle Clive said as we went in. Mission didn't have any bad women that I knew of and in a small town everybody, including the kids, knew everything about everybody else, sooner or later. There was a woman and her two daughters, who lived in an old house Bannister owned, right on Main Street, but they didn't look very bad. Everybody knew you could pay to sleep with the girls, and certainly on Friday and Saturday nights, when the loggers, mill workers and farmers came into Mission and visited that house, they sure didn't look like they expected a bad time, or had had a bad time when they came out later.

Anyway, if we had known any bad women, this wax museum would have scared us away from them forever. The models were all men, life sized, showing the terrible things that some diseases did to your private parts. One guy had great big red sores on his pecker, another with even bigger red open sores on his belly and another one with his balls all swollen up the size of grapefruits, all colored a vivid purple-green. It just about made me throw up right there, even though I knew it was only wax, and it sure made me determined never to have anything to do with bad women, should I ever meet any. Uncle Clive forgot to tell us how to recognize a bad woman if we saw one. It seemed important, if otherwise you found out only after your private parts started rotting away.

Driving back from Seattle at night was relatively relaxing, as Uncle Clive drove all the way. Even my iron nerves weren't up to driving at night at the crazy speeds people drove on those smooth roads.

Usually after May Day, the swimming season started, in creeks flowing through flat land between the hills and the Fraser River, as the river rose and held back clean water in the creek channels. The best place was called Second Prairie, a couple of acres of flat grassy land surrounded by cottonwoods a half mile down the railway track west of town. It was completely isolated, and had lots of dead branches for smoky fires that were supposed to keep the mosquitoes away.

It was like I imagined Huckleberry Finn's swimming hole

Second Prairie, the swimming hole, circa 1926. The fire discouraged mosquitoes, but not much.

might have been: not too clean creek water, no clothes, lots of sunshine, and lots of bare-assed noisy kids, smoke and mosquitoes around the fireplace.

But I don't think Huck had a problem like Ingo Riley to mess up his swimming. Ingo was a short heavy-built kid, real strong, walking sort of stooped forward, his long arms hanging loose, like in caveman pictures, except Ingo didn't have any hair.

He did have this awful dirty habit of suddenly grabbing a kid, hauling him off into the long grass, putting him face down, and buggering him, all the while sort of singing to himself, "In you go, in you go, in you go," like he was having a real good time.

I could have beaten Ingo in a fair fight—I think—but fair was about the only four letter word Ingo didn't know. It wasn't safe to be very near Ingo, so when we saw him coming down the trail, we kept on the creek side of Ingo, or close to the creek some distance away. If he got too close, a quick running dive and short swim underwater took you out of his reach, as he could barely keep afloat in water over his head.

Berry picking started about the same time that school let out, strawberries and raspberries. Berry farmers—the white ones— paid sixty cents a crate of twenty-four boxes, and I could pick four crates a day on good rows of berries. There were quite a few Japanese berry farmers too, but they did all their own picking, and had rather better crops than the white farmers, who farmed higher ground with sandy soil. The Japanese, who came last, had only heavier richer soil in creek bottoms and flats to settle on.

After the river went down in late July, the closest swimming was at Swan's Point on Hatzic lake. The catch was that it was a good five miles east of Mission. Berry picking was over by then, so I had plenty of time to bicycle out to Swan's, swim off and on all day in clean warm water, and bike home in time for supper. I had farmed out my paper route for the summer, so had nothing whatever to tie me down. Hatzic Lake was the closest swimming, but the lower canyon in Suicide Creek was the best, a mite cool, but with water so clear you felt like you were floating in free space when you dove deep under. But Suicide Creek was nearly ten miles east of Mission, a long ride each way on a hot summer day, though there weren't nearly as many mosquitoes.

One Friday night in late July when Dick Weatherhead and I, Ernie Catherwood, Jim Pearce and a couple of others were target shooting in the drill hall basement range, Mr. Eckhardt came in and said he wanted three volunteers, sixteen years old or older, to go with him and Mr. Stafford to militia camp on Vancouver Island for two weeks in mid-August. Ernie was the only one over sixteen, but Mr. Eckhardt said Dick and I looked big enough for sixteen, and could go if he couldn't find anybody else. Jim Pearce was even bigger, but he had a clubfoot, and couldn't go.

All our expenses would be paid, plus a dollar twenty a day. We would be trained as machine gunners, which sounded like pretty big stuff to fourteen-year-olds not yet in eighth grade.

We left Mission one Sunday in August on the evening train to Vancouver, to catch the night boat to Victoria. The officers had a cabin, but we soldiers travelled in the lounge, curled up in a chair, or stretched out on the floor with our small kit bags for pillows. An army truck picked the five of us up at the CPR wharf the next morning where the boat docked, along with another group.

The camp was at Heale's Range, on Vancouver Island— somewhere north of Victoria, we didn't know just where, but far enough from town that the army could shoot real machine guns. All six of us soldiers were issued blankets, led to a large bell tent, and shown how the army made beds, which were only very thin straw mattresses on the ground. Then we were issued army clothes: summer dress, caps, thin khaki pants and a shirt, not like the scratchy wool cadet uniforms, and, we were happy to learn, no puttees at all. The officers had separate quarters and we never saw them, much to our relief, as it is pretty hard to make like a real soldier with your seventh grade teacher looking over your shoulder.

After lunch we met our instructor, Corporal Black, of the Princess Patricia Canadian Light Infantry, an old-time regular who had survived lots of action during the war. The chief instructor was a Sergeant White, but we didn't see much of him.

The machine gun was the Vickers Maxim 303, belt fed, water-cooled, mounted on a big tripod. The gunner sat on the ground behind it to fire, while a helper crouched on the belt feed side. The instructions were really detailed. We learned how to dismount the gun, carry it to another location, set up, fill the casing with water, load—with dummy ammunition in the practice belt—and start firing again after clearing imaginary stoppages. The gun had four positions it stopped on, but the one I remember best, probably because it was hardest to clear, was the fourth position stoppage, with a cartridge in the barrel that hadn't fired (broken firing pin), or had fired but didn't extract (broken extractor).

Both those meant replacing the lock, which wasn't too hard if you had a spare, but was trouble if you had to replace the broken parts. Dick and I never did get the hang of it, though Ernie learned how after a while, with a little extra instruction on the side. The trouble was you couldn't see inside the thing. To get it apart, you had to press a couple of places hard, when presto it went *sproing* and you had a handful of springs and pieces that didn't look like they belonged together at all.

The first week was mostly talk. We liked the second week better, when we loaded belts with real bullets and were out on the range firing away, always so far from the target that we never knew how close we came to it, even when we could see it. In indirect fire we shot over trees and hills, using an aiming mark to hold the gun on a target we couldn't even see. The officers looked at maps, and told us how to set the gun, so I guess they knew where our target was.

Anyway, it was a pretty good two weeks, up around six, sunshine and work all day, and early to bed. It was about as far as you could get from my usual way of living. In the army camp, you didn't decide anything—when to get up, what to wear, when to eat, what to eat, how much to eat, what to do, when to do it —nobody asked your preferences. Two weeks was all right, but I thought it was about the least interesting way to live I had ever heard of.

Even so, we talked it up pretty big when we got back to Mission and started in the eighth grade. An army camp is a wonderful preparatory for hardening up seventh graders for the rigours of grade eight.

Grade eight started off quietly enough, but when my second report came home, I was way down to third place—behind Florence Rider and Marion Wren—and I couldn't do much about it. Those girls were good in everything, including painting and sketching, where I was hopeless; no talent at all. I worked out a deal with Wes James to do his arithmetic while he did my painting and sketching. The paintings and sketches I turned in were a lot better than my previous efforts, but not as good as Wesley's own. We didn't make them too good, as we figured anybody who had ever seen anything of mine wouldn't be fooled for a minute. In spite of all this, my art grades didn't improve. I would have thought my old army buddy, Mr. Eckhardt, could have helped out just a little to get me back to my rightful place—first in class. Wes did pass arithmetic though.

The Fraser River froze during the winter of 1926-27, and when the ice broke up, a dredge sank upriver, somewhere near Chilliwack. Two men on it escaped in a flat-bottomed boat, but were trapped in the moving ice floes coming down the river.

The police organized a rescue attempt from the Mission railway bridge, with ropes lowered from the bridge to hold the boat while the men were hauled up by other ropes. It was Saturday, so a whole lot of people were down to watch, as the boat was carried slowly down to the bridge. It wasn't really cold, just around freezing, but an east wind blew hard enough to make the telephone wires sing. Kids were kept off the bridge, so I was standing with Uncle Jim on the end span that ran over land.

"Can't see but one man," Uncle Jim said. We all looked, and sure enough, there was just one guy standing up, occasionally flapping his arms to keep warm. When the boat came closer, we saw the second man lying down all curled up in the bow, not moving at all.

The standing man caught a rope, and tied it to the boat

bow line. The lines tightened, and started dragging the boat up onto an ice pan, but the boat line broke right away. Nobody could get out on the jammed ice floes because of open water and small broken ice chunks floating near shore. The standing man kept on flapping his arms as they drifted downriver towards Matsqui Island.

The ice jammed on Matsqui Island about dark. Both men got ashore, we heard later, and started a fire, but one died anyway, probably the guy who wouldn't try. Uncle Jim just couldn't understand why anyone would lie down and die, when just flapping your arms would keep you alive.

The spring of 1927 saw the usual May Day dancing and cadet marching. But Dick Weatherhead and I, with our army qualifications, avoided that little kid stuff by playing hookey on Cadet days. Mr. Eckhardt thought that with our glorious army service we should be proud to lead marching cadets, but we felt the opposite.

That summer I worked as a skid greaser at Manzer's Mill in Whonnock. Mom heard about the job from Aunt Elsie Manzer, I guess, as they had been friends for years, and we often walked to Silverdale on Sundays to visit. So the last Sunday in June, at dawn, I walked to Silverdale with my pack, and left for Whonnock with Uncle Ernest, a great simple man who, with his two brothers, owned and managed the mill. Uncle Ernest's pride and joy were his four huge grey horses, the biggest horses I've ever seen, two beautiful pairs so much alike I couldn't tell them apart.

It is only six or seven miles from Silverdale to Whonnock Mill, but it took us until near supper-time. The only load that the greys were pulling was a farm wagon with a few bags of oats, and they ambled along at hardly a mile an hour. Uncle Ernest made it even slower—he was always stopping at the crests of little hills to "let the horses blow," or letting them rest to cool off, though that farm wagon couldn't have been a heavy pull, even for the knock-kneed old horse Morrison had pulling his grocery cart.

Because they had been friends for so long, Mom thought I would be staying with the Manzers, but after Uncle Ernest stabled the big greys and rubbed them down, he took me over to the bunkhouse and showed me a bunk at one end. There were three other occupied bunks, at the other end, and half a dozen empty ones in between. The mill had finished cutting its timber licence, so the woods crew had already gone.

Skid greasing is the easiest job in horse logging. The skid road is made of small logs about six feet apart, with notches cut in them spaced the same as the runners on a big sleigh. A good twenty-four feet long, the runners are shod with a hard wood called ironbark. The skid greaser fills a four-gallon can with heavy oil, rides back up the skid road on an empty sleigh, and then starts walking back, just before the next sleigh is loaded and ready to start for the mill.

The greaser has a three-foot stick with a rag mop tied on one end. As he walks the skid road, carrying the pail, he dips the rag in the pail and daubs oil on each skid, on alternate runner notches, right, left, right and so on all the way to the mill. A full pail of oil is heavy, so the woods end of the skid road is daubed much more generously than the mill end. Once back at the mill, the greaser refills his oil pail and waits until a sleigh arrives, unloads and heads back for another load.

A good greaser can grease fast enough that he has plenty of time for a cookhouse snack before the loaded sleigh arrives. In fact, if you were greasing ahead of Uncle Ernest, you had time for a full meal and a siesta, he was so careful not to overwork those enormous grey horses. The other teamster really hated Uncle Ernest, who would "rest" his big horses when only one sleigh was hauling by using the other four-horse team, with horses only half the size and not the best, one in particular being good only for mink food. But Uncle Ernest was an owner, along with his two brothers, so all the teamster could do was swear to himself—he couldn't swear at Uncle Ernest.

The teamster had my sympathy, particularly after Uncle explained to me that an owner's family couldn't invite a bunkhouse hand to visit their house. So I didn't get invited over for a meal —not even once. Fortunately, I made friends with the camp cook. This friendship was really accidental; I was really just looking for someone who liked fresh trout. I was damned if I was going to give the two dandies I had caught in Whonnock Creek to "Uncle". The cook, it turned out, liked fresh trout very much indeed, and to me a big slice of apple pie was more than a fair exchange.

And that was the summer of 1927, daubing skids, swimming in Whonnock Lake, catching trout, and eating like I never had before. It was a solitary summer but I really came to enjoy my own company, nobody yakking at you and nobody arguing. Man, it was wonderful, all that beautiful silence.

9

IN THE FALL OF 1927, I ENTERED FIRST YEAR HIGH SCHOOL; not willingly, but there wasn't anything else to do. Anyway, according to the government I couldn't quit school until I was sixteen, old enough to earn my own living.

Mission High School was about as close to a nothing place as you could get. The school had three teachers, and only one was any good: "Brick" MacMillan, a war veteran who taught French. He was rather nervous, and stuttered a bit, from bad shell-shock in the war we heard, but he was a good teacher, and we really did learn quite a bit of French, although it was not too relevant a subject in Mission.

We had one lady teacher, a Mrs. Jack, who used to be a missionary in China. I don't remember what she taught, but she spent most of her time sitting glaring at the class, mad as a hornet about something. She had hardly any self-control, and it was easy to stir her up—drop a desk lid, drop a book on the floor, cough real loud, anything. Jack MacDonald got her going easiest and oftenest, and she couldn't even keep him in after school since he lived in Ruskin and had to leave right after the last class when the bus pulled out.

Old Gamble, a dour self-important man who never smiled or spoke to us if he could avoid it, was the principal. He taught Latin or thought he did. He would come into class when the period started, write a bunch of Latin on the board in dead silence, turn to us and say, "Now write that out and learn it."

He would then leave the room until just before the period ended, when he would read out loud what he had written and that was that. Maybe he told us what it meant, I don't remember.

The big event of September 1927, that caused endless arguments in Mission and probably every other town in North America, was the Dempsey-Tunney heavyweight championship fight—the famous fight of the long count. Almost every boy in Mission immediately decided on a pugilistic career, where our failure to absorb Latin wouldn't matter. The high school acquired a set of pillow-sized boxing gloves from somewhere, and we whaled away at each other with enthusiasm every recess and noon hour. However, interest in a boxing career evaporates quickly if you lose all the time, and in short order only two of us were left, Wilfred Kennedy and me. Wilfred and I figured we were pretty good, and asked his older brother Brian who boxed senior amateur, or semi-pro, something big anyway, for lessons, free lessons of course.

Brian agreed, and we had two or three sessions in the back room of the printing shop where Brian worked—his dad owned the Mission paper.

"You got the general idea now," Brian said after these first sessions. "Now you come in at me and hit me wherever you can." We put on Brian's gloves—they sure felt short on padding to me—and I went at him. In a few minutes I was out of wind, and hadn't touched him. He motioned to stop.

"Okay, you're learning. Now defend yourself when I come at you." That wasn't so good. Brian had acquired about six fists, and he tapped me here, there and everywhere above the belt. Then one of those fists must have grazed my jaw—there was a great explosion of fire in my head and shooting stars by the million. When I came to, I was lying on the print shop floor, and Brian was putting wet cloths on my forehead.

"Jesus, kid," he said, "you must have a glass jaw or something. I hardly tapped you, and out you go. I don't think you should be a boxer."

A sound recommendation but quite unnecessary. I had made that decision five seconds earlier.

All the swampy places and wetlands around Mission attracted wild ducks by the thousands during the fall migration south, mostly big fat mallards, and local hunters shot a lot of easy meat without any real effort. With a rather large fraction of my skid greaser wages, I bought a Belgian double-barrelled hammerless twelve-gauge shotgun and set out to provide duck for our table. I blazed away steadily with shells that cost two dollars a box, and found that while I could win gold medals rifle shooting, I couldn't hit a flying bird once in a hundred tries. Even the lone mallard I did hit was a disaster.

Uncle Jim had taken me up to Harrison Flats late in the season, and a single duck came flying straight at me, so easy a shot even I couldn't miss. I brought my trophy home in triumph, and Mom plucked and stuffed it for the oven. But the wretched mallard had been feeding on dead salmon, and as it started to roast, it threw off such an incredible stench that Mom threw it out into the backyard, pan, stuffing and all.

So I would hunt deer instead. If I couldn't hit a flying barn with a shotgun, I could sure nail a stationary target with a rifle. At Lawrence's Second Hand Store I traded in my fine shotgun and a little more money for a Winchester .32 Special, and a box of shells. But we didn't eat any more venison than we did duck. There were no deer within miles of Mission. I never even found any tracks and went back to gaffing big jack salmon in Silver Creek.

The scarcity of deer around Mission was probably due to the always hungry stump ranchers living outside town, who shot any that wandered into their sight, in or out of season. When I mentioned this to Jack MacDonald, he said, "Deer? You want deer? No trouble, there are plenty around Devil's Lake. Come down to my place Friday after school and we'll hike up to the lean-to at the lake for the night. You'll have venison for Sunday supper, sure."

We reached Devil's Lake from Jack's place at Ruskin on the Stave River by walking the power company railway north to Stave Falls powerhouse, and the power line trail a couple of miles along the flooded river to the lake. At sunset, we arrived at the lean-to right where the trail crossed Devil's Creek just below the lake. Shortly after we got our supper fire going, a fellow and a girl showed up, but they weren't interested in hunting or fishing.

Jack and I stretched out for the night at one end of the lean-to, and we even got some sleep in spite of the hard ground and all the wriggling and giggling going on at the other end.

The next morning we started out at first light, no breakfast, north to the base of a ridge that had been logged a few years before, and started cautiously uphill. I had my .32 Winchester, a heavy gun, and Jack had his dad's great heavy .303 Savage.

We were moving east, and on the ridge crest, there was sud-

Opposite: "Room with a view," the lean-to at Devil's Lake, 1928. One room fits all, including our giggling company.

Left: Jack MacDonald, 1928. Mighty hunters but, "we ate no venison and we ate no duck."

denly a great commotion in the bushes ahead, probably deer, we never knew, as the commotion was directly in line with the rising sun, and we could see nothing at all.

"Not to worry," Jack said as we walked back for breakfast. "We'll get one this afternoon, sure." But we didn't even see any waving bushes in the afternoon. Sunday was the same, though we didn't try very hard that day. By then we were pretty short on sleep, what with the hard ground and our noisy company, and we had six or seven miles to walk home, mostly on railway ties which are spaced wrong for easy walking.

"So okay, we missed out," Jack said as we stumbled back down the railway. "But next time, we'll hunt the Frozen Cabin way up on Stave Lake. Country up there is crawling with deer, we can't possibly miss out again, sure. You can take your pick."

I knew Jack well enough by then to know he had the habit of providing imaginary details whenever he was short of facts.

My third gun episode Mom never knew about. I had the habit of playing with Dad's war souvenir Mauser Automatic. One day I found out how to load it, and had a full clip of nine-millimetre shells in the magazine, when somehow it fired, straight between my feet into the floor of my bedroom, with a most impressive bang. My dog ran for the basement, and I sat there holding a fully cocked and loaded automatic, and didn't know how to either unload it or uncock it, and didn't want to ask anybody who might know, like Uncle Jim, as he'd surely tell Mom.

The only way I could figure out to unload it was by firing off the other seven or eight cartridges. I wound a heavy sock between the hammer and firing pin, hid the gun under my coat and headed for a long deep ravine west of Mission where no one

Fraser Miles, 1928.
My pride, a 25-35
Winchester, and still
no venison.

lived. Picking the biggest alder tree in sight, I got behind it, unwound the sock holding the hammer back, held the gun on the far side of the tree with my left hand, and pulled the trigger.

Away she went—*blam, blam, blam, blam*—until I had an empty gun. I was rather pleased that I had thought to use my left hand, to leave me with at least a good right hand if something went badly wrong.

Winter sports in Mission included sleigh riding. Not plain ordinary little kids' sleighs, but a giant twelve-foot-long front-steering sleigh Vic Osborne had built that held at least eight kids, more if they squeezed up real tight. When the roads iced up enough, Vic dragged his monster out, polished the steel runners with sandpaper, and we all set out for an evening's fun.

The run started at the edge of Mission's third bench, went straight downhill at a fair angle, then over the edge of the second bench, a steep drop that ended on the moderate slope to the lower bench at the west end of Main Street. The sled with ten kids squashed in it would do fifty miles an hour or so—just a guess, but it was far too fast to make the sharp left hand turn at Railway Street. If the sleigh didn't make the turn, sleigh, kids and all went down the station steps, a drop of at least thirty feet, straight into the railway station.

To slow the sleigh down enough to make the Railway Street turn, we sprinkled the half block below Main Street with sand and gravel—rather more than sprinkled, as it needed a good solid coat for slowdown. The big sleigh would shoot out of the darkness, cross Main Street, hit the gravel, trailing sparks like a meteor, and just before the Railway Street corner, everybody yelled, "Lean, lean, lean!" and the entire sled load leaned hard left in unison. And usually got around home free. Once in a while our co-ordination was bad, or Vic didn't hit the gravel section quite right, and we only turned part way, ending up jammed under the heavy fence just east of the station steps. Nobody ever got hurt, and we never went down the steps. There was a lot of good luck involved in that, I think, as that sled was really going.

On a good night, with hard ice on the road all the way

down, we would sleigh until we were too tired to haul the sleigh back up the hill.

My baseball career lasted one whole spring, in 1928 when I was sixteen. In high school I was big enough and a good enough player to have the local senior team ask me to play for them. Mission was so small that getting nine players was difficult. Flattered, I agreed. I remember my last game. Mission was playing Hatzic on the Hatzic fair grounds, and I came up to bat. Pitchers were valued far more for speed than for control—no one was ever sure just where the ball was going to go, least of all the pitcher, only that it would go there with marvellous speed.

A pitch came straight at me. I ducked, but not fast enough; the ball bounced off my left shoulder, and took a further hard bounce off my head before taking off into outer space. I wasn't quite out, but saw as many stars as when my boxing career had

My baseball career was short and lumpy. That uniform sure was pretty though. 1928-29.

ended. I almost quit right then, but went up to bat again later, to show that I was not going to let a little bitty bump on the head, hardly bigger than a goose egg, stop me. I don't know how the game went, but I was rather pleased with my last hit, a long, hard foul fly ball straight through a window in the fair grounds hall.

After that, I didn't even play much high school baseball. I rather fancied my head, and hoped to make a living with it some day. The people around Mission I knew working with their hands weren't doing anything I wanted to do for a living. What else there was, I didn't really know, but there had to be something.

10

IN JUNE 1928, WHEN SCHOOL LET OUT, I FOUND MYSELF AT loose ends because there was no job at Manzer's again as Uncle Ernest had promised. It wasn't his fault. They had finished their timber at Whonnock and had not completely finished their new mill on Vancouver Island.

So it looked like a summer of berry picking, with girls and little kids of fourteen and fifteen. I asked Uncle Fred Solloway about the jam factory where he worked, but he said they had an on-call rehire list as long as my arm. Aunt Millie Cade, Uncle Bert's wife, saved the summer—she wrote Mom saying send Fraser over to stay with them at Youbou on Vancouver Island, as Uncle Bert could get me a job in the sawmill where he was steam engineer.

That sounded fine to me, job or no job, as Aunt Millie was a fantastic cook. Youbou was on Cowichan Lake, and the way to get there was by CPR train to Vancouver, CPR night boat to Victoria—sitting up in a lounge chair—gas car to wherever the logging railway joined the Island Railway, and another self-propelled passenger coach to Youbou. I picked a few berries to pay my fare, then left for Cowichan Lake.

Aunt Millie and Uncle Bert lived in a two-room shack on a log float moored in a bay west of the sawmill along with half a dozen other mill employees' shacks. The high-priced help lived on land, in houses on the lakeshore east of the mill—not the best place in summer, when the west wind started blowing shortly after sunrise and blew until near dark, smogging the houses with smoke, fly ash and fine unburned sawdust from the mill's waste burner and boiler house.

There was no job, but there was lots else very much to my taste. The bay water was clean, unbelievably clear, and warm, even in early July. I slept outside, on a narrow porch on the lake side of the shack, and swam half a dozen times a day, far out into the open lake.

Two float shacks west, "Cougar Charlie" Caldwell lived, with his wife and two cougar dogs. Cougar Charlie was seventy-two, worked at the mill as the night sweeper/watchman, and, in spite of a near-fatal fall into a moving conveyor two or three years before, was as active and opinionated as ever. They were Americans, from mountain backwoods country in the eastern states.

Charlie had maybe half a dozen teeth left and seemed always to have a week's snow-white beard, and a brown trickle of tobacco juice leaking from each corner of his mouth. We could tell meal times without a watch, just hearing Mrs. Caldwell holler, "Lunch time, Charlie. Go wash your chin."

Charlie and I got off to a poor start. He had the idea that everybody was just aching to do things for such a lovable old character as himself. When he found I was one of the idle poor, he asked me to cut firewood for him. I said sure, thinking he meant split wood. When I went over a morning or so later, he handed me a six-foot cross-cut saw and pointed at a three-foot diameter old growth fir log on his little bit of beach. I said forget it, in July, no way. He was quite put out, and expressed great regret that I had passed up this wonderful chance to change from a life of total idleness and poverty to one of useful work and poverty.

My conscience didn't bother me any, as I knew he could get all the wood he wanted from the slab pile at the mill, already sawed into stove length for anyone to help themselves. Charlie figured, rightly enough, that dry old growth fir sawed upon his own beach by someone else, was better than heavy green slab-wood he had to carry from the mill. Youbou had no roads. I don't remember even a path good enough for a wheelbarrow, or even a wheelbarrow. Everybody backpacked firewood, along the railway grade.

We became reconciled when he found out I was, or had been, a dedicated hunter, and a sturdy packer. Since his fall into the conveyor, he couldn't pack any weight, or carry his Winchester Thirty-Two Special. The Thirty-Two Special was a favoured rifle in British Columbia. I never knew why as the Thirty-Two Carbine was just as powerful and a lot lighter. I volunteered as packer.

Cougar hunting was mostly walking and listening, rather a lot of walking. We left Youbou at first light, about three-thirty, one morning in July with the two cougar dogs, Roy and Sam, and followed west on the logging railway half a mile to the abandoned railway grade running north up Cottonwood Creek Valley, then up to the end of Cottonwood Valley, near a low pass.

That was a fascinating walk—Cottonwood Valley had grown back after the logging stopped and was abundant with young scattered fir trees and a heavy growth of leafy bush, the best deer feed. As we walked up the grade, every hundred feet or so deer rose from their sleeping beds, and stood stiff-legged, staring at us. Roy and Sam paid no attention to them at all. Maybe, in the whole valley, there were a hundred deer. Sixty I know for sure, as I reached that many one morning before I stopped counting.

At the end of the railway grade we followed deer trails through the brush into uncut timber, and turned west up the ridge through stands of huge firs, on ground bare as a carpet.

"Okay boys, go find 'em," Charlie said or something like that. With his mountain country accent, and a mouth with more tobacco in it than teeth, he was a mite hard to understand. Away the dogs went, up the wide gentle ridge ahead of us, noses to the ground, silent except for an infrequent low-pitched baying. By this time Charlie was pretty well limbered up—he was a slow starter, being so old and all, and it took a couple of stimulating swigs from his hip flask to get him up to speed.

We followed slowly along the ridge as long as we could hear the dogs, but not later than eleven, by which time the summer sun had evaporated all traces of cougar scent, according to Charlie. Then we turned south, straight downhill in the wide open brushless forest, until we reached the railway along the lake and so back to Youbou, a stimulating twelve-hour stroll.

That first trip I was so thirsty I could hardly talk—Charlie hadn't bothered to tell me there wasn't a cupful of water on the whole ridge, or on the railway until we hit Cottonwood Creek, coming back. Later, even Cottonwood Creek was dry at the railway bridge, the tiny summer flow disappearing into the gravelly soil below the first canyon.

We hunted again, a few days later, over exactly the same ground. This time I had packed a double lunch and a half gallon of water—Charlie never bothered, except for his flask. He was already so thin and dried up he just didn't seem to need water. Charlie said cougar covered so much territory you could hunt the same area every two or three days. This second time we got lucky; hardly had the dogs left us up the ridge than they suddenly

Cougar Charlie Caldwell with the "ten-foot" cougar's little brother. Youbou, Cowichan Lake, Vancouver Island, 1928. Photo by Aunt Millie.

erupted into high-pitched yelping and yapping.

"Fresh trail, by golly," Charlie said. "Let's sit." Cougar hunting was a spectator sport, sure no test of hunting skill. We just sat and listened. If the cougar treed within our hearing range, we followed up and shot it. Sound carried a long way in the silent open forest, so we could still walk a couple of hours, if the cat treed after only a short run.

This trip the yelping and baying reached a sudden crescendo, then changed to a regular intermittent barking. "Cat's up," Charlie said, and we strode off towards the noise, downhill to the north, and shortly came to a growth of smaller trees, with the cougar sitting on a limb thirty feet up, switching its tail, keeping its eyes on Roy and Sam below. Charlie called the dogs and tied them to a tree uphill out of the way. He sure took his time shooting.

"Looks like a seven-footer at least," he said. I asked him if he was afraid the cat would jump before he knocked it down. "Cat's not afraid of anything, safe up a tree. She won't jump. I can get twenty-five bucks for a whole skin, not full of bullet holes or head not smashed up."

He moved around until he had a clear neck shot, just below the head, a relatively easy shot at forty feet. Down it came, dead as mutton. Roy and Sam leaped to get free and set up a fearful clamour, but subsided when the cat never moved. We were all set to skin it out, and head for home. So I thought, but Charlie wouldn't let me touch the body with my shiny new hunting knife, which hadn't yet tasted blood. He sure took a long time.

"A couple knife cuts, and they give you not even ten bucks for a skin this big," he said, while I rolled the body around and he skinned, ever so carefully. My guess was that Charlie's night watchman job in the sawmill was not in the big salary class—twenty-five bucks could well be a month's pay. Twenty-five bucks on top of the twenty-five dollar bounty paid for cougars by the game department, two months' pay sitting on a single shot. No wonder Charlie took his time.

Skinned out, the cougar had a lean, sinewy body, all muscle. Charlie cut a couple of chunks of very tough-looking meat for

Roy and Sam, who did a lot of chewing to get a mouthful. He rolled the hide, tied it on the Trapper Nelson packboard I carried, and we set off west, up and over the ridge and down to the railway, and were home just before supper.

And that was cougar hunting on Vancouver Island, a very tame spectator and listener sport. It might have been more exciting, I suppose, if the hunter only wounded the cat, and it fell out of the tree fighting mad. Maybe that was another reason Charlie took such care shooting. I never did ask if that ever happened to him. He would never have admitted missing a shot anyway.

About mid-August, Charlie mentioned that the game warden wanted him to take salt in to the elk herd in the Shaw Creek Game Reserve, a three- or four-day trip and did I want to come— I said sure, any number of days hunting out in the open old growth forest was fine with me. Knowing Charlie, I should have asked one question at least—how much salt?—and maybe another—do we get paid? The first intimation I had this trip might have a snag in it was when the game warden's launch pulled in to Charlie's float early one morning to ferry us up the lake to Shaw Creek. We didn't take Roy and Sam with us. When we off-loaded on the gravel delta of Shaw Creek, I learned the real snag, eight big blocks of rock salt.

Salt blocks are a bloody awful pack load, a heavy concentrated inert weight that dug into my hips at every uphill step, eighty pounds, plus the packboard, a huge cooked ham, the Thirty-Two Special Charlie brought along, dogs or no dogs, and some more food.

After a quick lunch we started up Shaw Creek on a good trail through a stupendous old growth fir forest, two-hundred-foot trees, four to five feet in diameter, growing almost side by side, ten to fifteen feet apart. Five-hundred-year-old trees, miles of them, a sight we will never see again in British Columbia.

I slugged it out for a bit more than an hour, four thousand plodding steps, I guessed from my Heale's Range military training, no more than two miles. I was more than a trifle worn, and stopped.

"How far yet to the cabin?" I asked Charlie. "Five or six miles," he said. That was comforting, as I had found his estimates of distances we walked were close to twice the actual—he just forgot he was taking shorter steps as he got older, I guess, in addition to his usual exaggerations.

"No sweat then, I'll relay from here," I said, sliding the painful pack down a big fir to the ground. Backpacking a heavy load is such grinding labour that nothing else you ever do in the future seems like work at all.

I dumped four blocks of salt, and carried on until we reached the cabin at Shaw Creek Forks, an elaborate twenty-four foot game department cabin on a small gravel bench above the forks. Two hours easy walking, hardly four miles from where I had left the salt. Supper was ready-cooked ham, bread, butter and jam and tea without milk. I turned in right after eating supper, well before dark, wrapped in musty blankets. The next morning I was away down the trail by sunrise, a beautiful silent walk through all those thousands of giant trees.

The silence was almost absolute, no birds, no deer, no wind and hardly a murmur from Shaw Creek.

That afternoon we went about four miles up the north fork of Shaw Creek and left four blocks of salt in a large natural meadow. We noticed lots of old elk tracks, but no new ones. The next morning I packed up the remaining four blocks. We walked through the meadow scattering salt blocks, then headed on into a forest of smaller trees beyond, less than a mile on an elk trail, with no new sign either, and sat down for lunch by a tiny stream, the source of Shaw Creek.

"No use going any further," Charlie said. "The elk stay away back all summer, higher up in the big meadows, where there's feed."

Late that afternoon, after a wash in clear cold creek water and more ham and bread, we walked up the south fork a couple of miles through the open forest, but still no signs of game. In those old growth forests, with no underbrush or small trees for browsing, no animals lived at all.

We slept again in the musty blankets, slept in, had a late

breakfast around eight, and were back down swimming and sitting on the gravel bar around noon when the government launch
arrived. It was a fantastic trip, in spite of the salt.

So what's so great walking yourself into the ground on a hot
summer day smelling fir needles and looking at a lot of trees, all
exactly the same? Well, you like something or you don't, and can
only find out by trying for yourself. Which nobody can do any
more—the big tree forests are all gone.

On the way back to Youbou, I asked Charlie how much the
game department paid for packing salt in to the elk meadows.
His answer was less intelligible than usual, but I think he said not
much, which may have been a fact, and that I couldn't expect a
share, which was certainly fact.

I went on one more cougar hunt with Charlie before I left
Youbou for school. We were well along our usual hunting ridge
before Roy and Sam, by then a good way ahead, gave out with
their "dogs on hot scent" yips and barks, but it soon changed to
the more relaxed "pussycat up the tree" baying, which they kept
up until Charlie and I were within a quarter mile, then suddenly
went back to the "hot pursuit" yipping.

"Son of a gun," Charlie said. "Cat's jumped—must be a big
one—the little ones don't never jump." The dogs were off down
grade to the northwest heading into the McKay Creek Valley,
halfway between Cottonwood Creek and Shaw Creek. The
cougar treed again, and as we got close for the second time,
jumped again, and we followed far down into Upper McKay
Creek, a long way from Youbou. Charlie was getting really excited, chomping away on his tobacco, dribbling juice out of each
corner of his mouth until it dripped off his chin.

"No cougar did this before," he mumbled. "Gotta be big,
real big. Keep moving." We moved. The cougar treed a third
time and stayed up as we reached the dogs. Even Roy and Sam
seemed awed by what they saw sitting above their heads.

"Holy Murphy," Charlie said, not real loud. "We got a ten-
footer for sure—biggest one in years." He tied the dogs back uphill, took a couple of long pulls on his flask of rum to steady his

nerves, and went into his shooting routine, slow and careful. I stood off to one side uphill, clear of both Charlie and the dogs. I figured a cat that had already jumped twice could easily jump again, and wanted it to have Charlie and the dogs as first choices in case it would rather fight than run. Kind of chicken, maybe, but from my failed experiment with Niggy, I knew how much damage even a determined housecat can do.

And man, that was one big cat up that tree. A big housecat is around thirty inches long—this big tom cougar was a hundred and twenty inches, give or take a few, and he was only forty feet away.

Charlie shot, and we had a dead cougar, which took us a long time to skin out. That huge skin, with head, paws, and tail, was heavy, not so heavy as eight blocks of salt, but heavy enough to tell me I would be very glad to reach Youbou.

When Charlie started back uphill the way we had come, he said, "Can't go down McKay Creek Valley—cliffs, rock slides, canyons and no trail."

After the long drag back up to the ridge we sat a spell, and Charlie sipped a little rum. I tried it, but preferred thirst. If there had been any water we would likely have stayed until morning, but the nearest water was upper Cottonwood Creek, not the shortest way home, but the easiest with a heavy pack and a big thirst.

People were getting ready for bed when we finally stumbled off the railway embankment, but everyone rushed out with lights to see us measure our trophy, Charlie saying over and over and over ten feet easy.

No amount of stretching got the tail beyond nine foot three inches. But a smidgen like nine inches didn't faze Charlie at all—it was a ten-foot cougar, to all who would listen.

A splendid end to an incredible summer.

11

IN SEPTEMBER OF 1928 AND RESIGNED TO ANOTHER PERIOD of limited freedom, I toddled off to enter second year high school, to learn stuff I saw no use for. But there was an immense improvement over the first year. Old Gamble had been made an inspector somewhere, and we had a new principal, a more friendly younger man, who actually talked to kids like they were people, not things.

There was still Latin to wrestle with, of course, but we were astonished to learn that people had actually spoken Latin, guys called Romans, who had ruled the whole western world for hundreds of years, built fantastic cities, road systems stretching for thousands of miles, bridges and water systems with aqueducts and siphons. Latin, now that it was a history lesson in disguise, was no longer a lousy memorizing chore and became more than interesting. We still couldn't see what good Latin would ever be to us in the unlikely event that we learned any, but we really looked forward to hearing more about those old Romans. We didn't absorb much more Latin, but we sure liked listening to that teacher. I wish I could remember his name, a real high type fella.

He got together with Mr. Eckhardt, the public school principal, and Mission fielded a basketball team, with Mr. Eckhardt as manager, coach and trainer, while the high school principal arranged games with other schools, in Abbotsford, Chilliwack and Haney. We practised hard and played harder, but the best you can say about our games was that we were totally consistent—we lost every game, by a large score, usually a three figure number, to nothing.

We were very much overmatched in playing the three larger schools. Larger schools have larger kids and more of them. We only spoiled our zero score record once, when we actually scored a basket. It was at a home game, and our faithful supporters—all twenty of them—made as much noise as if we had just won the provincial championship.

Jack MacDonald, who came in from Ruskin every day by school bus, and I finally got together again for deer hunting. After I had reminded him about my futile hunting efforts, he said, "No deer around Mission eh? I know where there's lots, around the Frozen Cabin on Stave Lake. Come on up with me next weekend. I can borrow Joe's gas boat."

Stave Lake ran to exotic names—Alligator's Point, Devil's Creek, and the Frozen Cabin. We left Jack's place at Ruskin early one Saturday morning with rifles and packs, and walked up the electric company railway line two or three miles to Stave Falls Dam and our water transport. We were a while getting away— Joe had apparently forgotten to give Jack a key to the padlock on the boat shed door, a stout affair that resisted our entry attempts for some time.

Once inside, we gassed up and headed up Stave River, a flooded river channel winding its way through an eerie forest of dead standing trees rising out of the water. There was a lot of driftwood, and it took us an hour and a half to reach Stave Lake, a fair bit of water ten miles long, maybe a mile wide. We ran up the western side, along a series of rock cliffs dropping straight into the lake, past a small powerhouse where it was possible to land, and on to our deer hunting ground at the Frozen Cabin, the only other place on the west side where a boat could land.

Here, the shoreline sloped a mere forty-five degrees to the vertical, heavily treed with young firs, and with plenty of brush. It sure didn't look like deer country to me, but I didn't say anything. The Frozen Cabin was an abandoned Japanese shingle bolt cutter's shack. The roof was still in place, but all the doors and windows had been removed, probably when the original owners left. Shacks were easy to build, but hinges, doors and windows cost real money.

The rusted-out stove worked, but we had to keep a close eye on the wooden floor underneath, where hot sparks fell once in a while. It was late October in a warm fall, so missing windows weren't a problem, even if we couldn't risk leaving a fire in the stove.

The next morning we set out hunting in this unlikely deer country. There were no deer, and no deer signs either, and it wouldn't have mattered even if there had been deer—we could only see twenty or thirty feet, and made more noise going through the brush than a threshing machine. We came back at noon, when it started to rain.

"We'll take the boat around the point tomorrow, up the inlet," Jack said. "The deer are at the head, up the valley."

Maybe they were, but we never found out. During the night Jack started moaning and groaning and at daylight was sitting up, holding his ear and complaining of the terrible pain in his head. It was also raining hard, a steady curtain of British Columbia fall rain that could go on for days. By noon there was no let up in either the rain nor Jack's complainings so I told him I was going to get him home, rain or no rain.

Fraser Miles on the floating shack on Stave River near Cedar Creek, 1927. Drowned Stave River bank in background.

Our boat was a beamy sixteen-foot clinker-built craft with a Briggs and Stratton air-cooled machine, a really simple, reliable engine. I rigged some poles across the bow section, tied a mattress down and a ground sheet over for shelter, loaded our gear and Jack, and took off south down the lake, running in close along the cliffs, huddled in the stern under another ground sheet, the tiller covered and dry.

There was no wind, but with the heavy rain and the low cloud, visibility was bad. There was so much driftwood floating around I had to stay alert. For good measure I ran about half speed—there was no place to beach a leaking boat. I lost a little time too, finding the outlet from the lake, a narrow opening in the flooded tree area south of the cliffs, so it was near dark when we landed at Stave Falls.

"I can't walk home," Jack groaned. "You can push me

Jack MacDonald
with the same fish,
Cedar Creek, 1927.

down the railway on the powerhouse hand car."

I carried everything up to the railway, found the hand car in an open shed, and loaded everything, including the mattress, on it by the power dam lights. Jack climbed on the mattress, and I pushed the hand car off into the darkness, with an ease I should have suspected.

Suddenly I found I wasn't pushing anything—the hand car had eased off into the darkness by itself, and was rattling away a few feet ahead of me. I made a stumbling run to catch up, hauled myself aboard on top of Jack's legs, and held fast to either side of the car.

In total, absolute darkness we ran down the easy grade from the dam, to the steeper section that went downhill all the way to Jack's place. I put out a tentative foot, thinking to slow us, but we were going far too fast to stop that way. How fast, I've no idea, I couldn't see anything, but we made lots of noise.

In the short cuts a rattling rumble reflected back from the earth banks. When we sailed out into space on the frequent high trestles there was only the thin tinny rattle of steel wheels on steel rails. On the trestles I held my breath. I knew from walking them that they were thirty or forty feet high—if the hand car jumped the rails we were dead ducks. It was the longest ride I ever went through—even though it could have been only a few minutes on such a short railway—until we started slowing down on the level grade past Jack's house.

Sheer fright had apparently cured Jack's earache, if there had been an earache at all. He was so bright and cheery when we entered his kitchen that I immediately suspected I had been conned into doing all the work.

For whatever reason, we didn't hunt or fish together again, and after Christmas Jack went back east to a private school and I never saw him after that. Jack's folks weren't the only ones with a low opinion of Mission High School, they were just the only ones who had enough money to do something about it.

That winter we rode Vic Osborne's sleigh again, but it was pretty tame compared with that paralyzing hand car ride in absolute darkness.

In the spring of 1929, our new principal talked to us about a track meet. We thought it was a dandy idea, and he went ahead and arranged a joint track meet with Matsqui, a town across the river, small like Mission, for some time in May. Mission had a three-room high school, with maybe a quarter of the kids coming in by bus from little settlements a few miles away.

Our athletic talent was scarce to begin with, and the bus kids couldn't stay after school to practise. For the boys' events, we could only hope for three winners, in the hundred-yard dash, the half mile and the mile runs. Our hundred-yard hopeful was Jack Simpson from Stave Falls, a bus kid. He smoked heavily, one of the few kids who did, and he could run hard for maybe ninety-five yards, but he was usually so far ahead by then he could do the last five yards on his hands and knees and still win.

John Windebank and I were the half-mile and mile hopefuls. For the runs in between, and the jumping, we didn't see any chance for Mission, unless the Matsqui entries were incredibly weak. We didn't know anything about our girls' chances. As far as boys could see, their main efforts went into making the huge baggy bloomers that our ex-missionary teacher, Mrs. Jack, insisted were the only sports costumes modest enough for Mission girls.

John and I were among the few boys who did any training. As soon as the spring rains eased off and the fair grounds dried up enough so we didn't have to run in gum boots, about mid-April, we set up a running program, three days a week. Monday, Wednesday and Friday mornings we walked up to the fair grounds by seven, after a training breakfast of toast and apple juice, and ran, sometimes three or four miles at an easy pace, other times a mile only, or our calculation of a mile, the best speed we could make.

We didn't have a watch, so didn't know how much faster we were getting, if we were getting any faster. And we really didn't care, it was just so much fun loping around and around the football field in the early morning sunshine. We ran, off and on, from seven to eight, then home for breakfast and off to hear more about Romans. It appeared those guys were strong on games too, really playing for keeps in a place called the Coliseum, with swords and spears and lions. They were rough on losers though.

Matsqui hosted the track meet. I don't know how that mistake was made. All they had for a track field was a big cow pasture from which the cows had only recently been expelled, leaving the soft ground full of holes and with lots of cow patties. A rough go for the runners, who had to watch where they put their feet.

The first event was the hundred-yard dash. Our hopeful Jack Simpson raced away ahead as usual for a sure win. Then almost within reaching distance of the finish line, the stupe turned his head to see how far behind the others were, and stepped into a hole. He came down so hard he was too winded even to crawl the last ten feet or so.

Dick Weatherhead was a surprise winner in the two-twenty, assisted somewhat by the fact the opposition had footing mishaps in that holy cow pasture.

In the half-mile, I paced John to an easy win, and in the mile he paced me for a walkover, so we boys ended up as anticipated, only three wins.

School honour was more than saved by the girls winning nearly all their events. The girls, in fact, turned out to be one girl, Nellie Weatherhead, Dick's sister. Nellie Weatherhead, the shyest girl in school, hoisted those baggy bloomers as far above her knees as she could get them, revealing a lot of skinny leg, and romped through every event, no contest at all. Our girls lost only the relay race, as we had only one Nellie. I don't suppose Nellie's legs were really that skinny, they were just skinny by Matsqui standards. Those Matsqui farm girls showed the results of eating too much wholesome farm food, and hadn't a hope against our lean, agile Nellie.

That June when school let out, I had a job lined up. Manzer's Sawmill on Vancouver Island was now running, and I went over to work in the mill yard, feeding the planer, quite easy work, but not very interesting. The mill had Chinese men working inside the mill, and turbaned East Indians working in the yard. No Chinese would feed the planer, if an East Indian was taking planed lumber away on the yard side, or bring rough lumber to an East Indian feeding the planer on the mill side. The feeder had to be white. Chinese and East Indians were both good workers, but wouldn't work together.

The mill was located on the Island Railway, the E&N, maybe a mile north of the Koksilah River bridge and a mile south of the camp and cookhouse, where the road from Duncan ended. Each morning started with a pleasant walk along the railway from camp to mill, and mill to camp in the evening. A flunky brought lunch from the cookhouse for the few white men who lived in camp.

It was much less fun than the summer before at Youbou, but I was earning some money, thirty-five cents an hour, which looked good until they deducted a dollar twenty a day, for board and room. Six days a week income, minus seven days a week expenses, net income, eight dollars and forty cents a week, less train and boat fare from Mission. It only looked attractive compared to the alternative, no income at all, and sitting around home, or picking berries.

The summer was hot and dry, no rain for weeks and weeks, with the dried-out forests a tinderbox. The sawmill was east of the railway, the mill waste burner east of the mill, so the prevailing westerly wind blew smoke, sparks and sawdust clear, towards a logged hillside covered with fine unburned sawdust. A mill hand occasionally hosed down the area close to the burner, where falling sparks started small smoldering fires from time to time.

Late one afternoon, a stiff westerly blew sparks as far as the brush line on the hillside above the burner, and a fire ran into the brush before anyone noticed. The mill shut down, and all hands, regardless of race, creed or colour, were handed shovels and mattocks and marched off around and above the fire to clear a fire line to allow backfiring—deliberately setting another fire that could only burn down-hill to meet the main fire, a standard and usually reliable way of stopping a fire on the ground.

We sweated away at this, the Chinese on one side, East Indians on the other, whites in the middle, at the highest point.

Sometime after supper the Chinese and the East Indians, not seeing any signs of food or drink, decided they had had enough, and
pulled out, tools and all, and the white men soon followed, without bothering to tell me. With smoke blowing uphill, I couldn't
see very far either side, and didn't miss them for some time.

The wind had increased enough to speed up the approaching fire when I decided it was time to leave, and I started off
walking uphill a bit faster than the fire, so I could detour to one
side or other of the blaze. I walked out of the low brush we had
been travelling through into a patch of young firs, and was just
entering an area of taller heavily crowned firs, growing close together, when I became aware the fire was overtaking me. When
the small young firs flared up, I started to run, easy enough in
the low salal brush. Even though there was a lot of thin smoke, I
was holding my own, when a great ball of fire flared behind me—
the fire had jumped to the crowns of the taller firs. This was real
bad trouble, the kind that can be fatal.

In the crowns, the fire spread fast—heat radiated from one
flaring crown fired the next like a chain reaction, and the cascade
of falling sparks fired everything underneath. So I ran like hell,
not a bad comparison, but I was fast losing ground when I suddenly found myself scrambling up a pile of small loose rocks, to a
level space, with a cave-like opening in the hillside beyond, and I
dived in a few feet, in ankle deep water, about five seconds before
the trees overhead flared up.

After I had recovered some breath, I felt my way further
back, where I figured the air would stay good, and scooped up
handfuls of water, sweet water, and lots of it. I went back slowly
towards the cave mouth—an abandoned mine adit in fact—and
sat down on a ledge just inside, where the air was still surprisingly
free of smoke, and was still cool.

It was warm enough outside, small fires on the ground and
air hot enough to explode small rocks on the dump, like twenty-
two rifle shots, for quite some time. After I realized that I was
neither going to fry nor suffocate, I began to enjoy the drifting
smoke, lit by occasional flareups and the continuing fusillade of
exploding rocks.

I even murmured a few thanks to the unknown prospector who had dug this most timely hole years before, and wished that I had something to eat.

So, unknown prospector—thanks—it was certainly through you that of all the firefighters ever over-run by a fire, I am one of the exceedingly small number who lived to tell about it. It was probably the time in my life when I needed good luck the most—and there it was, a simple hole in the hillside, a convincing answer to the question, "Has luck played any part in your life?" In this case, it was my life luck played with.

By daylight it was still smoky, but cool enough to stand out on the muck pile. There was no sign of fire anywhere, only wisps of drifting smoke. I gave it a couple of hours more, then soaked my canvas shoes and pantlegs and walked off uphill for some reason, looking for people and breakfast. After a bit I came to another fire line, where the fire had stopped after running through the high timber patch, and walked down the line until I came upon a firefighter, a stranger, just as he was finishing off the last sandwich in the breakfast box.

After the fire, I worked a couple of weeks more, then stuck a peavey point through my foot. We were loading a flatcar with heavy planed timbers, using cant hooks, except there weren't enough, and I was given a peavey with strict orders not to gouge the timbers with the steel point. A cant hook is just a peavey without the sharp point. I was stabbing the peavey down, carefully down between two timbers, to wedge one into place, when the hook struck a higher timber, deflecting the point clear through my foot into the timber I was standing on.

No pain at all when I pulled it out, but it soon felt rather squishy inside my running shoe. I walked back to camp, a bit woozy, but I only passed out a couple of times. After the first, I came to lying on the rails, which I thought was a real stupid place to choose to pass out. Next time I was careful to keel over in the ditch beside the tracks—all this nonsense with no pain and no loss of blood from my shoe—just shock or something, though I couldn't figure out shock without pain.

The timekeeper/first-aid man drove me into the Duncan

hospital for an X-ray—no bones broken, no sinews cut, just a nice clean hole, so the doctor said. I couldn't stand to look at it, even without any blood.

With this mishap I figured I had about used up my luck as far as Manzer's Sawmill was concerned, and quit. A couple of days later, out of hospital and allowed to walk on my heel, I caught the gas car north to Youbou for a few days on beautiful Youbou Bay before school went in.

The place was a disaster—a new sawmill built to the west was operating, sending as much smoke, fly ash and fine sawdust as a small volcano, coating everything, and covering the bay with a heavy sludge. Some log raft float-houses had moved out already, and the rest were going as soon as they could find a new mooring site.

Not my best summer, by a long way.

12

SEPTEMBER 1929, AND MY THIRD YEAR OF HIGH SCHOOL. MY summer earnings, after subtracting room and board, train fare, boat fare, and a schoolbook or so, were about gone, but not having much money was a circumstance I had adjusted to long before.

School actually cheered me up—I was feeling that low—and we had a new teacher, Miss Casselman, who replaced Mrs. Jack. She was not only a good teacher, but she also had this new idea that kids were people who you talked to, and who didn't sit glaring at us for half the period like Mrs. Jack. Miss Casselman didn't have anything as interesting as those old Roman guys the principal talked about. We sure liked those old Romans, though we still thought that they were rather rough on the losers of their games—after our basketball career, we had a great deal of sympathy for losers.

But Miss Casselman was real strong on a guy called Lawrence of Arabia, and told us what a wonderful man he was, and the fantastic things he had done. I got a book about him, and didn't see why she thought he was so great—just a whole lot of guys riding around blowing up trains and shooting up a lot of Turks. Not much different from wild west bandits who held up trains and stage coaches, and shot Indians, except these other guys rode camels instead of horses. But Miss Casselman was so emphatic about how this guy Lawrence had been so great, that it stayed in my mind for years, until Lawrence's own book came out, when I began to get an idea of what she meant.

Ed Kennedy was Wilfred Kennedy's older brother, and Brian Kennedy's younger brother—there were ten boys in that family—and the most independent, bull-headed kid in Mission. He didn't work that I knew about, didn't go to school, and roamed around the countryside most of the time, just living outdoors. He didn't care a hoot for personal comfort, and would walk miles and just sleep out anywhere under a blanket.

Ed and I would go on outings together, to destinations one or the other of us would choose. Neither one of us could ever persuade the other, so there was never any negotiating. Ed just said, "Think I'll go to Rolley Lake on Saturday," or I would say, "Think I'll walk up Suicide Creek in a day or so." Sometimes we went together, sometimes not. He was tricky though, and I learned to find out ahead of time how far it was to new places he said he was going to. He had the endurance of a pack mule, and a couple of times I was walked into the ground when I went with him, while Ed was still stepping right along.

Mom complained a lot about all the shoe soles I wore out and all the holes in my heavy wool socks, and finally made me learn how to half sole my own shoes, and darn my own socks.

We heard about a big sailing ship tied up in New Westminster, the four-masted barkentine, *S.F. Tolmie.* We decided to run away to sea. My extended reading of *Sea Stories Magazine* had filled me full of seagoing book learning—I was the expert, the enthusiast. What inspired Ed I don't know, but we hitch-hiked to New Westminster in late September, with a few clothes in our packs, all set to go sailoring.

The *S.F. Tolmie*, when we found her, obviously wasn't going anywhere, no sails on the booms or yards, ropes lying all over the deck, peeling paint, dirt, and clutter everywhere. We found a watchman, who told us what was obvious.

"No she's not going anywhere—just laid up here in the river away from the salt-water worms—you boys eat yet?"

We hadn't, and were glad of his bread and jam and coffee, before we started back home. Whether Ed was disappointed or not he never said—we never talked much anyway, but my disappointment evaporated quickly and silently once I had sized up the real height of the foremast, the one with square sails on it. *Sea Stories* hadn't quite prepared me for reality—a hundred and fifty feet of mast doesn't sound too bad in a story—but standing there on a real deck looking straight up to the highest yard where sailors actually climbed to furl or set the sail was a chiller. I had second thoughts about going to sea, but the ship herself saved me from the embarrassment of backing out.

On the way home we agreed that it was too bad the ship wasn't going anywhere, and decided we would go north to the Peace River country in the spring, and be homesteaders.

But for Eddie, spring never came. One day in November he and one of his older brothers had gone deer hunting far up Suicide Creek. They shot a buck, and were floating the carcass downstream in the creek—the valley sides were so broken and rough that even walking was hard, and carrying any weight impossible. Apparently Eddie slipped on a smooth rock, struck his head on another, and was swept unconscious downstream under a log jam. There was no way his brother could get to him in time, even if he had known where Eddie was.

That about finished me, coming so suddenly, the first death I had encountered close up like that. If death had come gradually, after a long sickness, I might have handled it better, but I just came apart. Then I made it all ten times worse by not going to his funeral. Sometimes I try to convince myself I must have forgotten about it, or was so confused at the time that I wasn't aware of anything, but I can't make it stick—I just couldn't face the funeral for lack of moral fibre or lack of something else important, I don't know.

Whatever, I knew it was a bad mistake almost right away, a mistake I have regretted all my life. If a mistake involves another living person you can try to make it right, but when the mistake involves only a dead boy and you, you are damned forever.

Uncle Jim Green had been in the war, as I told you before, being gassed like Dad, and I asked him how he could stand having his mates dying while he lived. He said war was different, you knew somebody in your company was going to die from time to time, nobody knew when or who, and after you got hardened to death, you were secretly glad that, once again, chance had taken someone else, and left you alive.

So for me it was a pretty bad winter. I played hookey from school a lot, and by February had stopped altogether. "Uncle" Jim said that since I wasn't going to school I had better start learning something useful like the garage business, apprentice mechanic, at forty dollars a month. If it was a cover-up for therapy it worked—being with Uncle Jim all day in the garage was far better than me more or less hiding away on my own.

I soon became aware I wasn't going to learn much about auto mechanics—Jim had a partner, and the garage had one mechanic, a Japanese named George, but in the spring of 1930, business was so bad none of them worked more than a couple of hours a day, and all I did was sweep up the floor and pump gas for the infrequent customers. Uncle Jim paid me the forty dollars a month anyway, but I was sure it was out of his own pocket, not from what the garage earned.

On my own I left and got a job as a whistle punk at Pete Bain's sawmill, away out north of Hatzic Lake. A whistle punk is the signaller who told the donkey man when to haul in, stop, and haul back while skidding logs in from the timber area to the cold deck or loading pile. I only lasted a couple of hours. I was stationed so far away from the donkey I couldn't hear the signals I made by pulling hard on a tightly stretched iron wire. That was dangerous for the choker man so they hauled me off and put me to building a railway with a big husky Hungarian who didn't know much English.

The railway was narrow gauge, and the rolling stock was one small log car pulled by a Fordson tractor fitted with railway wheels. Railway building was mostly carrying heavy fir ties and heavier steel rails, straight bull labour that came a good second to back-packing salt as the least desirable way of earning money. And not much money either, two eighty a day for five days a week, minus a dollar twenty a day board, for seven days a week. It was hard day-long work, and the first week I was so sore and tired I could hardly stay awake long enough at supper to eat a second and third piece of pie.

This life-saving labour came at the right time; when the job ended some three weeks later I had gained a lot of muscle and had pretty well come out of my long depression.

My next job only lasted a couple of days. "Uncle" Fred Solloway knew some people who wanted their septic tanks dug out, and lined me up. Easy work, compared to railway building, and only a little smellier than shovelling out after our cow, but not as messy, as the tanks were plugged solid, and had been for a long time.

Then Uncle Fred, who worked at the jam factory, told me they wanted some help for a few days to run through some stored strawberry pulp before the local berries ripened. Bright and early the next morning on a clear sunny day in late May, I showed up at the factory office with a half dozen other hopefuls. A short runty man came outside after a bit, looked us over for a few seconds and beckoned to me and another big kid.

"Okay, you two, we'll try you out. Follow me." We followed through the factory, to the boiler house alongside a railway spur, and were handed a big scoop shovel each.

"You unload that by five o'clock, you can have a job." "That" was a gondola carload of fine coal, parked on the rail siding above the nearly empty coal bin in front of the boiler house door. The boiler engineer unlatched the two side discharge doors of the gondola, and a few shovelfuls of fine coal trickled into the coal bin, a fine black dust rising from the miserable fall. There was sure one hell of a lot of coal left in the car. How much does a gondola car hold—thirty tons?—forty tons? We didn't know how much coal weighed, but there was some four feet of it in an eight by forty foot car, twelve hundred and eighty cubic feet, about forty tons if it weighed as much as water.

But weight didn't matter. We found the easy way to unload was to slide the scoop into the coal, pull it out, then slide the full scoop on the car floor, and tip the load out the car door. Not hard work, but hot and dusty—we soon looked like we were made up for a minstrel show. The other kid was a husky farm boy from Matsqui, and a steady worker. Even so, we didn't finish unloading until after five-thirty. The boss was real big about it.

"You didn't finish by five, and we only pay until five. But you can have a job anyway. Show up in the morning, eight o'clock."

My job was stirring strawberry jam in large cooking pans, about eight feet by three feet, and a few inches deep. It was good jam too. The old berries were all done before the new crop ripened. Maybe I could have hired on again when the new berries came in, but I got a better job at Osborne's Mill instead, three miles out on the road to Stave Falls.

This was good, still only thirty-five cents an hour, but I lived at home, not in camp. The job was outdoors, too, taking rough sawn lumber from the run out table, loading the selected sizes on a heavy hand cart, pushing a loaded cart across the road to the planer, and bringing an empty cart back. There were two of us, me and a big dumb clumsy kid who was always dropping his end of the plank at the wrong time, and bashing my fingers.

We could only work as fast as the planer size boards rolled out of the mill, which wasn't fast at all. When the other kid didn't show up one day I found I could keep up easy enough on my own, and saved a lot of pinched fingers. Ted Osborne, Vic's older brother who ran the mill, didn't even ask me if I needed a helper, as it was obvious I didn't. He was a real high type fella, always giving me a smile and hello when he went by.

Osborne's Mill was bigger than Pete Bain's, as they had more money to work with, what with the feed store and ice cream parlour to help out. Even so, things broke down once in a

while, either in the logging end where the trucks were home-
made, or in the planer, which was driven by an overloaded truck
engine rigged up by Jim Green for a belt drive. When the planer
was down I helped in the mill. When the mill was down I stayed
home, and studied a radio correspondence course I had started
after I found the garage job wasn't doing anything for me.

One morning about the end of July, with the mill down, I
was at home reading a Vancouver paper at breakfast. My reading
was limited to comics and the help wanted section, which seemed
full of ads for "Delivery boy with bicycle" but nothing useful.
This morning was different—"Youth wanted for half day garden
work, live in for free board, room and wireless telegraph course.
Start September. Apply Sprott-Shaw Wireless School. Sun Building, Vancouver."

That sounded fine to me although I had a steady job at Osborne's—when things were working—they shut down for the
winter when the bad weather started in November. I rushed
through breakfast, put on some unpatched clothes, and made it
down to the station for the eight o'clock morning train to Vancouver.

I was interviewed by an old fat guy who was nearly deaf, in a
dark gloomy old office, and can't remember much of it, except
that he didn't seem to hear my answers to his questions, judging
from succeeding questions. I suppose those were questions about
my gardening experience, but the only time he really seemed to
understand was when I told him about my radio correspondence
course, and found he didn't know anything about radio. I didn't
know what to make of the interview, though I was afraid I'd
messed it up, what with having to shout at the old guy, and him
asking the same question again right after my answer.

On the way home I just figured I'd wasted three dollars and
ten cents train fare. A couple weeks later I received a letter thank-
ing me for applying for the job, and telling me I had been second
choice this year, and if I wanted to apply again next year, I would
be seriously considered. Fine, but the invitation for next year
sounded like something to soften the blow, that I was second
choice this time, when second didn't mean anything.

But I was wrong. The first week in October, I received another letter from Sprott-Shaw. "Our first choice for a student gardener this year has been unable to continue with us, and we would like you to come in his place as soon as convenient, on Friday, October something, if possible. Please come into the school about noon, prepared to work and study starting on Monday."

The next morning at work, still not entirely convinced I was actually engaged, I asked Ted Osborne what he thought.

"Sure, go ahead, grab it. You can always come back here if things don't pan out. Leave at noon if you like, since tomorrow is Friday. Let me know if you ever need help."

A real high type fella, Ted Osborne.

Though I was a bit dubious about suddenly reducing my income to zero for an unknown period, I left for Vancouver the next morning with most of my worldly possessions in Mom's old suitcase, and my life savings of one hundred and eighty dollars, reported in to Sprott-Shaw, and was duly driven out to Sprott's house at 3351 Marine Drive by the fat deaf guy who turned out to be Sprott himself.

My room was in the basement, quite a good replica of a dungeon cell, with its one small high window, but it was dry and clean and had a mirror and washbasin in a corner closet with real hot water.

I met Katie, the work-worn cook/housekeeper, Mrs. Sprott, and a Mrs. Willis, who was Mrs. Sprott's daughter from her first marriage. I shared the basement with Mutt, an ancient Airedale, with more fleas than I thought possible one dog could feed. He slept in the sawdust bin near the furnace, and the fleas stayed with him. I was shown the second floor bathroom, and was told my bath night was Thursday night, when everyone else was out. It was no surprise to find out I ate in the kitchen. As a matter of fact, I was quite happy not to have company at mealtime.

The setup looked okay to me, and for the first time in my life I lived in a house with central heating, running hot water, and a bathroom. I had really come up in the world, if you ignored the fact of the basement room.

On the next morning, Saturday, Sprott showed me around the garden, which was big, but even in October it looked as though the previous gardener had been neither very expert nor very industrious. My chores, in addition to so-called garden work afternoons and Saturdays, included tending the sawdust burning furnace, and washing and polishing two cars every Sunday morning that it wasn't raining—not many in a Vancouver winter.

On Monday morning I rode in to school with Sprott and took a streetcar back out at noon. After a week I decided this was no good. School started at nine, but it was an exceptional morning when we arrived as early as ten-thirty. I asked Sprott if it was okay for me to ride the streetcar both ways, and he said fine, and he surprised me by saying he would pay me the fifteen cents a day return fare. He was really a nice old guy, living in his own deaf world like Uncle Bert, and it was soon evident that the women really decided what went on in the house, not that that affected me at all.

When I returned Monday afternoon for my first half day of work, I looked around, as nobody had told me what to do, and decided the large scruffy lawn around the tennis court out front was the place to start. It was about three-quarters covered with weeds, the kind with long deep roots, enough weeds to keep me digging all winter. When I wanted a change, I sawed up small dead trees from the wooded ravine east of the house, and piled wood in the basement for the fireplace. On rainy days I polished furniture, floors and silverware, lots of platters and ornaments with fine detail you could only clean with an old toothbrush.

When I asked Katie why the other kid quit, I was quite shocked at her answer. His mother had come down from Powell River to visit him, and was so horrified at the dreadful conditions he was living under that she ordered him home with her immediately. And the poor spineless chump went home—imagine an eighteen-year-old being told what to do by his mother! Mom hadn't bothered me like that for years. He had my sympathy, rather shallow sympathy I guess, since his sudden departure made way for me.

The Sprott-Shaw Wireless school had two good instructors,

Bruce Arundel, a genial six-footer, and Jack Holmes, who put on an act of finding fault with everything and everybody, but it was so clearly an act nobody paid any attention. We practised Morse code every day, and learned how to operate a standard marine long wave transmitter, and a home-made—by Jack Holmes—fifty-watt short wave transmitter, just a plain Hartley circuit, with a motor generator, and one thousand volts DC for the plate.

Neither Bruce nor Jack told us who used this type of transmitter. As it was tuned to the low end of the amateur forty-metre band, we thought it was just to give us actual practice working other amateur stations. I soon started building short wave receivers, as I found I liked building better than just operating. Although my expenses were very close to zero, my income was even closer, so these sets were self-financed. I would build one, sell it to another kid for a little more than the cost of parts, build another, and so on. Then I got big ideas—instead of a small three-tube set using triode tubes, I built a four-tube set using the new screen grid tubes, from a circuit in *QST Amateur Radio Magazine.*

Then came disaster. The screen grid tubes needed a high positive voltage on the screen grid, and a low negative voltage on the control grid—I mixed them up, and four high technology screening grid tubes flashed and died, changing my self-financing project to non-profit in a microsecond. I bought new tubes—five dollars each wholesale—and sold the set to Fred Heathecote, a classmate, then returned to the much safer construction of triode tube sets.

Otherwise, it was a quiet winter—Marathon Dancing and Six Day Bike races were big in early 1931. Katie was a dedicated marathon dance spectator, and every Friday lunch I was given a detailed description of her Thursday night out, how the brave, suffering dancers kept shuffling round and round, barely conscious of their swollen feet. Flat-footed Katie felt strongly for others with painful feet. It all sounded rather revolting to me.

I took in one bike race for a couple of nights, mostly to see two local boys, Torchy Peden and his brother Doug, but bike racing was dull watching, and expensive.

Dad died in Shaughnessy Hospital in June. It was a small funeral—Mom, Lloydyboy and me. I thought he looked more relaxed and peaceful lying there in his coffin, than I'd ever seen him before.

In July I wrote my second class wireless telegraphy exam, twenty words a minute plain language, sixteen words a minute coded groups. My wireless class was fully aware that job prospects after they wrote for their ticket were as near hopeless as makes no difference.

At the end of August I left Sprott's as the new boy was starting after Labour Day, and went home, which was now 2133 Yukon Street in Vancouver, just south of the acetylene plant, with my new ticket, but otherwise back to square zero—living at home, zero prospects, near zero expenses and absolutely zero income.

I decided to stay in Vancouver for the winter, and go back up to work for Ted Osborne when he started up in the spring, if nothing showed up before then, almost a certainty.

II

Rum Running

13

THE MORNING OF DECEMBER SEVENTEENTH, 1931 STARTED like every other rainy, windy morning that fall. After Mom had gone to work and Lloydyboy had gone to school, I pulled out my box of radio gear and started working on a partially completed three-tube shortwave receiver I was building. The tubes and parts had taken most of my remaining money—I had started at Sprott's in September of 1930 with one hundred and eighty dollars, and hadn't earned a nickel during all that time. And the way things were in Vancouver in 1931, it was going to be a long time yet before the nickels began to roll in. And believe me, I had lots of company in that situation.

Then the telephone rang and startled me, as hardly anyone ever telephoned us.

"Hiya Sparky, this is Fred. Doing anything today?" It was Fred Heathecote, my friend from the radio school and like me, broke, unemployed and living at home with his mother and two sisters. I never knew whether there was a Mr. Heathecote around or not, but I guess not; Fred never mentioned him.

"Nothing at all, Sparky old buddy. Why, you got something lined up?" I asked him. We called each other Sparky since we had written for our second class wireless telegraph tickets in May, though neither of us had any operating experience on a ship, and the way things were, never would have any.

"Well, sort of," Fred said. "Bruce just phoned me to say they want someone to help load stores on a boat at Coleman-Evans dock. Longshore work isn't my thing, you know, especially in all this rain and wind. It's only a day's pay. Want to try it?"

"Sure, why not?" I said. "Which boat?"

"It's a boat called the *Ruth B.* Bruce says she looks like a fish packer."

"Okay, thanks. I'll let you know how it goes."

So I piled all my radio stuff back in the box and headed over the Cambie Street bridge towards the harbour. Fred was a brainy little guy, but in order to pose for a ninety-eight pound weakling picture, he would have had to put on some weight.

I never did let Fred know how it went as I never saw him again.

At Coleman-Evans, the *Ruth B* was the only boat at the pier, a typical fish packer, sixty feet long, a big dory in chocks at her stern, a battened down hatch, a mast, winch and boom, a small cabin and wheelhouse and an anchor and large coil of line lashed down on her foredeck. A typical fish packer, except for one thing—how clean her decks and paintwork were, and not a spot of rust on any of the ironwork. She wasn't a riot of colour though, dark red decks, dark grey paint with black trim, seeming

Ruth B out of the water at Vancouver Shipyard, sixty-one-foot fish packer type, one 100-hp diesel engine. November 1929.

even darker in the dim light. The southeaster was just making up, gusty, but not much rain yet, but with the cloud blowing just above the sheds on the pier.

A ladder led from the dock down to the small deck space beside the winch—the deck aft was filled with oil drums lashed to ring bolts in the bulwarks on both sides. I scrambled down the ladder and went forward and knocked on the wheelhouse door, then tried the doorknob. The door was locked, so I knocked on the scuttle door just forward of the wheelhouse, and the doors opened immediately and a round merry face looked out.

"Bruce sent me down to help load stores," I said.

"Don't know any Bruce, but if you're gonna help load, I shouldn't worry. Truck ain't showed up yet. Come below and warm up, while I get the coffee going."

When we got below the guy laid out hardtack, butter and jam and, a few minutes later, coffee.

"I'm Jasper, the cook," he said. "What's your name?"

"Fred," was all I said, as I didn't want to explain why Fred hadn't come, supposing someone had told the cook a fellow named Fred was coming down to help load.

The galley of the *Ruth B*, lit by a single low-powered bulb, was dark, painted in the same exotic colours as the top sides, and made even darker by the thick grey paint on the four glass portholes. A small kitchen oil stove was bolted to the deck amidships just forward of a bulkhead, with a kitchen sink to port and work boards either side of the sink and cupboards underneath. Forward, two bunks right in the bows could be reached by climbing over a narrow table, with dividers spaced a plate diameter apart, a bench two people could sit on to eat, and more cupboard doors in a low bulkhead forward of the table, underneath.

Above the smell of fresh coffee, there was a definite aroma of diesel oil, but not the slightest trace of fish smell, something my stomach was always sensitive about. So the *Ruth B* had not packed fish in the recent past and was riding high in the water, so there could be little in her hold. She could hardly be a rum runner, as in the popular concept these were all long low boats capable of thirty knots or more loaded. Had she been deeply loaded,

I would have guessed at a rum runner's supply ship. So I didn't know what, not that it made any difference to a day's pay.

Then somebody leaned on a truck horn on the pier and we went on deck. The truck panel said "Campbells Boat Supplies," and two men were opening the rear doors of the covered van. They hauled out a wooden chute and slid it down to the *Ruth B's* hatch cover.

"Okay, what do you want first?" one of the men asked.

"Doesn't matter," Jasper said. "Just as she comes." We soon had a quite surprising pile of groceries on the hatch and deck, quite enough, I figured, to feed several men for three or four months, though I couldn't see how that tied in with a boat that had no cargo. When the supplies were all on deck, one of the men climbed down and handed Jasper a paper.

"Here's your supply order. Want to check it?"

"Hell no, we gotta get this stuff out of the rain right away," Jasper said, and signed another paper without even looking at it.

"Okay Fred, we get this tarp over the stuff that shouldn't get wet, before we start stowing."

The supplies that stowed topside were first, eggs, potatoes and crates of fresh vegetables went into the dory, under the tarp cover. A side of beef, one of pork, and a side of bacon we hung in the shrouds, wrapped in small tarpaulins, and lashed tight so they couldn't swing when the ship rolled.

"Good enough," Jasper said, after the last side had been lashed securely. "Now I go below and you bring all the dry stuff to the scuttle—sugar, coffee, and flour, stuff like that. When that's all done, bring me all the cases, then come below and help me stow."

All easy enough, except the cases of canned stuff, which all went into the large locker under the two bunks forward, through the small doors under the galley table.

A clock in the wheelhouse struck two bells as Jasper leaned the last case into the big locker.

"Five o'clock," he said. "Not bad going at all. And nobody likely to show up for hours yet. If you could stick around, there's things I could be doing up town. How about it?"

"Sure, why not?" I said. I didn't figure I was going to get paid any more by staying, but I was on a real ship, that would sail to real places, though without me, and I liked the change. Jasper hacked off his two days of whiskers after we had eaten, biscuits and jam again, plus a good sized slab of cheese, and coffee.

"Okay, anybody shows up, tell them I'll be back at ten o'clock. Leave the deck lights on, and look around outside once in awhile," Jasper said as he climbed the scuttle ladder.

So not only was I on a real ship, I was also in sole occupation, with nothing much I could do to get into trouble. The only real disaster I could think of was the boat burning or sinking. Jasper had set the oil stove on low heat so fire didn't seem likely. On deck I tried the manual pump I had seen by the winch, and after a dozen strokes the pump sucked air. I should have remembered, with the hull riding so high, that there could be nothing in the hold, neither cargo nor water.

I dozed in the galley while the wheelhouse clock chimed through eight bells and went on into the next watch. Except for the odd gust of wind moaning down the ventilators, it was quiet and warm, although not very comfortable as the galley table bench was the only place to sit down. Shortly after five bells there was a thump and tramping on deck, and Jasper slid down the scuttle ladder.

"Well, well, got company," he said, looking generally in my direction, and weaving around. "I'm Jasper the cook. What's your name?"

"Sparky," I said. "I helped you load stores."

"Sure, sure, good boy. Stay around eh, I don't feel too good." He stuck out his hand and we shook on the deal. Then he pulled off his shoes and coat and slid into a bunk behind the stove, pulled a blanket up, and was snoring away by the time the clock chimed six bells.

Well, what now, stay or go home? I didn't like the idea of leaving "my" boat, mine for a few hours anyway, with a sleeping watchman who could get into trouble, whether the boat did or not. I decided to stay around, perhaps the luckiest decision in my whole life, or close to it.

After seven bells—eleven-thirty—I went on deck to pump out again, for something to do mostly, and noticed four big guys and one shorter fat guy standing on the pier under the wharf shed overhang. I climbed to the dock and went over towards the men, to see about my pay.

They were all looking at the *Ruth B*, and arguing. "But dammit Frank, we can't go out without an operator," one big guy with a quite soft voice was saying to one of the others. "I got Louie, Jasper and Charlie, but can't reach Slim on the island—telephone's out."

"You go tonight Harry," the big guy who was Frank said. "I've set up a meet with the *Ragna* for the twentieth—Charlie you can operate some, can't you?"

"Sorry, Frank but no can do," the short fat guy said.

Another big guy spoke up, one whose voice I knew, Bruce Arundel, head of the Sprott-Shaw Wireless Telegraph School.

"I sent a kid down to help load stores. He's a good radio operator. Looks like he's still here. Hey Fred, come here."

"You want to go out and work wireless?" Big Frank asked, without even bothering to look me over very closely, in the kind of voice like he wouldn't be at all happy with a no answer. He didn't need to worry. In late 1931, asking anyone if he wanted a job was about as relevant a question as asking the pope if he wanted to go to heaven.

"Sure, I'll go, but I don't have any clothes with me."

"No worry, Fred. I'll run you home and bring you back," Bruce said, and away we went.

"So what happened to Fred?" Bruce asked as we drove through the rain to Yukon Street.

"Decided he didn't want to work in the rain."

Stuffing all my warm clothes into a suitcase was a short job, and left room for the box holding my partly built receiver and the wire and pieces needed to finish it.

"I got a job on a boat," I told Mom when she looked in to see what I was doing. "This is Bruce Arundel, from Sprott-Shaw."

"What kind of boat, and when will you be back?" Mom

asked, and all I could do was look at Bruce.

"Just a small cargo boat running up and down the coast. He'll be back some time after New Year's," Bruce said, and we headed back to Coleman Evans. I shook hands with Bruce and climbed down to the *Ruth B* with my suitcase, and down into the galley. Harry, Charlie and Louie were drinking coffee.

"Okay, Sparky," Harry said. "I'm the captain—Charlie here is engineer, and Louie is mate. You stand watch with him. Your bunk is the port side there forward. Wind her up Charlie, so we get to sea tonight, like Big Frank ordered."

"Real deep sea, or just deep sea enough so you become the boss?" Charlie asked.

"Deep sea is anywhere outside Vancouver Harbour. Snug Cove on Bowen Island clearly qualifies. The whole crew needs a good night's sleep, to face winter in the North Pacific. It gets bumpy, as you may remember."

I gave Louie a hand with the lines, and we ran out through the First Narrows, a lively southeaster pushing us along. After an hour, the *Ruth B* pulled into a small cove and we tied alongside a moored fishboat, our tire fenders squeaking slightly as the boats blew together. I was at sea, technically speaking, but I didn't actually know very much for a fact.

I had a job on a boat, a boat called the *Ruth B*, a fish packer that hadn't carried fish in years. That was all I knew, or could guess. What I didn't know didn't seem important, like what the boat carried, where it was going, when I would be back, the name of the company, and not least what I was being paid for my as yet unknown duties.

Harry, Charlie, Louie and Jasper all looked like real high type fellas; I dropped off to sleep, no worries at all.

14

WHEN I WOKE UP, THE TEMPERATURE WAS ABOUT A HUN-
dred degrees, and I smelled coffee and bacon as Jasper
rattled away around the stove. Louie was still asleep in the starboard bunk. The bacon and coffee smell reminded me I hadn't
had a good meal since yesterday's breakfast at home. I was about
to crawl out over the table and sit down, but Louie made no
move, so I decided to wait and see what the system was before
showing my ignorance. It seemed likely that the captain or engineer ate first.

Sure enough, after a bit Jasper went into the engine room
aft, banged a jingly little bell a couple of times and Harry and
Charlie slid down the scuttle and sat down on the bench, eating
in silence. Harry finally spoke up.

"Hey Louie, you awake yet?"

"Sure, Cap, any time you say," Louie mumbled.

"Okay, break it up now. After you and Sparky eat, you rig
the aerial, rig the wheelhouse window screen, and get the sail
ready to hoist. Then we'll head over for Gabriola Pass."

We ate a splendid breakfast, hotcakes as well as bacon and
eggs, and went on deck just as the clock chimed out one bell.
Eight-thirty, low cloud, windy, but not much rain, and just about
enough light to see our way around, as it was only a few minutes
after sunrise, so close to the shortest day of the year.

The radio aerial ran from the wheelhouse roof to the mast-
head, a couple of minutes' work. The canvas wheelhouse window
screens took a few more minutes, and made the wheelhouse look
like a masked, five-eyed bandit.

Louie poked his head inside the wheelhouse door after we
had cleared the sail gaskets, and said, "All done on deck."

"Okay, Charlie, let's move along," Cap said. "Give me a
couple of minutes to warm the engine and show Sparky how to
make it go. Come on below, Sparky. You're second engineer as
well as radio operator, you may be surprised to know."

Surprised, but not wishing to show it, I followed Charlie through the galley into the engine room, where a black four-cylinder diesel engine, the cylinder heads about waist level, took up most of the engine room, except for a big steel tank on the starboard side and a long workbench on the port side. The engine had two wheels on the port side, and had no valves in the cylinder heads, or any gauges that I could see. Charlie started his recital.

"This is a two-cycle Fairbanks-Morse diesel. A two-cycle engine is direct drive, no clutch, no reverse gears. Remember, when the engine goes, the boat goes, if it isn't tied up. This small wheel is the throttle—set it at slow to start up. This big wheel is the starting wheel. Turn it ninety degrees left and you start ahead, ninety degrees right and you start astern. The wheel is spring return, so you just let it go after the engine fires. That's all you do when the engine is warm.

"Not quite so simple when the engine is cold like now. You take out these four plugs, these things that look like rifle bolts, and hang them in this rack over the bench, and put one of these white punks into the hole in the bottom of each bolt."

Charlie hammered the handle on the top of each plug, giving it a half turn, lifted them out, and installed the short punks, three-inch lengths of what looked like hard braided cotton rope.

"You are now ready to start. If you are not tied up, you ring the jingle like this..."—he sounded the same jingle Jasper used to call Cap and Charlie for breakfast—"...and wait for Cap's orders. We are still tied up solid to Bowen Island. Now, the careful part. You light those punks with a match, like this, and let them burn enough so you get a good red glow on the end. Now quick, you take this gas can..."—a small pump type oil can—"...and squirt once into each cylinder through the plug hole, and shove the plugs back in."

Charlie did a quick squirt, shoved the glowing plugs into the cylinder head, hammered them tight, and shoved the big wheel ninety degrees left. A swish of compressed air, and the engine went *crack-crack-crack-crack* like four high power rifles fired in a closed room, then settled down to a low steady *lub-lub-lub*.

The *Ruth B* surged gently ahead, and snubbed on her lines. Charlie let the engine run for a minute or so.

"You stop by turning the throttle counter-clockwise until the arrow points to Stop. Okay, now stop, and we'll let you make a couple of warm starts, since we can't make any more cold ones.

"Let's try starting astern," Charlie said. "Your bell goes *bong, bong.*"

So I turned the throttle up to slow, turned the starting wheel ninety degrees right, and the engine fired, nothing to it.

"Bong," Charlie said. "When you are running slow, either way, that means stop." And I stopped.

"Bong," Charlie said again. "When you are stopped, that means slow ahead."

Away we went again, a couple more times. Pretty easy, this second engineer bit, I thought.

"Now we tell Cap we are ready to roll," Charlie went on when I stopped the engine again. "You reach up and whack the jingle and wait for bells. Cap has control, so you don't do anything on your own after you hit the jingle. I'll take her out now, my watch anyway. You give Louie a hand on deck with the lines and sail."

So I became a ship diesel engine operator in one easy lesson. We eased away from alongside a couple of small fishboats tied to a dock, nothing showing ashore through the mist but trees and a couple of small buildings. At Cowans's Point we changed course to starboard, bringing the wind on the port beam but with the riding sail hoisted, the *Ruth B* was steady, except for the continuous up and down motion as successive waves passed under us. My stomach took rather a poor view of this up and down bit, though it was only four or five feet.

Louie and I turned in for the rest of our watch below, and my stomach relaxed when I was lying in my bunk, much to my relief. I knew people got seasick on the ocean, but surely I could avoid the disgrace of seasickness crossing the Strait of Georgia. Cap and Charlie stayed on watch until we were through Gabriola Pass and were running south through islands on the Vancouver Island side, in smooth water. In the rain and mist the shorelines on either beam were just a dark blur.

During the early afternoon, Louie rang the engine room jingle so I went up into the wheelhouse. "You take the wheel for an hour each watch when we're running steady. Now while we are running through the Gulf Islands you can practise steering by compass, while I stand by." There wasn't much to it, after I relaxed and didn't over correct for each small swing off course. Just before supper, around five o'clock, Charlie came into the wheelhouse.

"Come on below, Sparky, and I'll show you the rest of the engineer chores before we eat."

There wasn't much; how to start the electric generator, and charge batteries, how to pump out with the electric pump, and how to pump up starting air pressure with the gasoline-driven compressor. The diesel had an automatic compressor on it, so the gasoline set was hardly ever used.

So that was most of December eighteenth, 1931, and all of the good part. After supper, Louie and I turned in, but a while after, we must have entered the Strait of Juan de Fuca, off Victoria. My last thought, as I turned in was, "Gulf Islands—Louie said we were running through the Gulf Islands. Now how could you have gulf islands in a strait?"

But I never found out why, for as soon as we hit the rough water, my stomach went crazy—I made it to the galley sink, and heaved up all my supper in short order, then kept heaving, trying to unload an empty stomach, until I was exhausted. I think I washed the sink clean, but don't remember for sure before I hauled myself back up over the galley table into my bunk and passed out cold, dead to all the wild gyrations of the *Ruth B.*

All I remember for the next while was several more short painful efforts to heave my guts into the sink, then sinking into quite painless oblivion in my bunk. I tried drinking water, but threw it up right away, though with much less pain than the effort to heave empty guts. Actually, being seasick wasn't really that bad for me—five or ten minutes of painful heaving into the galley sink, then hours and hours of painless oblivion.

One morning—I only knew it was morning because I could

smell coffee and bacon—I lay, semi-conscious, quite relaxed, listening to Cap and Jasper.

"How's Sparky doing, Jasper, eating yet?"

"Still out cold Cap—can't eat, can't even drink water and hold it. Worst seasickness I've ever seen."

"Not good at all," Cap said. "If he doesn't come to by tomorrow morning, we better get him ashore."

I slid off into unconsciousness again, but maybe my subconscious recognized some threat to my future, and took control. When I woke up again, it was afternoon, maybe the same day, maybe the next day, I didn't know. Cap and Charlie had just finished lunch and were still sitting at the table. Something was different, and much better. I was really awake, and my stomach had the strangest feeling—I was hungry! I thought being hungry was the most wonderful sensation in the world, and wriggled myself out of my bunk, down to the shelf between the bunks where there was enough headroom to sit up.

"Well, well, look who's come to life. Welcome back to the world. How do you feel?" Cap asked.

"A bit hungry," was all I said, as I figured they would realize someone conscious was better than someone unconscious.

"Okay Sparky, we want you to hold the seven-thirty radio schedule tonight. What do you think?"

"Sure, I can do that," I said and really meant it.

"Good enough," Cap said. "Jasper, you get Sparky some porridge and hotcakes too if he wants, but no more. His stomach must be shrunk to nothing, with no food all this time. Then you turn in for the afternoon, Sparky, and sleep if you can, and we'll see about supper. Charlie can connect the radio for you."

I ate and turned in again, and slept. But somebody owes me nearly four days that 1931 cheated me out of. At supper I found that it was the twenty-second of December.

15

W HEN I WOKE UP I HEARD THE WHEELHOUSE CLOCK
strike eight bells—four o'clock. I had slept only three
hours, so it was still daylight, or what passes for daylight in mid-
December north of latitude 49. Five days at sea and I hadn't yet
seen the ocean. The *Ruth B* was stopped, not rolling much, but
lifting away up and dropping again, every seven or eight seconds.
My stomach said okay, let's look at the ocean, so I stuck my head
out of the scuttle.

No land in sight for miles, but man, that water. The whole
sea surface was a churning mass, big patches of foam, and all between long streaks of foam running down wind, and the steady
moan of the wind was a dismal accompaniment. The horizon
dropped from several miles as the big rollers slid under the *Ruth
B*, to a hundred yards or so in the troughs.

"Well Sparky, that's the Pacific Ocean. What do you think of
it?" Cap said as he looked out the wheelhouse door. I couldn't
think up anything clever to say but made a mental reservation
that while I could tolerate a seafaring life, I was most certainly
not going to like it, aside from whatever it paid.

After supper, Cap, Charlie and I went up into the little cabin
back of the wheelhouse. It was about eight feet long, with two
bunks on the port side, and a low locker to starboard, leaving a
floor space about four feet wide. There was also a chart table
with a radio receiver and telegraph key on it, and a single tube
short wave transmitter on the shelf above, everything screwed
down solid against the continuing efforts of the *Ruth B* to throw
everything around, crew included. Louie told me afterwards the
seas were about thirty feet—quite enough in a sixty-foot boat.

Charlie pointed at the transmitter.

"She's all hooked up, but better check anyway. Here's the
wave meter—our frequency is this mark on the dial—you set the
pointer to the scratch mark."

The wave meter coil had been broken and glued back together again, and presumably the scratch mark took this into account. The mark said 6950 kilocycles just below the forty-meter amateur band between 7000 and 7300 kilocycles, where I had my amateur transmitter.

The motor generator set buzzed away happily when I pushed the starting switch, and the 203 tube filament glowed. When I pressed the transmitting key the plate current meters indicated lots of plate current, so I held the key down, set the frequency to the wave meter mark, rotated the antenna tuning until we had a good antenna current, and shut down. We were in the transmitting business, with the same type of home-made fifty-watt transmitter Jack Holmes showed us how to set up at Sprott-Shaw, one fifty-watt 203 tube in a Hartley circuit. I think Jack made them up as a sideline to teaching, but the transmitter was the only good news.

The battery-powered receiver would do nothing but make loud popping and crackling noises, like bacon in a too-hot frying pan.

"Got any spare tubes?" I asked Charlie. We had, but the spares made exactly the same racket in the earphones.

"Maybe she's a bit damp," Charlie said. "Let's heat it on the stove."

So we heated for an hour at least, and connected the batteries again. Still lots of frying noises, but nothing even remotely like a signal, no matter where I turned the dial.

"She's just dead," I said after a while, as I put the earphones down. Nobody spoke, we all just listened to the sorrowful moaning wind.

"Blast the bloody thing," Cap said. "Sparky gets better, and now the damned receiver won't work. We'll have to get a new set in Victoria. The *Ragna* crew will sure be pulling their hair out, not hearing from us on the twentieth at all. They won't make Vancouver for Christmas now, no way."

We sat some more, and listened to the wind. Then I remembered.

"Say Cap, I have a receiver in my suitcase that can receive on forty meters."

"Well well," Cap said, his ruddy face glowing with relief. "Bring it here and set her up."

I hauled out my box of radio stuff, and took it up to the

Above and opposite: *Ruth B* in heavy weather off Cape Beale, January 1932.

cabin. Nobody seemed much impressed by the small aluminum box I showed them.

"Well, try it out," Cap said. He didn't sound convinced that the little box would receive anything.

"Trouble is, Cap, it's not quite finished. A few joints to solder yet, and I have to wind the coils."

Cap didn't say anything, just looked disappointed. Charley had picked up my small electric soldering iron, and was looking at the nameplate.

"This iron is a hundred and ten volts, Sparky. No good here, we only have thirty-two volts."

It was my turn to look disappointed. Rather more than disappointed, more likely badly depressed, as we would now run in to Victoria for a new receiver. It was a fair guess they would also pick up Slim, the operator who was supposed to go originally.

"Are we downhearted?" Charlie said to no one in particular. "We sure as hell are. But cheer up, everybody, genius to the rescue. I can make a gizmo that will solder small wires."

So we went back to smiles again, like traffic lights changing.

Charlie's gizmo was the carbon rod from a flashlight battery, sharpened to a pencil point at one end, and a pair of wires, with spring clips on each end. The two clips on one end gripped the connections of the thirty-two volt battery, but only two or three cells, giving four or six volts. On the other ends, one clip held the carbon rod's blunt end, and the other held whatever metal wires needed soldering.

Charlie clipped on to a piece of copper wire and touched the carbon tip to it. The tip glowed a dull red, and the soldering wire he held at the copper wire/carbon tip melted off onto the wire. Money for jam.

"Just be real careful only the carbon tip touches the soldering part—you touch it with the clip, everything burns up," Charlie warned.

We went back up to the cabin. By this time it was after nine o'clock.

"Well Sparky, can you finish your set? How long do you need?" Cap asked.

"Charlie's gizmo is fine—maybe a couple of hours on the set, then another to wind the coils—not more than four hours," I said and almost added, "...with good luck." Good luck was the only kind I could use, as this was certainly my last chance to get the *Ruth B*'s wireless going—and to keep me in the crew. What luck to have a partly built forty-meter receiver with me. What luck to have Charlie's gizmo.

"Good enough," Cap said. "We can't make the midnight schedule, so you turn in until midnight. Then keep working until you're finished, call Louie and turn in. We can try the radio again after breakfast, and can hold the nine o'clock schedule in the morning. I hope, I hope."

Hope was what I had a lot of too.

Judging from the *Ruth B*'s motion, and the endless moan of the rigging, the gale still hadn't eased off when Charlie called me at midnight. We had toast and a coffee mug-up, then I was on my own in the engine room with my box of radio gear. For the first time in my life, I was into a situation only I could resolve, by working all night while everyone else slept warm in bed. The first time, but not the last.

As a workshop, the engine room of a small boat riding on endless successions of twenty-five foot waves has its drawbacks.

But with my right foot jammed against the diesel, holding my left hip under the edge of the workbench, and elbows hard against the bench, I had two hands more or less free to hold the small radio on the bench. The *Ruth B* did a very inconvenient flip-flop just as she crested each roller, quickly uphill one instant, and an even faster drop downhill a fraction later. But there were some five or six seconds of relative quiet in between, about time enough to solder a joint if everything was ready.

Anyway, the carbon rod of Charlie's gizmo only gave me three or four seconds before it got too hot to hold. But it did solder, when everything went right. I took a long time checking each connection before I soldered. The disaster to the last receiver I built still haunted me—a high voltage plus lead was crossed with the low voltage negative grid lead, and presto, four radio tubes that cost five dollars each wholesale, flashed into instant junk. I was very conscious of tubes.

And tubes again were possible trouble. My circuit was fine, as I had copied it out of *QST Amateur Radio Magazine*. For tubes though, I had substituted a new two-volt battery which had been claimed to improve set performance over the old five-volt type. Tubes incorrectly connected had been blow-outs before, and I couldn't help wondering about substituted tubes.

Finally, it was all done except for winding the coils, where the worst thing that could go wrong was letting the coil form slip before I had the ends soldered, meaning I would have to start over again. Anyway, every three or four turns I daubed on shellac, which dried fast and held the wire already wound on the form, while I added a few more turns, and added more shellac.

It was around four when I called Louie and turned in. Cap let me sleep until seven-thirty. While hove to, the *Ruth B's* regular watch schedule, six hours on and six hours off, twice a day, slipped. Cap and Charlie weren't called for their normal five-thirty breakfast—Jasper took over at six for a couple of hours after Louie turned in, and we all had breakfast after seven-thirty.

"So Sparky, how did it go?" Cap asked when I climbed out for breakfast.

"It's finished," I said. Nobody congratulated me. It was definitely a wait and see atmosphere. The final act was a total anti-climax—the blessed set worked perfectly and I said so. But there was unspoken doubt.

"That's fine, Sparky. You stay up for the nine o'clock schedule," was all Cap said in a way that suggested he would not be totally convinced without some real evidence, like receiving a message.

Nobody else could receive code—all they knew was the set made dot and dash sounds. The doubt was not about the set, I realized after a bit, it was about me. The new kid had a receiver he said worked, but was he able to operate for real after such a wearing introduction to life on the high seas?

I didn't worry about that—failure on my first real operating job was much too unpleasant even to think about. And I was too tired to think about anything.

16

W HILE I WAS WAITING FOR NINE O'CLOCK, I TUNED UP and down the forty-meter amateur band. I couldn't reach the top end because I had put one extra turn on the tuned circuit coil to bring the low end of the band up enough to cover a fair range below. I hoped this would include 6950 kilocycles, our approximate transmitting frequency. Just before nine, Cap slid back a concealed panel above his bunk, and hauled out a flat canvas bag. From a loose-leaf binder he handed me a sheet of paper that had two rows of ships' names, one vertical and one horizontal, the same ships, and rows of two letter groups between.

The list was similar to the one shown here *(overleaf)*. I never did succeed in getting a copy of a real call sign sheet; this one is approximate from memory.

"Here's your call sign list," Cap said handing it to me. "Either Vancouver or the *Lillehorn* will call us, LL or LG, most likely the *Lillehorn*. Vancouver's signals skip over us most of the time."

Right on nine—I found out later the Vancouver operator was a stickler for time and a nine o'clock schedule meant nine o'clock, not a minute after and, not by any means, four or five minutes after—I heard a weak but clear call "LK LK LK, *Lillehorn* calling Vancouver" then silence, nothing from Vancouver. After half a minute LK came back, signed off, then called "LG LG LG" a number of times, like he'd called without any answers many times before and he didn't really expect one this time.

He signed off and I came on "LH LH" and by golly the *Lillehorn* heard me, and came right back, not a strong signal, but easy to read.

"Glad to hear you at last. Any trouble?" he asked.

"No, no trouble. Very bad weather," I said.

"Okay, okay. Take this," and the *Lillehorn* transmitted a series of four-letter word groups, maybe ten.

"Message from the *Lillehorn*, Cap," I said, like I'd been

handling messages for years, not the first real message in a radio operating career just one message old.

"Good man, Sparky. Tell *Lillehorn* to stand by," Cap said, taking the message and looking up the letter groups in the code book. He handed me a three group message and said, "Get this off to *Lillehorn*, then try to raise the *Zip*."

But I didn't need to try *Zip* because at the moment *Lillehorn* signed off, a powerful signal blasted in my ears "OW OW OW, I have a message for you."

I took the message and Cap decoded, and looked quite cheery.

"Good news," he said, "*Zip* won't arrive on position until noon tomorrow. So I don't have to explain where the hell we have been since the twentieth. Okay Sparky, just tell him 'see you tomorrow' and sign off."

Cap put the call sign sheet and code book back into the canvas bag that handled heavy as if it had a lead weight inside, and slid the hidden compartment door back into place.

CALL SIGN TABLE

Called Ship

Calling Ship	Vancouver	Lillehorn	Ruth B	Malahat	Querida	Zip	Ragna	Hurry Home	Old Maid	Chief Skugaid	Audrey B	Ryuo	Taiheiyo	Kagome	Prince Albert
Vancouver		LR	LL	LD	LA	LC	LB	NA	NB	LX	NC	ND	NE	NF	NG
Lillehorn	LK		LG	LN	LO	LP	NH	NI	NJ	NK	NL	NM	NO	NP	NQ
Ruth B	LV	LH		LE	LF	LI	LJ	LS	LT	LU	LV	LW	LX	LY	LZ
Malahat	NR	NS	NT		NU	NV	NW	NX	NY	NZ	OA	OB	OC	OD	OE
Querida	OF	OG	OH	OI		OJ	OK	OL	OM	ON	OP	OQ	OR	OS	OT
Zip	OU	OV	OW	OX	OY		OZ	PA	PB	PC	PD	PE	PF	PG	PH
Ragna	PI	PJ	PK	PL	PM	PN		PO	PP	PQ	PR	PS	PT	PU	PV
Hurry Home	PW	PX	PY	PZ	GA	GB	GC		GD	GE	GF	GH	GI	GJ	GK
Old Maid	GL	GM	GN	GO	GP	GQ	GR	GS		GT	GU	GV	GW	GX	GY
Chief Skugaid	GX	HA	HB	HC	HD	HE	HF	HG	HI		HJ	HK	HL	HM	HN
Audrey B	HO	HP	HQ	HR	HS	HT	HU	HV	HW	HX		HY	HZ	JA	JB
Ryuo II	JC	JD	JE	JF	JG	JH	JI	JJ	JK	JL	JM		JN	JO	JP
Taiheiyo	JQ	JR	JS	JT	JU	JV	JW	JX	JY	JZ	KA	KB		KC	KD
Kagome	KE	KF	KG	KH	KI	KJ	KK	KL	KM	KN	KO	KP	KQ		KR
Prince Albert	KS	KT	KU	KV	KW	KX	KY	KZ	FA	FB	FC	FD	FE	FG	

"So far, so good," he said. "We still got a small problem. We don't know where we are, and can't get a sight today in this muck. Tonight we do a coast crawl until we find a lighthouse to fix our position. We'll start in now, Charlie, since we may be pretty far offshore."

We stopped for the noon radio schedule on December twenty-third. Nobody had anything for us, and the *Zip* still said, "See you tomorrow." Early in the afternoon, Louie picked up a dark line on the horizon that was land. We hove-to (at a standstill with our head to the wind) until four, and then ran in closer to shore, and turned northwest, running slow, looking for lights. Cap and Charlie picked up Pachena Lighthouse before Louie and I came on watch at midnight.

"Keep in sight of Pachena until four," Cap told Louie. "Then run out towards position, fifteen miles south-southwest of Cape Beale, by daylight."

The clouds had lifted a bit, bringing visibility to something like three miles. At four, Louie started up, and after breakfast we stopped on the Cape Beale position, a vast expanse of heaving ocean. On the nine o'clock radio schedule *Zip* came blasting in so loud she must have been nearly on top of us, and by noon the grey hundred-foot sub-chaser hull first showed on a wave crest. *Zip* stopped fifty feet to leeward of the *Ruth B* and a husky man stepped out of her wheelhouse.

"We have eleven hundred for you, Harry," he shouted to Cap. "We want to see Vancouver tomorrow. No transfer out here. What about San Juan?"

"San Juan's okay," Cap shouted back. "Follow me in. We'll run down to Swiftsure by dark. If my deck lights come on at any time, it's trouble. You run back out."

He shouted to Louie next, "Sort out our anchor gear while there is still light. We won't need much line. San Juan is only forty feet deep on the northwest corner under the bluff. Check our following light too." The "following light" was a small electric lamp mounted on the boom in a tin can, showing a three-inch beam directly astern and totally unnoticed from any other direction. About four p.m. we spotted the Swiftsure lightship, as we passed south showing no running lights, just our weak following light. After an hour's run, we dropped the lightship astern, and the heavy swells began to ease off. Cap opened both wheelhouse doors, and he and Charlie watched out port and starboard, as with the canvas screen covering the lower three-quarters of the wheelhouse windows, visibility was reduced to near nothing from inside. Cap had me looking out astern, by the winch just behind the cabin.

Jasper relieved us each in turn for a quick supper and some time after that we approached the Port San Juan whistle buoy, and slowed down. Port San Juan is three and a half miles long, a mile wide, with high steep land on the northwest side, and steep to the southeast, but only half as high. On the high northwest ridge the wind made a steady high-pitched roar, rather more cheerful than the very tiresome moan our rigging made. Inside the port, there was hardly any wind, and only a gentle surge rolling the boat.

"Okay Sparky," Cap said coming aft like an invisible man. "Give Louie a hand sounding."

Man, it was dark—no lights, no stars, nothing. The clouds overhead showed lighter than the hills, and our night vision was

M.V. Lillehorn at anchor on Rum Row. *Zip* loading alongside in rough weather.

good enough to feel our way around. I found Louie on the foredeck, and he put a small line with a lead weight on it into my hands.

"We do it this way, Sparky. You heave the lead over when I say 'sound,' let the line run through your hands and yell 'bottom' when she touches. I'll get the depth."

In complete blackness, I couldn't figure out how he was going to read depth, but it was simple, when you knew how.

He yelled "Sound" just inside the whistle buoy and I threw the lead overside, and yelled—rather a quiet yell—"Bottom" when the line stopped running out. Louie stretched his arms out a couple of times, and then called out to Cap in the wheelhouse, "Nearly fifty feet, Cap."

"Okay, we'll run in close under Pandora Peak and anchor in thirty feet."

We sounded several more times on the way inside, and Louie went through this arm waving business each time before he called out the depth; and I finally figured the system. He had a short line whose length he knew. He simply measured the line left slack on deck by the arm waving business, added maybe six feet from me to the water-line, and the difference was the depth. He had certainly done it before, and it was quite accurate, even in total darkness.

When Louie said, "Forty minus," Cap stopped the *Ruth B* and came out of the wheelhouse.

"Okay Sparky, you stand in the wheelhouse out of the way. Louie and I'll handle the anchor."

I was glad to hear that. Being told what to do with a lead line in the dark was one thing, but shifting a large anchor and many feet of two-inch line was not an appropriate chore for a new seaman in the dark of night. After a big splash and some slithering noises, Cap came back into the wheelhouse and ran the *Ruth B* slow astern until Louie called, "Dug in Cap," when we stopped. The only light showing was the red flasher to the southeast, a good mile away at the village of Port Renfrew.

Almost immediately a vague shadow showed to starboard, and the *Zip* moored alongside with a squeak of tire fenders. The hammering and rasping sounds I then heard were hatch covers coming off on both boats, and finally Charlie called me.

"You stand inside the hold, on the oil drum. When I pass cases to you, lower them down to your feet, and hold on until Jasper pulls them away."

The hold was lit for Louie and Jasper. If you could call a single small bulb forward lighting. Anyway, I could see, and slid down onto the upended oil drum, my waist level with the hatch combing, my body blocking the small part of the hatch that was open, except for a couple of spare feet behind.

Somebody said, "Okay, let's get going," and then Charlie pushed an oblong sack against me, a solid sack about sixteen by twelve by eight inches, burlap covered over what felt like stiff cardboard packing. I slid my hands up the smooth burlap, and found a large burlap ear on top at each corner, making the sacks easy to lower down to Jasper.

After a time I heard a voice on *Zip* say, "Harry, we have to speed this up. Can we give you a hand to stow?" Cap agreed, and another man slid down into our hold, and things went faster—nobody complained anyway. We transferred eleven hundred cases in four hours, at a fair guess. Two bells struck just before the last case came over, one o'clock Christmas morning.

Zip's crewman crawled back aboard, and threw off our lines so fast we were startled by the sudden blast of diesel exhaust. As *Zip* backed away and turned out towards the whistle buoy, a big rumble came back to us, and then another as she fired up her two Liberty gas engines.

"The boys sure are in a hurry to see Santa's rosy cheeks," Charlie muttered to no one in particular.

"I don't think Santa's cheeks are the ones they have in mind," Cap said. "More likely the assorted cheeks at Celestine's place will get more attention than Santa Claus."

Jasper disappeared into the galley and soon called Louie and me for a quick mug-up, then Harry and Charlie, while Louie closed the hatch and battened down. I just watched, if one can watch a totally unfamiliar job in near total darkness.

When Cap and Charlie came on deck again, we hoisted an-

Transferring Johnny Walker in boxes from *Marechal Foch* to *Malahat,* 1933.
Boxes were removed before sacked cases were loaded on distributor boats
Ruth B, Ryuo II, Ragna, etc.

chor, a chore involving Charlie at the winch with Louie and Cap handling the two-inch line. Anchor and cable all ended up behind the hatch.

"Just tie the whole bundle to the bulwarks," Cap told Louie. "We'll tidy up later. Charlie and I are turning in after we pass the whistle buoy. Run out south-west for an hour to get offshore, then west by south for the lightship."

Away we went, rumbling along at *Ruth B's* hottest pace, almost eight knots. Cap and Charlie came on watch at six before we sighted Swiftsure. Louie and I turned in and slept until Jasper called us for lunch at eleven thirty. The *Ruth B* was stopped, rolling in the never-ending swells, and we heard again the moaning wind.

"There's a message for you to send to Vancouver on top of the radio set," Cap said when he came below to eat. I got it away via *Lillehorn*, and so, at noon, December twenty-fifth, 1931, we advised all interested parties that the *Ruth B* was ready for business, with eleven hundred cases of something that was probably not lemonade.

17

CAP AND CHARLIE CAME INTO THE CABIN JUST AFTER THAT and climbed into their bunks, the only spot on the *Ruth B* where you could relax. We all had high bunk boards that kept us in place in even the worst rolling.

In your bunk you were also warm. The *Ruth B* had no heat, except close to the galley stove, so we existed at outside air temperature, somewhere between freezing and forty degrees in the winter. Louie and I and Jasper didn't even have bunk lights to read by.

"Damn, damn, damn," Cap said, suddenly sitting up in his bunk. "I was going to take *Zip's* receiver in trade for our bad one but clean forgot last night. So your receiver has to keep going, Sparky, we can't run inside now."

Well that was good news, in a way, as I couldn't be replaced by their regular operator Slim, not for a while anyway. The bad news was spare parts.

"The receiver is okay," I said. "Except I don't have any spare tubes."

"Not to worry, we can get tubes sent out. Give me the numbers for our seven o'clock schedule tonight. And say, now that you are going to live and be with us for this trip, you better tell me your name so I can put you on the crew list in place of Slim. I'm Harry Slattery—Charlie is Charlie Smith, and Louie, Louie Seabaun."

All high type fellas, those. Harry Slattery was a real old time rum runner, aged twenty-eight, at sea on various rum ships since he was twenty-one. I didn't know that then, or learn anything else about him while I was with him. Rum runners, I found, just didn't talk about themselves, their business, their previous ships, or anyone else either.

Charlie was about fifty, short, a bit stout, going bald in front, not an especially cheery type, a resigned guy. A seafaring life at his age couldn't be good. Louie and Jasper were in their late twenties too, I guess, a mark I was still short of.

Jasper served up quite a respectable Christmas dinner at six, ham and assorted goodies, but no liquor. Our table only sat two, so it was not quite a party, but real good anyway, especially compared to the next two or three days. The wind picked up early on December twenty-sixth and we had immense rollers by suppertime.

The *Ruth B* rode not badly, port side to windward, except for the occasional quick flip-flop as a sharp crested sea lifted and dropped her. By dark, the sea was almost covered in foam, long streaks running to leeward, as the sea crest broke, rolling an avalanche of white water down the wave face.

After dinner, while Jasper cleaned up, we were in the small cabin, Cap in his bunk, Charlie and I sitting on the deck playing crib, and Louie in the wheelhouse.

"Jeez, listen to that," Cap said all of a sudden, and Charlie stopped his hand in mid-air. A great roaring sound drowned out the wind, like we were fast moving towards a great waterfall. Before anyone said anything, solid water hit the *Ruth B*, knocking the ship flat on her starboard side. Cold water poured down the cabin roof ventilators and squirted in around the wheelhouse door. I slid over on top of Charlie as water washed our cards and crib board into the corner.

"Haaah," Cap said, letting out a long sigh. "One of those could hurt something. We'll run into the wind until the seas ease off. Start her up, Charlie, and run slow."

We ran slow ahead into the wind and the increasing sea all night and it was bad. My bunk and Louie's were right forward in the bow, about three feet from the stem post and two feet below the deck. Even at slow ahead, the *Ruth B* did a fearful dive down the back of each sea, and tons of water fell on deck right above us. The bow dropped so fast we lifted clear of our mattresses, and we pounded down hard when the dive stopped.

It was impossible to sleep, not that the pounding bothered me, but lying there, awake, nerves tensed for the next plunge, there was no way I could relax. The gale lasted two and a half days more. The galley fire went out, and we ate tinned stuff and biscuits, what little we wanted.

The ocean was a heaving waste of foam and flying spray, the half mile we could see to the horizon. I timed the waves. At the worst, near the end, seven huge rollers passed under us a minute, over four hundred an hour, more than ten thousand a day, endlessly riding up the front of a white wall of water, and diving down the back. The novelty of this wears off pretty fast.

After about the three-thousandth plunge, I had decided that somehow, sometime, as soon as I could make it, I would abandon my new seafaring career for something else. This was the only time I ever felt really affected by conditions while I was at sea. It was a combination of miseries: the long night—Louie and I only saw daylight four hours a day; the completely shut in feeling below decks, especially in the coffin-like confines of my bunk; and the damp cold when the galley fire was out. And it all went on for so long, seemingly forever, when so little time was passed in sleep.

I wouldn't admit to being scared, maybe I wasn't, but I will admit to a state of high apprehension, the last half day or so.

None of the others looked like they were enjoying the ride either; even Cap had bags under his eyes, and a pale spot in the centre of each normally rosy cheek.

The wind went down as quickly as it had risen, and we hove to as soon the seas stopped breaking, and were back to regular rolling again, up and over the now rounded crests, a motion that had previously seemed quite uncomfortable, until we encountered absolute discomfort.

The next morning, on the nine o'clock radio schedule, we received a message from Vancouver via the *Lillehorn*.

"Business at last," Cap said when he decoded it. "We have a release. We'll run up toward position this morning and hope for a noon sight. Fire up, Charlie."

Cap didn't get a noon sight, and we did a lighthouse hunt after dark that night, and evidently got close enough to position the next day that around three Louie picked up a speedboat as it crested on the big swells. It soon stopped alongside, fifty feet to leeward, a low fast boat painted the usual dark grey. I couldn't see any name on the bow and never got a good look at the stern.

"I can't come alongside in this, Cap," a figure hollered out of the speedboat wheelhouse door. "Want to try your dory?"

"The dory's no good either," Cap shouted back. "We'll run into San Juan. About ten o'clock, away in close under Pandora Peak." A misty rain had set in, not too much wind, but big rollers still, as we ran down to Swiftsure lightship and were in San Juan and anchored a bit after ten. It was quieter than our previous trip in, but there was still enough wind in the trees overhead on the ridge and wave wash on the beach, that we could work without worrying about noise. After waiting for about half an hour, we heard a low engine rumble approaching from the Port Renfrew direction. There were a few uneasy moments until a black shape pulled alongside and stopped.

"What did you do, Smitty, run over to Port Renfrew for a quick beer?" Charlie asked.

"No, just took a look around checking for trouble," a voice

said in the darkness. "My order says two hundred cases, you check?"

"That checks," Cap said, and he and the voice went into the *Ruth B*'s wheelhouse for a minute.

Louie already had the hatch open when they came aft, and we worked the same as before, Louie and Jasper in the hold, me standing half out of the hatch and Charlie and Cap out towards the rail. This time I lifted out, and in no time at all Cap said, "Okay, that's it," and Smitty pulled away into the darkness.

We battened down, lashed the anchor, and were away ourselves half an hour later, and were out past the lightship before Louie and I turned in around six-thirty. When I was called at eleven-thirty for lunch and radio, we were drifting again, in very large swells, but only a little wind.

Two or three days later, we received another release and this one said "Proceed to position San Juan." We ran in again, the same route, and loaded Smitty with another two hundred cases or so. A third trip in to San Juan left us with only four hundred-odd cases left.

"Sure nothing to this rum running business," I thought. "Get a release by radio, meet and load a speedboat and run back out to sea. Like shooting fish down a well."

Our fourth release came along four or five days later, just about time for our speedboat man Smitty to complete his delivery and rest up for a couple of days. It was a noon radio schedule release, also for San Juan, so we didn't start up right away. After an hour or so Louie poked his head down the scuttle and said, "Hey fellas, we got company."

A great white ship was almost alongside, just running past very slowly. She looked at least two hundred feet, and her deck was above our mast-head. It was *Chelan*, a big U.S. Coast Guard ship. Cap and Charlie were looking out the starboard wheelhouse door when I came on deck.

"Well now, Captain Slattery, sir," Charlie said, "what are you going to do about that? Tell him to go away, so we can meet Smitty in San Juan tonight?"

Cap thought for a minute or so.

"No problem, Charlie, no problem at all. We can bluff him into thinking we are empty, by running in towards shore; we usually run offshore when we are loaded and a cutter shows up. Louie, start up and run in slow on a course for Pachena Lighthouse, and let's see what the cutter does."

Sure enough, after we had run in slowly towards Vancouver Island for a couple of hours, the *Chelan* turned away, picked up speed, and disappeared towards Neah Bay in Washington directly across the Strait of Juan de Fuca from Port San Juan.

"See, just like I said. He fell for our bluff. Okay Louie, change course to pick up the Carmanah light. We'll pick up Carmanah, then run in close to the beach to the whistle buoy—in case that guy looks around before heading home."

We picked up Carmanah after supper, and were anchored in San Juan again before ten, in quite clear weather, though the only lights showing were the San Juan whistle buoy and the Port Renfrew flasher.

The afterdeck of the *Ruth B* was a silent place for maybe an hour, as we all sat out on the hatch, stared into the darkness, and

US Coast Guard cutter *Haida,* the large size, similar to *Chelan.*

listened for Smitty.

"He's late—I wonder if he had engine trouble," Cap muttered, more or less to himself.

"Maybe he had to bluff somebody too," Charlie said, but Cap didn't seem to hear.

And then, all at once, we weren't staring into darkness, but at two searchlights that flared up away out in the Strait. As an attention getter, two searchlights on a dark night, suddenly appearing in the middle of illegal activity, are hard to beat, even if they were miles away.

"Look at those two bluffers," Charlie said. "Who do they think they're fooling?"

"No worry at all," Cap said. "American cutters away over in American waters can't bluff me out of here. We'll give Smitty until midnight, then we'll have to blow, or we won't have enough night left to clear the coast by daylight."

He had hardly stopped talking when a bright green light, with a white light above it, came into sight past San Juan Point,

The *Principio,* later called *Tooya,* was at sea from 1924 to 1927, and again from 1931 to 1933.

moved rapidly across towards Owen Point and disappeared to the west. "Another bluffer and a much closer bluffer, like fleas on a dog," Charlie said. "Now what, Captain Slattery, sir?"

"Now what is right. That seagoing hot-rodder was doing twenty knots, and he's not fishing. If he suddenly smartens up, and looks in here, there are a few hundred things in the hold we couldn't explain. We move out fast. Anchors aweigh, and no fooling."

When Louie and I and Cap got the anchor aboard, Cap went into the wheelhouse and started away slow, towards the southeast side of San Juan, as far away from where our speedy friend might be expected if he turned back from the west and looked around inside.

The two searchlights were still sweeping back and forth, away over near Neah Bay, but not moving fast. As we approached the San Juan whistle buoy from the east we relaxed. After we had battened down and secured the anchor Louie and I grabbed a quick mug-up below, then came up to relieve Cap and Charlie. We were nearly clear of San Juan and home free, running along the southwest coast of Vancouver Island close in against the black hills.

We then rounded Owen Point and saw ahead of us, several miles towards Carmanah, not one, but two sets of red, green and white ships' lights, maybe two miles offshore.

"Heh, heh, bluffer boy," Charlie said. "For a minute there I thought I saw two ships' lights. A mirage surely, only one ship went west."

"I wonder where the hell he came from," Cap muttered to himself. "No problem really, as long as they don't use search-lights. We stay close to the beach, especially past Carmanah. The light is a hundred and seventy-five feet above sea level, away over our heads and they'll never see us looking against the light. Sparky, you watch astern."

The *Ruth B* ran along about six knots, three-quarter speed, with probably the most alert lookout she ever maintained. The two Canadian cutters moved slowly offshore towards the international boundary.

Nearly two hours later we passed close under Carmanah, feeling rather nervous in so much light, but with no risk that anyone looking shoreward would see anything through the blinding lighthouse beam. By then the cutters were on our port quarter, sliding astern.

"See, no problem at all," Cap said, though we were still about as far inside the twelve-mile-limit as we could get. The Neah Bay cutters were not in sight, as their searchlights had flared out about an hour after we left San Juan.

Half an hour later, Cap put the wheel over, and the *Ruth B* swung nearly ninety degrees to port, bringing the Canadian cutters on her port beam, a long way to the southeast. "Louie, you run off southwest for the rest of the watch. Charlie and I are turning in—see you all for breakfast."

18

CAP LET ME SLEEP THROUGH TO NOON, AND HAD A SHORT message for Vancouver.

"I am on position Cape Beale."

"They've heard already we didn't meet Smitty last night, and they don't need to know the rest."

We rolled gently—every motion of the *Ruth B* now seemed gentle compared to the antics she'd performed in the big storm —for another twenty-four hours, and received a release the following noon, which also read: "Proceed to position San Juan."

"Ah no," Cap said when he decoded. "Not that box trap so soon again. Tell him to wait, Sparky." He looked at the chart, and scribbled a message.

"Query San Juan. Suggest Sombrio River. Confirm."

I got the message away, and Vancouver came back after a few minutes with: "Sombrio confirmed tonight."

We moved off a bit later, running down to Swiftsure lightship as before, under a heavy cloud cover that was beginning to break up, as the wind dropped to a modest twenty knots from the northwest. After we left the lightship we held straight east down the international boundary, until we had the San Juan flasher to port and Neah Bay lights to starboard, each some five miles off. Shortly after, we changed course to northeast, and stopped at what must be Sombrio River.

It was a bright night. The moon had risen a couple of hours earlier, and shone through breaks in the clouds from time to time. We didn't anchor, but drifted close to shore, in a shallow bay.

"Louie, you keep an eye on the beach, see that we don't drift too close," Cap said. He didn't need to tell us to keep a sharp eye to seaward. There was so much light a really sharp eye wasn't necessary.

Smitty gave us a bad moment by coming in from the west, close in so we were silhouetted against the moon.

"Sorry about that," he said, "but I wanted a clear look at your outline before I closed up. So many cutters moving last coupla days I couldn't keep track where they are now."

We did a real fast transfer, just drifting with Smitty tied alongside, and cast him off as soon as he stored the last case.

The *Ruth B* moved out to sea, retracing her inbound course, and at noon when I sent the position report, we were drifting near Cape Beale in quite the best weather we had had since we left Vancouver.

After the radio check, Cap turned to Louie. "Only one load left. You and Sparky fix breakage this afternoon."

So I was to see at last what we had been carrying. During transfers to the shore boats, Louie had put to one side any case that rattled with broken glass. "Fixing breakage" was simply cutting open the case that rattled and replacing the broken bottle or bottles with a full one, an easy chore since all the bottles were completely wrapped in cardboard. After we opened the hatch completely, we let it air out for a time—the atmosphere below was noticeably alcoholic—before we lowered ourselves into the hold. We had to walk on the cases during earlier transfers, when the hold was nearly full, which no doubt caused some damage.

The cases were clean, brand-new burlap. Some had a picture

of a Kentucky colonel on them and the words "Kentucky Colonel, Rye Whiskey" while others had a picture of a raccoon and the words "Coon Hollow, Bourbon Whiskey." That was all; nobody claimed to have distilled the stuff, and no country claimed the unknown distillers. Canada got all the credit without advertising. Each case contained twenty-four small flat bottles. I don't remember seeing any of these bottles with a label. Later, when we loaded European whiskey, cases were all twelve bottles with original labels—Johnny Walker, Teacher's Highland Cream, Haig's, as well as French champagne and other expensive goodies, destined for the quality trade.

Our breakage wasn't bad, and we closed up and battened down well before dark. The next morning we got our release, went in to Sombrio and transferred to Smitty for the last time, and, even though we were all clean and legal, were back outside the twelve-mile limit by daylight.

Legal except for the radio that is—none of the smaller boats were allowed a licence for short wave wireless. The bigger ships—*Lillehorn*, *Malahat*, *Mogul* and others—were probably licensed for standard shipboard wireless telegraph sets, but at a guess I would say highly doubtful for forty metres. And I never asked Al Magee on the *Lillehorn*. By then I had found out that while I sometimes asked questions of other rum runners, I seldom got a relevant answer. Most times, no answer at all.

At noon the next day we received a short signal.

"Proceed to position Vancouver."

"Well, surprise, surprise," Cap said when he had finished decoding. "We were supposed to go south next. Most likely they want us to load oil. We'll run in easy to William Head, as those quarantine birds won't clear us until eight in the morning."

Right after clearing quarantine Louie and I turned in, and the *Ruth B* was running quietly somewhere in the Gulf Islands when Jasper called us for lunch. We docked at Menchion's Shipyard in Coal Harbour in Vancouver well after dark.

"All ashore what's going ashore," Cap said. "The shipyard watchman will be enough for tonight. Show up by ten in the morning and we'll run up to the office."

Where, presumably, we would be paid. And, I wondered, would I be replaced by the unknown Slim that the *Ruth B* couldn't find when we sailed in December. While life on the *Ruth B* wasn't a joy, there was money to be earned by staying, and money was the key to getting into something better later, like going back to school.

I caught an eastbound streetcar on Georgia Street and was home in short order, suitcase in hand.

"Well, I was wondering when I was going to see you," Mom said when I came in. "How was the boat?"

"Fine, just fine, a sailor's life is the life for me," I said with the mental addition, "until I can get the hell out of it."

"What were you doing?"

"Just running along the coast. I'm second engineer. Good food, and some real high type fellas to work with."

"You need a bath. You tell the captain you should have a bath every week."

I was about to tell Mom that the *Ruth B*'s life-style didn't run to baths, but then hesitated. Baths were a minor matter, but the less anyone knew about our other activities the better, and I followed instinctively the rum runner's motto: "Don't never tell nobody nothing, nohow."

This creed allowed the business to flourish in obscurity at the time, but left an impossible job for later historians trying to research Pacific Coast rum running, especially as the active participants didn't write anything either.

The next morning—the twenty-sixth of January, 1932—we left the *Ruth B* at ten when Cap showed up, and took a taxi to the office on Homer Street.

"We're not paying off," Cap said in the taxi. "We load oil day after tomorrow. The shipyard will replace the guard plank tomorrow. Show up at eight the day after. We'll leave that night."

The *Ruth B* had pounded a section of guard plank loose just at the bow in the horrendous three day storm. Not serious, as the guard plank just protected the hull planks from the continuous wear of our tire fenders, and the occasional smash when we were alongside another boat. A two-by-ten-inch plank, well fastened, takes real force to remove.

At the Homer Street office I met a Captain George Ford and Captain Charles Hudson, and also learned that I was working for the Atlantic and Pacific Navigation Company, and that I was being paid a quite satisfying hundred and twenty-five dollars a month. Then a thin, sort of bookish chap who looked like he thought well of himself, came up to me.

"I'm Jimmy," he said as we shook hands. "Captain Slattery wants me to look at the *Ruth B's* receiver, to see whether we need a new one."

We drove back to the *Ruth B*, and Jimmy looked at the *Ruth B's* dead set, simply said, "Junk," and then looked at mine.

"You taking this out with you again?"

"Sure, it works fine and I've got spare tubes."

"Good, we won't need to buy a new receiver," Jimmy said.

Cap laughed when I told him about it later. "Our Jimmy's not a big spender," was all he said. Cap told me later he was the Vancouver short wave operator, but whether for all of the west coast mother ships, or only the *Lillehorn*, he didn't say, and probably didn't know.

I spent some of my new wealth on more clothes—even if I couldn't wash, clean clothes would feel good—and a whole day's pay on a book on vacuum tubes written by a guy named Van der Bijl. The store clerk said the book was "sufficiently elementary" and the first few chapters "very elementary" which fooled me into buying it, but unfortunately what was elementary to Van der Bijl was Greek to me. Cap was impressed when I showed it to him, but it was far beyond my high school drop-out level.

The *Ruth B* had a new mate when we came aboard at eight the day we were to sail. Jack Harwood, a dark-eyed man of about my build, good looking, high type fella, with grey hairs in his crew cut, and a ready laugh. Louie had been a bit on the moody side. I never knew why Jack took his place. After introductions, Cap said, "Jack, you and Sparky and Jasper load stores when the truck shows up, then run over to the Imperial Oil dock in North Vancouver and load diesel oil. They have a crane, so all you do is stow. We'll leave about eight tonight. If anything goes wrong, don't call me. I'm going back to Celestine's."

The supply truck had only a small load for us, mostly fresh meat, eggs, fruit and vegetables, and we were at the oil dock shortly after ten. Loading diesel oil in drums took all three of us in the hold. The big drums were heavy, and the metal ends hard on the hands. At noon we ate at a cafe near the dock and by three we had battened down, and crowded four more drums alongside those already lashed to the bulwarks. Back at Menchion's, Jack said, "Shore leave until eight, since I seem to command."

I went home for supper, and another bath.

At eight we sailed in clear cold darkness, but only to Bowen Island, for a good night's sleep before we again faced the *Ruth B*'s version of the perils of the deep.

Once out of the Strait past Cape Flattery, we turned south-southwest, at first in cold clear air and gradually, into cool clear air, with a following north-west wind of twenty knots or so, hardly a stiff breeze. Every day at noon we stopped for the radio check and a noon sight. About a week out, we received a message.

"Proceed to position Guadalupe."

Guadalupe is an uninhabited Mexican island some two hundred miles south southwest of Ensenada, Mexico, and a hundred and fifty miles from the Mexican mainland.

"Well, okay," Cap said. "Ours not to know why, but if we have to lay over a spell, much more agreeable than the Row." The "Row" was the name given to the California coast, where much of the rum running activity was centred.

So, ten days out from Vancouver, in a complete calm, we sighted a high bare rock dead ahead, and were cruising the east coast of the thirty-mile-long island of Guadalupe by mid-afternoon. It was bare, rugged, composed of red and yellow rock, and had no vegetation at all.

"A dead volcano, I think," Cap said as we ran under the high cliffs. "Guess how high, Sparky."

I looked and said, "Four thousand feet."

"Quite close, for what you can see. But the ocean is twelve thousand feet deep here—you are looking at the top of a sixteen-thousand-foot mountain."

Just before dark we rounded the south end of the island and entered a wide round bay, three quarters closed in by black vertical cliffs, with a noisy, echoing surf rolling up on a narrow sand beach. A boat that looked like a subchaser was anchored well inside.

"*Ragna*," Cap said looking through his binoculars. "We'll run by and say hello and see what they know."

"Been here a week," *Ragna* answered Cap's hail. "Orders to leave for the *Lillehorn* tomorrow."

"Maybe good news," Charlie said. "Maybe a week in the sun for us too."

We anchored clear of *Ragna*, in about fifty feet of nearly transparent water, rolling gently in the ground swell. The overhanging cliffs echoed and re-echoed the surf until it became a continuous sound, like the roar from a sea shell held to your ear, amplified a thousand times.

After dark there were stars like you wouldn't believe, millions of them, that you can see only in the absolute darkness far from city lights. Around the ship, shoals of small sardines gathered in the glare of our deck lights, until we switched them out to let the stars shine clear and bright. In Vancouver, during the winter rainy season, if you can see one hazy star a week, you're lucky.

My birthday must have passed on our way south, so I was now a full twenty years old. After the midnight radio schedule—I could work Vancouver direct—I then stood watch to three, and Jack took three to six, letting me sleep through to a late breakfast and the nine o'clock radio schedule. We heard odd roaring noises from time to time, apparently coming from some great sea animals on the beach.

"Okay, give me a hand to launch the dory," Cap said after breakfast. "Jack and I are going ashore for a look at the sea elephants."

They looked, rather briefly, then swamped in the surf coming off the beach. Charlie and I watched through Cap's glasses.

"Two live bodies walking the beach so nobody hurt," Charlie said, but it took them most of the morning to clear the dory, and move it south where there was less surf, before they tried again. This time they washed back, but didn't swamp and on the third try they came through easily.

During the intervals between dory watching, I pumped diesel oil into our tanks from the drums on deck, with hand pump—slow going but not hard work. After lunch we sunbathed, soaped up in a half bucket of fresh water, and rinsed off with buckets of warm sea water. Charlie and I rowed the dory in close to the surf, and looked at the sea elephants through glasses, but didn't fancy our chances getting the eighteen-foot dory through the surf, either way. The sea elephants disappointed us, not one raised its head so we could see the big hooked snout.

The *Ruth B* was returned to reality six days later by a message on the PM radio schedule.

"Proceed to position *Lillehorn*."

Heading north by northeast, we left Guadalupe at daylight the following morning.

Ragna off the Island of Guadalupe, Mexico. 94.5 feet long, one 200-hp diesel and two 450-hp Liberty gas engines. Top speed 18 knots, hold capacity 1800 cases.

19

A T DAWN THE NEXT MORNING THE *RUTH B* WAS RUNNING
in a smooth sea under a low layer of thin misty cloud, and
soon picked up the *Lillehorn*. We tied alongside about seven. Cap
climbed the rope ladder up the bigger ship's side, while Jack and
I knocked out the batten wedges and opened the hatch. Cap
called down to us from the *Lillehorn*'s bridge.

"We'll start unloading oil at eight."

The *Lillehorn* was anchored five or six miles off the Mexican
coast, thirty-five miles down from Ensenada, off Punta San
Isidro. About five miles further down, a small two-masted
schooner, a big five-masted schooner and a large freighter were
anchored in a group.

"The big five-master is the *Malahat*, and the other ship is
the *Mogul*," Jack said as we cleared the lashing from the oil
drums along either bulwark. The *Lillehorn* was riding high in the
water, so high that a few feet of keel at the bow just touched the
top of each small wave. The ship's bridge, living quarters, and
engine were all right aft. She was one half of Rum Row as it was
in 1932. The *Malahat* was the other, better known half.

Promptly at eight—the *Lillehorn*'s deck crew worked a
straight eight-to-five day—there was a rattle of winches above us,
and a cargo boom swung out directly overhead, lowering a section of chain. A second line led from the chain to another boom
amidships over the *Lillehorn*'s after hold. The chain had two steel
clamps sliding on it. Jack and I heaved an oil drum on its side
and Jack grabbed the slack chain with the clamps, shaped like
very flat "C" clamps.

"Now watch this," Jack said. "You slide the clamps apart,
hold one under each end of the barrel, pull the chain tight and
hold the clamp until the barrel lifts clear. And keep your fingers
clear of this bloody chain, just hold it with your knuckles. All
set?"

Jack signalled a man at the *Lillehorn*'s rail, who waved to the unseen winch man. The line tightened the clamps with a heavy *thunk* and the barrel jerked straight up, fast. Jack jumped back a few feet, and I did the same, so if something went wrong and the barrel dropped, we were clear. After the deckload was lifted off, we opened the hatch, and unloading went on, rather slowly, like we were all doing a job we liked, but with nothing to do after we finished.

And we didn't. Cap came back aboard around three, after we had tidied up and put the hatch covers loosely in place.

"We hang on astern tonight, and load in the morning," he told us.

We tied astern of another fish packer, the *Ryuo II*, which was tied astern of another boat, all tailing out astern of the *Lille-horn* like little ducks, kept mostly in line by a current flowing steadily down the coast. There were no signs of life on the other boats after we tied on. Someone must have taken our line, but I was below in the engine room, and didn't even see the boat names.

No visiting aboard other ships was allowed. A funeral home would have been livelier, it would have at least had music. After supper Charlie and I had a couple of games of crib, but Jack and

Malahat, a five masted schooner, built in Victoria, B.C.

I turned in before nine, as we had been going since midnight the previous night.

By eight the next morning we were back alongside the *Lillehorn*, hatch open, a landing cushion rigged in the bottom of the hold with a few tires, with the canvas hatch cover spread on top. The *Ruth B* was rising and falling maybe two feet in the small running sea, so nothing could be set down gently on deck or in the hold. Shortly after eight, the first sling load, maybe forty cases, came down, with Cap and Charlie holding the load clear of the hatch combings. This was all different from our Cape Beale load, cases of twelve bigger bottles, well-known brands of Scotch mostly, and some gin and champagne and liqueurs.

Five sling loads which we—Jack, Jasper and I—stowed against the forward bulkhead, when Cap said, "Okay, no more here. We take the rest from the *Valencia*."

The *Valencia* was the two-masted schooner anchored close to the *Malahat* and *Mogul*. We tied on her port side, so that a

Lillehorn docked at B.C. Marine Ways October, 1930.

landing stage slung over her rail was even with our hatch, and started loading after lunch, a thousand cases of Old Colonel and Coon Hollow, in about equal quantities, one case at a time, hand to hand, Cap at the rail, Charlie at the hatch and Jack, Jasper and I in the hold.

We were loaded about five, and the supercargo, the only man aboard the *Valencia* who spoke English, invited us aboard to the captain's cabin for a drink. The captain was a young Frenchman—the *Valencia* was up from Tahiti—as was the mate. There were introductions, but no conversation. In lieu of talk the supercargo brought around drinks in large mugs, and circulated frequently topping them up, with special attention to his own. I had looked in vain for a convenient means of dumping mine, as a mug of whiskey before supper, or any other time, was away above my capacity of a small teaspoonful.

But it was wine, quite pleasant wine, not whiskey, so dumping wasn't required. After smiling at each other happily for half an hour or so, and listening to a young native crewman play the guitar and sing, Cap excused the *Ruth B's* crew so we could sail by dark. For a farewell party it was rather a good one—no conversational chores, agreeable music and a most pleasant refreshment. The rum runners could learn something from the *Valencia*.

As we passed the *Lillehorn* going north after dark, Cap tooted our whistle, but the mother ship showed no more life than a tomb. The *Ruth B* took nearly ten days to reach the Cape Beale position, as we were slowed down for a couple of days off San Francisco by a stiff northwester, for us a direct headwind and sea.

Once on position, we got a release the second day and Smitty showed up before noon the next day. The weather was fairly good, by Cape Beale standards, but it was still too rough for the thin-hulled speedboat to load alongside. The wind waves and the swell waves seldom coincided unless the wind picked up enough to overcome the swell, by which time it was too rough to transfer, by dory anyway.

Launching our eighteen-foot dory was easy. Unlash, slide it onto the stern-roller, wait for a smooth spot, a quick heave and she was in the water. Transferring by dory was slower than transferring alongside and was more work, but far easier than the long overnight run into San Juan and out again.

"Okay Sparky, you come with me in the dory," Cap said the first time Smitty's boat showed up. I never did know her name, if she had one.

Cap and I stood in the dory, tied alongside the *Ruth B*, while Jack and Charlie passed some forty cases previously stacked on deck down to us, one at each end. Cap rowed quickly down wind to Smitty's boat, tailing down to leeward of the *Ruth B* on a couple of hundred feet of line. We unloaded just as fast to Smitty and his helper, who stowed the cases below while I rowed back to the *Ruth B*, standing up, facing forward fisherman style, pushing on the big oars, knees braced against the center thwart. Hard work only for a few minutes, as the *Ruth B* was drifting downwind rather faster than I was moving.

Two hundred cases, five quick trips with the dory, and Smitty was away, heading east for the Strait at slow speed, waiting for darkness before running into Canadian waters. His boat was still in sight after we had battened down and rigged the dory for hoisting aboard.

The winch line ran up the boom, braced up over the dory chocks, to a long sling fastened to either end of the dory. From the bow and stern, sway lines led straight aboard through ring bolts in the deck and forward to towing bitts behind the winch. Cap and Jack had a sway line each, with a turn around a post on the bitts. In a trough, Charlie lifted the dory a foot or so clear of the water, Cap and Jack hauling in slack and tying off. Charlie then inched the dory up the *Ruth B*'s side when the hull was more or less upright, until the keel slid over the bulwarks, and the flat-bottomed dory was sitting one side on the chocks and one on the rail.

Cap and Jack tied the sway lines, and the four of us slid the dory's stern, then bow, into the chocks and lashed down. No trouble, as long as the sway lines had no slack while the dory was suspended alongside. And we returned to "normal" until the next transfer. Normal, on a rum runner offshore, was about as close to zero activity as a human being can get, mostly eating and sleeping.

A day's routine started with the twelve o'clock radio schedule, and the noon sight for latitude. If Cap got a sun sight, he gave Jack a time and distance to position fifteen miles south-southwest of Cape Beale. If Cap didn't get a sight, it was the same, except the time and distance to run were dead reckoning, not at all accurate off the Strait of San Juan, as wind drift combined with currents that changed direction and strength with every change in tidal flow, and they normally changed four times a day.

Every other day, on those days with no sights, a good number of them, we ran in after dark until we picked up the Cape Beale light, and ran up to position. The Cape Beale light is high, and has an official range of nineteen miles, only of academic interest when weather visibility was four or five miles. Off Cape Beale in winter it was often much less.

Then, if Smitty showed up, we transferred, the big event of the *Ruth B*'s day when it occurred. After the noon sight Cap and Jack turned in, and often Jasper too for a couple of hours. With two or three people sleeping at any time of the day or night, the two on watch were limited to quiet activities, which most of the time were watching goonies or watching waves or watching. That is, in daylight. At night, hove to almost all the time, the watch stood in darkness in the wheel house, on lookout for other ships' lights. In fair to good weather, we split the six-hour watches, only one man on at a time. These night watches gave you plenty of time to think, if you were so inclined.

After a supper and the seven o'clock radio schedule, Charlie and I would usually have a short cribbage game, sitting on the tiny cabin floor, with Cap in his bunk and Jack standing in the wheelhouse door watching. Charlie was really fond of crib, and got quite upset when he lost. Cribbage or any other card game meant nothing to me, so I let Charlie win most of the time.

Jack and I turned in around eight, and I was called at eleven-thirty for the midnight radio schedule and the graveyard watch. If we were splitting the watch I stayed on until three in the morning, then called Jack.

I was called again at six for breakfast, then turned in, called at eleven-thirty for lunch, and the beginning of another fascinating day on a rum runner.

There was only one potentially exciting event per day—if your bowels moved regularly—and that was the daily visit to the *Ruth B's* head. The head was a tiny cubicle on the port side, opening only on deck. On calm days, you did your business and dumped a bucket of sea water down to flush, no problem at all. On windy days, after the wind waves had built up to six or eight feet, there could be trouble.

The head discharged through a vertical pipe to an outlet through the hull just below the water-line. The ship always hove to port side to windward and the wind waves struck the port side with force enough to reverse the flow, giving any one seated an upside-down shower, almost fully dressed, in forty degree North Pacific sea water. Water on the head floor meant there had been reverse flows, so you judged the seas, waited for a series of smaller waves—if you had a choice—and went in fast and out fast. This was the exciting event of most days in the right—or wrong—weather.

I think this was the trip the transmitter aerial came off the mast-head sometime during the night. I couldn't get any antenna current on one morning's radio schedule, and found the aerial trailing off the wheelhouse roof into the water. The quarter wave forty-metre aerial was thirty-three feet long, putting the mast-head over forty feet above the *Ruth B's* water-line, flopping from port to starboard with every roll, far beyond the ship's side.

"Can you get it back up?" Cap asked, looking up at the weaving mast, as though to ask did I have the guts to climb that crazy upside-down pendulum.

"Sure, no sweat," I said, accepting the challenge—if that was what Cap meant. "But I need someone on the wheelhouse to pay out wire as I pull up."

"Good enough," Cap said, "I'll do that—unless Charlie wants to volunteer."

"No way," Charlie said, patting his rather generous stomach. "I'm not the acrobatic type."

Cap found a short piece of half inch line for a safety belt, and a heaving line for hauling the aerial up. From *Sea Stories*, I knew that in a gale or strong wind, a sailor climbed the ratlines on the windward side. In sailing ships, the sails held the ship heeled to leeward—the *Ruth B* made it more exciting by rolling as far one way as the other. The wind pressure helped me to hold on, but even so, it was a bit hairy hanging out over the water on the rolls to windward, when my feet had a perverse tendency to swing away from the ratlines on their own.

I climbed fast on the leeward roll, and once tied on to the mast-head, had two hands free to work during the downwind roll, and it was a short job to haul the aerial up and secure it.

We got rather a lot of sleep, in bits and pieces. Our only contact with the outside world was Smitty, and he never talked. It was as though five unambitious men, of quite amiable disposition, had taken vows of celibacy and near silence and renounced the world to punish the flesh by living in fair discomfort on a small ship at sea out of sight of land. If we had taken vows of poverty as well, we could have stayed ashore in a comfortable

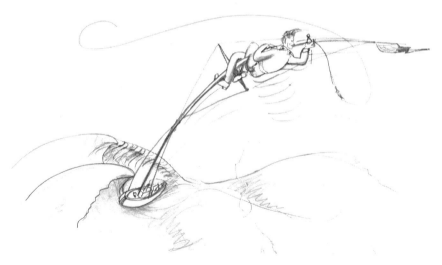

Repairing the aerial, sketch by Gallistel.

cave somewhere, and slept on beds of nails like the Indian fakirs, to punish the flesh anytime we felt the urge. On the *Ruth B* there was no choice.

Since most of us had already had enough of poverty without the necessity for vows, a voluntary return had no appeal.

The shore system for receiving Smitty's loads seemed to be a smooth operation, from our viewpoint anyway, with Smitty showing up every three or four days for another load. Transferring our remaining thousand cases took us to March sixteenth and we were back in Vancouver on the eighteenth, total deliveries to date, twenty-three hundred cases, since December seventeenth.

"The *Ruth B* isn't paying off," Cap said when we received our cheques in the Atlantic and Pacific Navigation Company office on Homer Street. "Show up at eight, day after tomorrow, to load oil."

For three months' easy work I had been paid three hundred and seventy-five dollars, risking life, limb and liberty on the high

Nick Gjengsto in the *Ruth B*'s dory off Cape Beale, 1932.

seas, and enduring endless hours of tedium and discomfort, all for sixteen cents a case, which, the rumour was, sold in Seattle for two hundred dollars.

While the discomfort was real enough, the risks in rum running were, so far, very close to zero, so even sixteen cents looked good to me, especially when compared with the alternative, permanent unemployment.

20

THE *RUTH B* STAYED IN VANCOUVER ONLY LONG ENOUGH for us to get a bath or two, get clothes washed and take on stores and another load of diesel oil in drums from North Vancouver. And a new mate, Nick Gjengsto, a Norwegian. He was on the thin side, blond and good-looking, but as close-mouthed as every other rum runner, so that's all I know about him.

Cap Slattery stayed ashore to take out the *Skeezix*, and Jack Harwood took over as skipper. Our three-day stay in Vancouver and an eight-day run down the coast brought us alongside the *Lillehorn* late one afternoon near the end of March, in the usual hazy mist that seemed to hang a couple of hundred feet over our heads. There was another ship, heavily loaded, at anchor half a mile down from the *Lillehorn*, an old rusty steamer with a long thin funnel set amidships, and empty oil barrels piled everywhere.

"*Prince Albert*," Charlie said as Cap climbed aboard the *Lillehorn*, which was even higher in the water than before.

Cap came back before supper, and we tied astern of the last boat in the string behind the mother ship. Cap told us the program.

"Tomorrow we discharge oil to the *Prince Albert*, and the day after load firewater. Sorry, no holiday in Guadalupe this trip."

This trip turned around so fast on Rum Row I never noticed which other ships were further down the coast. We transferred our load of oil to the *Prince Albert* by winch like the *Lillehorn*, except the winches were steam, and leaked an impressive amount.

At eight the second morning we were alongside the *Lille-horn*, loading first thirty small kegs of malt, maybe five gallons a keg, then three hundred cases of brand whiskey, mostly Scotch, before we dropped back alongside the *Albert* for slingloads of our main stock in trade, Old Colonel Rye and Coon Hollow Bourbon.

"Nine hundred," somebody said when the hold was full. "Two hundred more for your deckload."

This was just before dark, so Jasper got supper while Nick and I battened down. The *Albert*'s deck lights gave us some illumination, a rather ghostly sort of glow filtering through rising steam. Sometime during the day, a "polecat" cutter—a seventy-five footer—had arrived, and kept circling the *Lillehorn* and *Albert* all afternoon, less than half a mile off. We piled the deckload on the hatch, covered it with tarpaulins and lashed down. When we were finished Cap called up to the *Albert*.

"Keep your winches making steam until I move away, just in case the cutter intends to follow."

We waited while the cutter moved up our port side, then turned to pass down the starboard side of the *Albert*. Cap ran the *Ruth B* a bit offshore, keeping the steamer between us and the

SS Prince Albert anchored on Rum Row, fully loaded 1932.

cutter, then headed more inshore, as the cutter came around the *Albert*'s stern, to find us gone away in the night. The cutter apparently couldn't care less about our disappearance, no searchlight blazing through the darkness, no sudden rush to windward at speed, no reaction at all. We felt let down; all that clever manoeuvering for nothing.

For about a week we ran steadily northward, in good weather, keeping regular watches six hours on and six off, nothing to do but eat, sleep and steer. We stopped for a noon sight about the end of the week, and a radio schedule. There were no messages and all Nick said was "Nearly up to 48° north latitude."

The Cape Beale position was about 48° 30' north, but we kept on steadily northward in a dead flat calm, though the swell waves moved under us in a steady procession, a smooth gentle roller coaster ride. The next day at noon Nick pointed to a dark line away on the distant eastern horizon. "North end of Vancouver Island," and the next day at a similar far-off horizon, "Queen Charlotte Islands," and a day or so after that, to a faint dark smudge to the northeast, where the grey flat sea met the grey flat sky, "Alaska."

"You are really seeing the world, Sparky," Cap said from the wheelhouse door. I couldn't care less about the world but I was quite happy to enjoy calm seas.

This far north I could work Vancouver direct, and we received a release the second day, and the third morning, around seven, Charlie sighted a fishboat heading our way. It was an Alaskan fishboat, at a guess, as the names were covered over and no flag flew at the mast-head.

"Halibut boat," Nick said, pointing at the swan-neck longline chute on the boat's stern. And it smelled strongly of fish, once it was alongside us. There were two men aboard, dressed alike in brown wool shirts and heavy brown wool pants held up by broad suspenders, regular fisherman's gear. One brown shirt jumped to the *Ruth B* and went into the cabin with Cap.

A few minutes later they came out, and Cap said "Okay, let's go; two hundred cases of firewater from the deckload, two hundred more from the hold, then two hundred special brands from

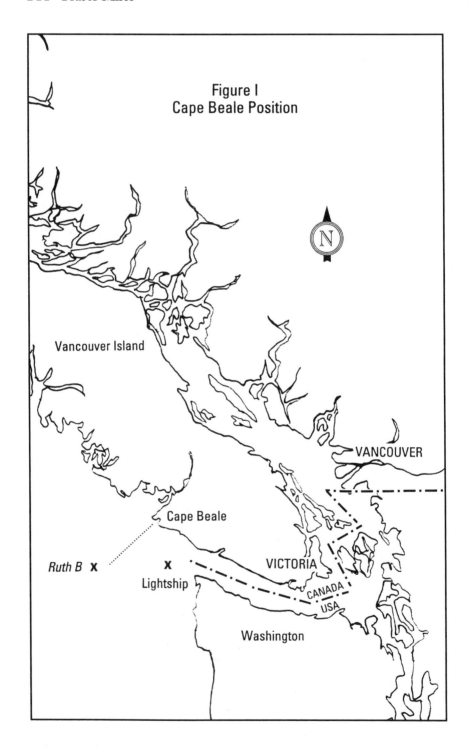

Figure I
Cape Beale Position

the quality—six hundred total."

Transferring alongside in a smooth sea is fast work. We had all six hundred cases across to the fishboat by one o'clock. The two guys on the halibut boat never said a word the whole time, not even at the end when one brought out a fine halibut from a small dory lashed on deck, and handed it to Jasper, with almost a smile.

On the seven-thirty radio schedule after supper we sent Vancouver a signal. The next morning at nine we received one.

"Proceed to position Cape Beale," Cap said. "Light the fireworks, Charlie, we shall proceed."

The lighted punks needed to start the cold Fairbanks-Morse diesel weren't exactly fireworks, though the resulting engine detonations made an impressive series of bangs in the still air.

We arrived off Cape Beale two or three days later in the same calm weather, and received a release right away. The next day, Smitty's boat arrived around three in the afternoon, and took a hundred and some cases and the thirty kegs of malt; then two days later, on another release, he took another two hundred cases.

After this rush of business we had a slump for a few days. My recollections of time elapsed are certainly general; every day was exactly the same routine, nothing changed at all. We had no newspapers and no radio except the short wave sets, and had no problems like deciding what show to see on Friday night, or what to do on the weekend. Our life-style required not the least amount of mental effort.

Cap let the *Ruth B* drift off position when we had no release. Most of the time he kept us near La Perouse Bank, in about two hundred feet of water, where Nick bottom fished for red snapper, a helpful addition to our stores. We had eaten all our fresh food even before the Alaskan fishboat gave us the halibut— and red snapper is tastier than halibut.

One day while we were drifting on the windless sea, I heard Cap and Charlie in what seemed to be a serious argument. Cap would point at the mirror-like water surface and say, "At least Force 10," then Charlie would say, "Hardly Force 9—those waves aren't over thirty feet," and Cap would shout, "Forty feet at *least*—certainly Force 10," and so on for several minutes, deadpan.

"What was that all about?" I asked Nick later when we were fishing off the bulwarks.

He laughed. "Just a dumb sailor's joke. They make believe they are two sailors on a ship sinking in a gale, arguing how strong the wind, how big the waves. Just like two guys drowning arguing how deep the water is. Crazy nonsense, all it is."

Our freshwater tank was evidently losing its cement lining, but Jasper just made the coffee stronger, and you could hardly tell it was made with wash water from a cement mixer.

After the lull, Smitty's boat resumed loading, taking on our last five hundred cases in three loads, two or three days apart,

75-foot US Coast Guard cutter nicknamed "Polecat" by the rum runners for no known reason. They never bothered the offshore Canadian ships.

and we were back in Vancouver on May tenth, again staying only long enough for a couple of baths, laundry, filling fuel tanks, and cleaning and re-lining the fresh water tank. And most important, receiving our fresh food stores.

My score now, thirty-seven hundred cases (and thirty kegs of malt) in five months. Not counting the kegs, my average pay was now almost seventeen cents per case.

From time to time I have mentioned that life at sea, and life on the *Ruth B* in particular, was at best tolerably uncomfortable, and at worst, like in the long January gale, was nerve-racking. I had already decided to end my seagoing career as soon as I could afford to, or find something better, meaning, I suppose, something more comfortable.

On this trip I realized that there was some other reason. Discomfort was the excuse, the real reason was that I had, for all practical purposes, lost control of even minor matters in my life— what to eat, when to get up, what to read, when to go to bed, when to do anything on the ship, you name it, somebody else had control. It was the same feeling of frustration that I had felt in my brief army career at Heale's Range a few years earlier.

Probably I should have understood sooner, given my early avoidance of any group of kids at school who decided what everyone in the group would do. I had always decided what I wanted to do, and did it, most of the time on my own, as a lot of things I did, like long hikes in the rain or snow, had no popular appeal whatever. With no father around and an understanding mother, I had been quite free of restraint in my school years, as you may have inferred from earlier chapters.

Now, of necessity, I had volunteered into a life-style that was about as far from my early years as it was possible to get, far beyond the moderate restraints of a plain ordinary shore job. The *Ruth B* was not unusual, all ships are like that. The sacrifice was for a noble purpose, my future education and return to a life with much more freedom of choice. I knew I could not again be really free, say, as the year I was sixteen. Man, that was a year to remember. It could never be that good again.

I was quite tolerant of discomfort when I was younger, and

frequently exposed myself to short bouts of self-inflicted pain, blistered feet, hunger, and wet blankets, and thought I was having fun. The *Ruth B*'s miseries were as much mental as physical, but went on day after day, month after month. My toleration level dropped steadily with time, and there was no end in sight.

That was good in a couple of ways. It was a splendid experience in self-control, very useful in later years, and the money was rolling in at a rate I had never known before. I didn't know how much I would need for an education, but suspected it might be rather a lot.

So I couldn't quit the sea yet. It had been an accident I had gotten on the *Ruth B* at all, after a lucky wind blew down some telephone wires, leaving the former wireless operator, the unknown Slim, totally unreachable. In 1932, it was rare good luck that I had even one chance to earn for future learning, and it would have been complete folly to gamble on a second.

Skeezix, Spring 1933. Canadian shore boat 56 feet long, one 80-hp diesel and two 450-hp Liberty gas engines.

21

THE *RUTH B* LEFT VANCOUVER ONE MORNING IN MID-MAY with an empty hold.

"Somebody bringing a load north for us?" Charlie asked when we headed straight out through the First Narrows, instead of over to North Vancouver for oil.

"*Ragna*'s coming in for a refit—she's been out for a long time," Cap said. "Saves us a long drag down and back, not to mention fuel."

We arrived out on the Cape Beale position in a light southeaster, and received messages from Vancouver and the *Ragna* on the noon schedule. Vancouver told us: "New position twenty-five miles south-southwest Cape Beale tomorrow." So we moved over to shallow water—thirty fathoms—on the south end of La Perouse Bank, and fished for red snapper until dark.

The *Ragna* arrived punctually at noon the next day and stopped fifty feet to leeward. Somebody hollered from her wheelhouse door.

"We transfer right away. We've been out since January."

"Okay," Cap hollered back. "We'll pull alongside you."

It was my watch so I automatically went below to the engine, lighted the punks, and banged the jingle.

"Bang, bang, slow astern," Cap rang down, and with the usual cold engine rifle-shot start, we moved astern and held for a couple of minutes, Cap making sure the engine was warm enough to start without punks, I guess. The southeaster was hardly blowing fifteen knots, but the swell waves were rolling in from the Pacific, big as ever.

Cap rang "stop," then "slow ahead" for a time, then all of a sudden, "stop," and "full speed astern." I swung the air wheel over to reverse, and as soon as the engine fired, spun the throttle wide open. The engine first revved up to full speed when there was a tremendous thump astern, and the engine just took off. It was turning over so fast the noise just made me slam the throttle off without waiting for any signals, because something sure was wrong.

In the dead silence of the engine room I could hear a lot of shouting on both the *Ruth B* and *Ragna*, then we hit the *Ragna* with a force that threw me against the engine and there was even more shouting. The engine signals came later, "slow astern," "stop," and then a jingle, "through with the engine," and I went on deck.

"Sorry for the inconvenience," Cap was telling *Ragna*, "but we have lost our propeller. Can you tow me up to La Perouse so we can anchor? We should hold in two hundred feet."

The *Ragna* said okay, we'll tow, and it was damned careless of us to lose a propeller, and other things not as polite. Cap and Nick rigged the big anchor to our hundred-fathom cable with an empty oil drum on the other end, and from that drum another cable, three or four hundred feet back to the *Ruth B*, like she was riding to a buoy on a long bow line. By supper-time we were riding comfortably to leeward of our oil drum buoy, out of sight of land. The *Ragna* disappeared to seaward.

Vancouver got the bad news on the seven o'clock schedule.

"Propeller lost. Anchored La Perouse Bank, southwest Cape Beale, magnetic. No cargo aboard."

On the eleven-thirty schedule that night we received a signal that said simply: "Sending tug tomorrow."

"Good going," Cap said. "With a little luck, we'll be back out in two or three days."

"With a little good luck, that is," Charlie said dourly. "With a little bad luck we could sit here for a couple of weeks."

By daylight the next morning, visibility was down to a hundred yards in drizzle, mist, rain and low cloud, just enough for our buoy to show through once in a while when it surfaced. When the *Ruth B* surged back on a swell wave, the buoy pulled completely under. A couple of days later, the visibility was the same, with slightly more wind, not enough to trouble us. We all spent a lot of time watching that buoy to windward, all except Charlie.

"Waste of time looking," he said. "If the line breaks, we

swing beam on right away. Why look?"

But we looked anyway. It was the only thing in sight.

"I would feel better in a westerly," Cap said. "If the line went then, we could rig a tarpaulin jib and sail straight downwind into the Strait. In a southeaster, we just blow ashore. Nick, you and Sparky clear the junk from the dory, just in case."

With the swell waves coming in at their regular intervals of seven or eight seconds, the *Ruth B* was surging on the anchor line over four hundred times an hour, and had been for two days now. If the line was chafing, it could go any time. Seven or eight days later, at ten thousand surges a day, it still held, and the weather finally cleared. Before noon, we heard away inshore, a faint screaming sound that increased and decreased with the same time interval as the swell waves.

"A boat, and a damned noisy one," Charlie said.

The high scream grew louder almost by the minute and a small tugboat pulled up to the *Ruth B* and cut its engines. All of twenty-five feet long, it was.

"*Ruth B*?" a figure asked from the minute wheelhouse. "Tow you to Victoria. Take a line?"

"Okay for Victoria," Cap said. "Stand by and clear our anchor."

Cap and Nick rigged a couple of snatch blocks to bring the

Ragna in Vancouver harbour, 1938.

buoy line to the windlass. Charlie ran the winch, while I tailed off, and Cap and Nick coiled down on the port deck between the hatch and bulwark. After we retrieved our oil drum buoy, Cap fed the anchor line through a block on the boom end to a snatch block, and away we went again at the slow windless speed, everybody handling the line soaking wet in no time. We had over half the anchor line in when the winch ground along slower and slower.

"She's pulling hard on something," Charlie said. "Looks like the anchor's really dug in. We'll have to take it slow until she breaks out."

After quite a few minutes more, alternately winching and waiting for the *Ruth B* to pull up over the anchor, we ended up with the anchor line vertical, and tight as a bow string, not even the surging rise and fall of the ship doing anything but squeeze water out of the line.

"Well damn me," Cap said. "First boat I ever knew anchored solid with the anchor line straight up and down. No wrecks this far from shore. I wonder?"

He stopped talking and went into the cabin for a minute. "Chart shows two submarine cables run across the eastern end of La Perouse Bank. For a nickel we're hooked onto one of them. Can you lift any more, Charlie?"

Charlie started up and I hauled tight on the tail. We gained a couple more feet, just stretch in the line and the winch stalled.

"Okay, ease off," Cap said. "Nick, the axe. We cut and run, just in case we are on the new cable, and maybe kinked it a little."

After Nick chopped the line we took the screamer's tow line, and were on our way towards the Strait some time before supper. Cap sent a last signal on the seven-thirty radio schedule.

"I am proceeding to position Victoria."

I then, as usual disconnected and stowed the sets away in an engine room cupboard. We stopped briefly at William Head, then towed in to a shipyard in Victoria's inner harbour. Cap went into the shipyard office, and found they had received a replacement propeller, and were going to haul us out at seven in the morning. He also found out something else.

"Big Frank brought over some of Celestine's little kittens on last night's boat. Sparky, you sleep aboard as watchman tonight. You can go ashore when she's hauled out in the morning."

Cap, Charlie and Nick changed into shore clothes and left in a taxi presumably to visit Celestine's "little kittens." Jasper stayed aboard with me that night and left sometime in the morning after I did, so I didn't see him go.

To me, Victoria consisted of a fantastic indoor swimming pool called the Crystal Gardens. There was also an impressive hotel and huge stone government buildings near the CPR steamship wharf. I bought a bathing suit in the Hudson Bay store, and walked around in the warm May sunshine until the pool opened, swam for a couple of hours, picked up lunch somewhere, sat on a park bench, and thought about things. Mostly about myself, and what I could do about getting back to school, or at least learning something that I could study on land. My radio magazines were full of advertisements for wireless telegraph schools, showing handsome young men in immaculate uniforms on decks of enormous ships. Maybe some made it like that, but for me a leap from rum runner operating to passenger lines operating looked impossible. And anyway, as I have said, a seafaring life had lost its appeal, dating back, I think, to that bloody awful January gale.

The ICS radio correspondence course I had been studying had helped me through Sprott's, and I knew the government education department had correspondence courses for students who were off in the back country. So let's find out, I thought, since my own effort, Van der Bijl's book, wasn't helpful at all, except to emphasize just how much there was to learn, and all that incomprehensible algebra too.

So I wandered over to the stone government buildings, and found my way in to the man in charge of high school correspondence courses.

"What would you like to find out?" he asked, a cheerful, interested high type fella.

"I never finished high school, so can't get into university," I said.

"What high school, and when did you drop out?"

"Mission City High School, third year, February."

"What do you want to take in university?"

"Engineering, electrical engineering."

"Well, Mission High School wouldn't have done much for you even if you had finished. What you need for engineering is elementary physics. We have a good correspondence course, including experiments. Where are you working?"

"Second engineer on a small boat."

"So you wouldn't have a room to yourself. And the boat would roll, so no experiments. And maybe not even any place to sit down and write?"

"No, just the engine room workbench."

"Well, I'm sorry, but a regular correspondence course looks impractical. The best I can suggest is you buy this physics book. You can start on your own, studying, until you can manage a regular course. But it's going to take you years to make university. It looks difficult."

Difficult, hell, it was impossible, even in my present circumstances and at my fabulous rate of pay, where saving was easy. I would be an old man like Charlie if I got through at all. My advisor must have read my thoughts.

"For you, regular university is out, I'm afraid. But there is a way out of this high school/university corner. In the United States there are several small colleges that offer a Bachelor of Science degree in two years, and let you take the high school courses you need. Their degree doesn't rate with M.I.T. by a long way, but it would get you out of the hole you are in now, and give you a college base for transfer to a university later. These colleges advertise in *Popular Mechanics* and *Popular Science*. I recommend you write for a catalogue or two."

It was probably the soundest recommendation anyone ever made to me. I bought his physics book anyway, *The Ontario High School Physics* for a dollar thirty-five, thanked him, and left to look for a magazine store. In my excitement I never did remember his name, but I sure am grateful to him, that department of education man in Victoria.

Popular Mechanics had the advertisements I was looking for. There were three or four, all more or less the same.

"B.Sc. Degree in two years. Aeronautical, Civil, Chemical, Electrical, Mechanical Engineering. Make up high school work. Low tuition, living costs. Write for Catalogue."

And write I did that same afternoon, to two of them, Tri State College in Angola, Indiana, and another one in Chicago. I finally had something to look forward to.

The *Ruth B* was back in the water when I arrived at the shipyard around five. When I went below to dig up something to eat I found a note on the galley table.

"Went to Vancouver to see a doctor. Jasper."

Cap, Charlie and Nick showed up around eight.

"Damn Jasper to hell anyway," Cap said, when I showed him the note, but he sure didn't sound upset at all. "I'll phone Vancouver for a new cook. He can come over on the night boat. And Big Frank and the kittens can go back on tomorrow's boat, instead of tonight. Damn Jasper, damn, damn, damn—another night of playtime. Thank you, Jasper."

They all disappeared again. I read my new physics book on deck until dark—after nine o'clock in late May in Victoria—pumped out, and turned in. That physics book sure had a lot of real interesting looking stuff in it. I could even understand some of the elementary electricity part. From then on, book learning was what it was all about.

22

WHILE I WAS SITTING ON THE HATCH THE NEXT MORNING in warm sunshine, drinking my after breakfast coffee, a taxi entered the shipyard, and a little guy carrying a small cheap suitcase got out. He paid the taxi driver and came over and looked down at me.

"Hey, chum. I'm looking for a ship called the *Ruth B.* Do

you know it?"

"You're looking at it," I said. He just looked a minute more.

"Well, love a bloody duck, another goddamn fishboat. Well, beggars can't be choosers. Show me around."

I showed him his bunk in the black hole that was the *Ruth B*'s galley, and he said a few more things, though I guessed he'd been on boats before as he didn't sound surprised. He poked around in the galley cupboards, and I showed him where the big food locker was, under my bunk.

"A bleeding pepper-and-salt cook—when do we sail?"

"Cap said ten this morning, but no sign of anyone yet. By the way I'm Sparky, second engineer."

"The name is Butts," he said, sticking out a small bony hand. "George Butts. And if you call me Limey you eat salt pie. I need an hour to get some stuff to cook with—got any money?"

"Twenty bucks. That enough?"

"I'll make out with that," George said, and scuttled off up the dock.

He came back about twelve, lugging a couple of cardboard boxes. I didn't see what was in them. I showed him the fresh stuff that was in the dory, then we went up the street for a shore lunch.

Cap, Charlie, and Nick returned about one.

"We are very weary," Cap said. "Nick, you and Sparky take her out. Charlie, let us old men sleep."

Nick wasn't so alert either, so after the *Ruth B* was out in the Strait, I took the wheel and Nick slept sitting in the sunshine on the foredeck, his back against the wheelhouse.

At five-thirty I called Cap and Charlie, who went below for supper. They came back up later, most pleased about something.

"Where'd you dig him up, Sparky?" Cap asked.

"He just showed up. Was he the wrong guy?"

"Hell no, he's terrific. You and Nick see for yourselves."

Nick and I went below and ate, and all the while George kept up an ill-tempered monologue on how could anyone expect to cook good meals in a hell-hole like this and so on.

We didn't say anything, but we soon realized we had a real cook, probably the best in the rum fleet. Damn Jasper, damn, damn, damn. It was all his fault we ate so splendidly for the next year.

George Butts was probably the worst-tempered cook in the rum fleet too, but that didn't matter much, since most of the time he had only himself to talk to.

After supper I reconnected the radio sets and the aerial to the mast-head and raised *Ragna* on the seven o'clock schedule. Cap arranged to transfer the following morning on the Cape Beale position. When we were close by the *Ragna* the next morning, her skipper warned us off.

"You shut that damn thing down. This time we come alongside you. We don't want another accident that lets you go in, and leaves us sitting here."

Ragna pulled neatly alongside, but after that, it was a sham-

George Butts in
the "bathroom",
spring 1933.

bles. Nick and I had the hatch open, ready for our usual one case at a time transfer, but the *Ragna*'s crew just started throwing cases our way. Charlie and Cap were both catching, but *Ragna* threw even with no catcher, the cases landing on deck, with brown liquid trickling out. We all worked on deck, dropping cases into the hold any old way, in a heavily alcoholic atmosphere.

Eight hundred cases came over in maybe an hour, probably a record for time as well as broken bottles.

"Nick, you and Sparky sort this out and start fixing breakage right away," Cap said as the *Ragna* pulled away to the east. "Get two hundred good cases ready for Smitty tomorrow maybe."

And tomorrow it was. We received a release on the seven o'clock schedule, and Smitty eased up to us about five in the afternoon. With the long days of June, he only loaded three or four hours before sunset, to run most of the Strait in the dark. We had been fixing more breakage, and ended up with maybe sixteen cases of broken bottles, a piddling two percent loss. During the transfer, it sounded more like fifty percent.

Shore side was working smoothly, and Smitty took off the three last loads during the next eight days. After the last load, we received a signal.

"Proceed to position *Malahat*," so we headed off on the long run to Mexico. Our deliveries now totalled forty-nine hundred cases, less a little breakage, but including the four hundred cases with the *Ragna*'s help, but so what. It was a summer cruise, good weather, sometimes whales to see, and almost always goonies, the brown north Pacific albatross with their long thin wings. Some of those birds spanned over ten feet, wing tip to wing tip.

We pulled alongside the *Malahat* late one afternoon in the usual thin overhead mist. Cap just climbed aboard over the low rail, she was loaded so deep. There was no one in sight so Nick and I climbed aboard and sat on the bulwarks; there was no clear deck space, the whole open waist of the *Malahat*, from poop to fo'c's'le, was filled with sacks of firewater level with the bulwarks.

"Quite a load," Nick said. "She stows about eighty-five

thousand cases in the hold, and with this lot on deck she's carrying a hundred thousand cases, maybe more."

Cap climbed back aboard after a few minutes and announced, "We load first thing in the morning."

We dropped back and tied astern of another smaller boat for the night. First thing in the morning for the *Malahat* was eight o'clock, the same regular working days as the *Lillehorn. Malahat* rigged a stage overside and we loaded hand-to-hand one case at a time at a good pace, as the mother ship gave us an extra man to help Nick and George in the hold, the slow point when the *Ruth B* was nearly empty. After eleven George climbed out to get our lunch going. The hold was maybe half full by then, so Nick and the *Malahat*'s sailor kept up easily.

After a rather long lunch hour, we loaded again, twelve hundred cases in the hold, and another two hundred on deck, covered and lashed down on top of the hatch. Fourteen hundred cases was the *Ruth B*'s limit—the after-deck had about two inches freeboard, and small seas washed through the scuppers while we were still alongside the *Malahat*.

We pulled away before supper, running up past the *Prince Albert* before heading away offshore. There was no sign of life on the rusty old tramp. Working on Rum Row, on the mother ships anchored off the Mexican coast for months on end—the *Malahat*'s last trip lasted twenty months—looked to me like the world's most boring job. Life on the *Ruth B* was not entirely fascinating, but it did involve movement, and we saw shore boats once in a while.

After an easy run of a week or so, we were back off Cape Beale, riding the never-ending swell waves comfortably in a dead calm—not a ripple to be seen clear to the horizon. Shoreward, at night, hundreds of fishboat riding lights flickered like a Japanese water festival—salmon trollers just drifting after dark, now only five or six hours, last light to first light.

For the little trouble he had, Smitty could have been delivering milk. We arrived off Cape Beale about mid-July, and Smitty cleaned us out in seven trips. The short nights didn't seem to slow operations in the least, and we were back in Vancouver on

August seventeenth, eight months from the day we first sailed. Our deliveries had now reached the impressive total of seventy-five hundred cases. My total pay would be a thousand dollars even, my rate per case down to thirteen and a third cents. It was more than a living in 1932 in Vancouver—it was damn near close to prosperity.

Cap went ashore to telephone when we pulled in to Menchion's Shipyard.

"Come in to Hamilton Street at ten in the morning. The *Ruth B* is paying off this trip."

"Well," I thought, "it was good while it lasted."

When I got home I immediately dived into the two American college catalogues that had arrived. There was no discernible difference to me in what they offered, and I simply picked Tri State

Five-masted schooner *Malahat* from the masthead.

College, Angola, Indiana, because being in a small town it was more appealing to me than the college in Chicago.

Money was the key—how much for two years? Tri State was very detailed on costs: board—$5 per week; room—$2 per week; tuition—$50 per quarter; books for engineering—$12.50 per quarter. The college ran full year, four semesters, so it added up to around $160 a semester; $640 a year—$1280 for two years, plus a few things, like bus fare from Vancouver to Indiana, personal expenses, and some clothes.

Why hell, I had enough money for at least a year already.

Then I found the page on prerequisites—meaning the courses you had to take if you had no high school, or had forgotten it all, before starting the two year college work. That page was a jolt—two full semesters—half a year—even if I could learn, or re-learn, enough algebra to eliminate Elementary Algebra A. So it looked like $2000 minimum to finish—American dollars. I learned about foreign exchange much later—a dollar was a dollar to me then wherever you were.

Regardless of whether I could finish or not, I decided on Tri State. Even if I could only make it through a year, on the money side, that was enough to get me out of high school, and a quarter of the way through college. I dug out an old school book on elementary algebra, and felt good.

And I could start right away—it was still three weeks before the fall quarter started in September. At the Hamilton Street office the next morning there was even better news.

"The *Ruth B* is laying up for a while," Captain Ford told us when he handed us our cheques. "But Charlie, Sparky, and George will be going out on the *Ryou II* in about three weeks." In 1932 nobody asked you if you wanted to keep on working.

Thus, all of a sudden, I had it made, either way, a full college course if the *Ryou II* stayed out long enough, with a full year minimum already in the bag.

I felt so good I even had a few kind thoughts for the *Ruth B*, especially now I wasn't going back out on her. The *Ryou II* had to be better.

23

WHILE MY BANK ACCOUNT AND EDUCATIONAL PROSPECTS had improved immensely, I found that I had slipped a rung on the social ladder.

At Cowichan Lake in 1928, the summer I was sixteen and couldn't get a job, I met the Farley family on holiday in a floathouse at Youbou, next to Aunt Millie's. Once in a while I phoned them at their place in North Vancouver while I was at Sprott's—every two months or so—and got invited over for Sunday dinner. They had a daughter, Karen, two days older than me. The best you can say about our relationship is that we tolerated each other. Sunday dinner was more than tolerable as Mrs. Farley was a splendid cook. While at Sprott's I dined on leftovers from the great table.

So I phoned them this time, bubbling over with good news and good cheer, and Mrs. Farley invited me over for dinner.

After previous dinners, I had been subjected to lengthy lessons in contract bridge. In 1932, in North Vancouver, if you couldn't play contract bridge, you had no social future whatever. Learning bridge was all for my own good, Karen said. Karen was real helpful; in addition to endless pointers on playing better bridge, she had a lot of suggestions on my grammar, my choice of ties, my clothes, my conversation, my haircuts, my table manners and my inability to dance well—you name it, she was right there with helpful hints. All for my own good.

This Sunday in August was different. There was something in the air. Mrs. Farley was abnormally anxious that I eat lots of everything, fussier than usual, while Karen said nothing and couldn't seem to look at me. Mr. Farley was his normal patronizing self, the genial squire condescending to dine with a member of the aspiring lower classes.

I was clued in right after dinner, when Mrs. Farley said, "Mr. Farley wants to talk to you privately in the living room."

Talk, not a bridge lesson! So something was up.

She only called him Mr. Farley in his presence when something difficult had happened, or was about to happen. We went into the living room and I listened.

"I have great respect for you, Fraser," he stuttered, "but we can't invite you over any more. We can't risk our daughter's future by having her associate with a rum runner, a law-breaker. We expect her to marry well, and we can't allow you to spoil her chances."

Karen was in training to be a nurse, and her parents thought a rising young doctor would be just fine as a son-in-law.

Mr. Farley talked for quite a while. He was really worked up. I didn't say a thing, as I didn't want to spoil Karen's chances to snare a suitable husband, if knowing me did that. I never did find out how well she married, or whether she married at all. But she was such a helpful girl. I hope she did well.

So I left without my bridge lesson, more confused than annoyed. Everybody does a little law-breaking when it suits their convenience, like jay-walking or driving over the speed limit. Anyway, breaking the law isn't really damaging. It's getting caught that causes all the trouble.

I was a bit depressed even so, but it soon wore off, as my good news far overshadowed this trifle of bad news.

I bought a railway ticket to Mission and went up to see "Uncle" Jim Green, the garage man who had been gassed in the war like Dad. He had it worse than Dad did, so the lung troubles showed up sooner, before he was discharged, in time so the doctors could leave him with one sound lung. The garage business was finished—his partner did the book-keeping, much to his advantage—and Jim now lived on a stump ranch north of Hatzic Lake, and with his war pension, was making out. He was glad to see me, as always.

"If you have a couple of days, let's go up to Stave Lake fishing," he said as soon as I arrived. He liked fishing a lot more than work, which hadn't helped the garage business either.

We hauled his flat-bottomed low-sided skiff to the lake, and with the old outboard motor we had relocated from Sprott's, rode in some insecurity to Vic Osborne's shack on a log float, tied to the shore where Stump Creek joined the upper Stave River. We fished and did well, four and five-pound Dolly Varden; Jim shot at a wolf, and missed, and shot a mountain goat, which wouldn't fall off the mountain. Getting a mountain goat off a cliff is almost as hard as getting down off the cliff yourself.

The two valleys, Stave River and Stump Creek, had not been logged, and the great old growth firs and cedars cut the light, so little underbrush grew, and we wandered in a splendid park of tall pillars along the deep clear pools. It was good just to be there, even better with Jim's company.

We started back at noon of the fourth day. A north wind blew down the valleys under a cloudless blue sky, but as soon as we rounded the last river bend into the open lake, we knew we were in trouble. The wind was rising noticeably, while we hugged the eastern shore of the lake, looking for easier water. The overloaded skiff wasn't doing well, and after a while, waves began breaking over the stern, momentarily shorting out the spark plugs.

I shifted our goat so I could row, but just as a forced landing on the rocky shore appeared necessary to avoid swamping, we found a minute bay with a log raft and a shack on it and quickly hauled out. The raft was big, but by daylight the next morning the waves had built up enough to roll the raft. When the shack began to break up, we moved ashore to an abandoned shingle bolt cutter's shack, which in fact was only a roof, no windows, and only two walls.

The second morning the northerly still whipped down the lake, and I tried to count days, to see when the *Ryou II* was supposed to sail. I couldn't remember just what day I had come to Mission. I had lost the calendar habit on the *Ruth B*, where all the days were exactly the same, and we weren't going anywhere anyway. There couldn't be more than two or three days margin, and by the night of the third (or fourth) day of that infernal north wind, I was worrying.

Sure, I had a year of Tri State in the bag—it never occurred to me that they might not let me enter—but with times so hard, I just couldn't condition myself to miss any available work. I had my eye on the whole course, now that the beginning was assured.

Last December I had joined the *Ruth B* thanks to a southeaster that cut telephone lines to the unknown Slim; now it looked like this big north wind would maroon me on Stave Lake long enough for some lucky fellow to receive an unexpected offer of employment. And there was nothing I could do about it, in time.

We could walk out the east side of Stave Lake, as the hills were relatively low and rounded, not the sheer cliffs like the west side, dropping almost straight into the water from the six-thousand-foot peak of Robie Reid. But Jim wasn't a strong walker, with his single lung, and we would have spent four hungry days bushwhacking out. We had ditched our smelly goat and fish the second day.

MV Ryou II, spring 1933. 60 feet long, one 100-hp diesel, maximum speed 8 knots.

During the third or fourth night the wind dropped as fast as it had risen. Jim and I shoved off long before sunrise and were home in no time. Jim drove me into Mission for the morning train west, and I was home before twelve.

Mom was working, but there was a note on the kitchen table. "Call from Captain Ford. Come into the office tomorrow," with no date on it. Not wasting any time, I cleaned up in a rush, had some toast and coffee, and made time to Hamilton Street.

"*Ryou II?*" I asked the office girl. "Captain Ford called me."

Captain Ford came from a back office. "She's down at Benson's Shipyard," he said. "The cook, Charlie and Jack will be loading stores after lunch. You go down too. Sleep aboard if you want to. You'll only be out a couple of months this trip." Jack, it turned out, was the mate.

Two months or two days, no matter, I still had a ship.

Benson's Shipyard was near Menchions in Coal Harbour. The *Ryou II* was another fish packer, sixty feet long, like the *Ruth B*, but beamier, with less draft. The wheelhouse was smaller, but there was a large galley, with three windows to port, two portholes aft and a dutch door and another window on the starboard side, a splendid improvement over the black hole that served as living quarters on the *Ruth B*. She was painted a cheerful light grey.

Charlie and two younger men were sitting in the galley. The youngest of the two spoke when I came in. "I'm Jack Wolf, mate—you know Charlie, Bennie here is cook. Your bunk is the upper one, aft, port side. Throw your suitcase in and eat. Stores should be here soon." I shook hands with Jack Wolf and Bennie. Jack was a pleasant looking man of maybe twenty-five, rather dark from a lot of sun, about my build, on the medium side. Bennie was my height, heavier built, probably over thirty. He was dark too. Charlie looked up, but didn't say anything or shake hands. I never had Charlie figured—was he always like that, or was it just to me he gave the distant treatment?

Loading galley stores was the same as on the *Ruth B*, fresh meat lashed in the rigging, fresh vegetables and eggs in the big dory, everything else in the fo'c's'le, which had four bunks port side, full-length food lockers starboard side, and a canvas-covered cubicle aft against the engine room bulkhead. I looked inside—wires and a telegraph key, my wireless office. I found the sets in an empty food locker. There was no heat.

The engine was a green three-cylinder Atlas-Imperial diesel, as high as I was. The engine room had a workbench on each side of the engine, and an auxiliary battery charger and air compressor. It was probably no better lit than the *Ruth B*'s engine room, but painted white, it was far brighter.

After the food was put away, we loaded sacks of coal for the galley stove, quite a lot, four sacks in the dory, the balance in the hold. Charlie had disappeared early in the afternoon. Jack, Bennie and I ate aboard the boat, and slept aboard. I wasn't letting this one get away. Bennie was a genial easy-going guy who tried hard, and was a better cook than Jasper, but he was no George

Jack Wolf.

Butts.

After supper I went home for a quick bath—loading coal in sacks was a poor way to resume a life-style that did not include baths.

Before I turned in I connected the radio sets for a try-out—everything worked. I checked the spare tubes—okay. Anyway, I had brought along my lucky home-made short wave receiver that had saved my rum running career on the *Ruth B.*

The next morning, September eighth or ninth, Charlie came aboard about eight-thirty.

"Okay Sparky," he said. "Come below and I'll show you the engine. This one's four-cycle, and starts without all the *Ruth B's* nonsense. First you have to bar the engine over so one of the flywheel notches is at the arrow on the crankcase. Here, try it."

I stuck the long steel bar into a hole on the flywheel, and a strong pull turned the wheel to the next notch.

"Check that the clutch is in neutral—this is the lever. Pull ahead for ahead, shove back for astern. Try it."

I pulled, and nothing much happened.

"You gotta put some real beef into it. Throw your body forward for a hard pull just as your arms are straight."

The clutch lever was head high, and needed real beef, as Charlie put it. The trick was to jerk, not pull.

"Okay, now, flywheel set, clutch in neutral, you pump fuel pressure to two thousand pounds like this, set the throttle line at slow, and open the starting valve."

Air hissed into a cylinder, and away she went, at a much slower speed than the Fairbanks-Morse, but just as quiet. Charlie called up to Jack, still sitting in the galley.

"Ready to move off. You handle her, Sparky."

We slipped out of Benson's to the North Vancouver oil dock, and topped up our fuel and fresh water. I started to knock out wedges to free the hatch battens.

"We aren't loading drums, Sparky," Jack said, so I hammered the wedges tight again. We returned to Benson's and Jack phoned the office after lunch.

"Skipper's on his way," he said.

Jack and I hoisted our gaff-headed riding sail, checking out sail and halyards. Not new, but okay.

We were re-tying gaskets when an old skinny hump-backed guy in a faded blue wool jersey, faded wool watch cap and heavy brown wool pants walked down the dock, carrying a duffel bag, and stopped where Jack and I were sitting on the hatch in the sunshine.

"I'm Captain Harry Lind," he said. "Take my bag and put it in the cabin. Are we ready for sea?"

"All ready, Cap," Jack said. "Oil, water and stores all complete, crew complete. Shall we move out now?"

"No hurry," Cap said, not shaking hands with anybody. "After a mug-up, and a look around."

He must have been well over six feet, but he was so humped over he didn't stand much taller than Jack. His small round eyes were a pale blue, close together, riding astride a long thin over-

Prince Albert on Rum Row.

hanging nose made for dripping. As the junior crew, I took his bag into the tiny cabin. If he had slept in similar cabins, his humpback was explained—the bunk looked all of five foot six long.

We left Benson's around four, and the next afternoon were again riding the swell waves in a dead flat calm off Cape Beale. I had rigged the radio in time for the eight-thirty morning schedule, and received a message.

"*Prince Albert* arriving tomorrow," Cap said.

24

AT DAYLIGHT THE NEXT DAY, JUST BEFORE JACK AND I WENT below for breakfast, a great blot of smoke rode the horizon to the southwest.

"Only the *Prince Albert* could make that much dirty smoke," Jack said, and sure enough the rusty old tramp soon pulled up to us and stopped. A small cargo door opened on her port side, a few feet above the water-line.

"Start up Charlie," Cap said, and we moved alongside under the cargo door, which now had a small stage slung outboard below it. Jack and I took their lines, and our fendered starboard side lay alongside, but too far out to receive cargo from the stage.

"Haul in tight," Cap called to Jack and I. We pulled in and tied off, and undogged our hatch battens. The old *Prince Albert* rolled on a swell wave, jerked our lines tight, and pulled the *Ryou II* against her steel sides with a crash that knocked us off our feet, and did it on every wave, pulling us in like a yo-yo, then bashing us away again.

"Slack off, slack off," Cap yelled, but when we had slacked enough to stop crashing into the rusty old hull, we were out of stage reach again.

"Launch the dory when we pull away," Cap said. "Let go both lines."

We moved away a quarter mile, slid the dory over the stern after removing the coal, eggs, vegetables and spare lines we stored there. In the windless sea, transferring by dory was easy, but slow, forty or fifty cases a trip. Loading from the *Albert* meant waiting under the stage until the ship rolled our way, taking the case held down from the stage, and waiting until the next swell brought the stage low again. Only the dory man was working steady, but not very hard. Jack and I spelled off every couple of loads. Everybody else sat around except for the few minutes needed to unload at the *Ryou II.*

Nobody seemed pressed for time—there was no action on the *Albert* to launch a lifeboat to speed the transfer, but maybe her crazy rolling prevented a safe launching. We finished shortly before dark, the *Albert* disappearing to the east, spouting black

Captain Harry
"Hot Pants" Lind, of
the *Ryou II* near
Santo Tomas
Mexico.

smoke like an erupting volcano.

We had twelve hundred cases aboard, all firewater, Old Colonel and Coon Hollow.

Smitty's delivery system had almost become a schedule, two loads, two hundred cases each, every seven or eight days. We worked a couple of hours twice a week loading, and loafed in the sunshine. There was hardly any breakage to fix and we couldn't work at noisy jobs in the afternoon, like chipping rust or scraping paint or Cap would yell at us to be quiet so he could sleep.

During the first days Charlie made several mumbled remarks to himself, loud enough for us to hear, about, "Reduced to the fo'c's'le, sleeping with the common people." Maybe it was supposed to be funny, but after a couple of days seeing Captain Lind we didn't hear it any more. In good weather, Cap didn't use the head, but stuck his bony ass out over the ship's side and opened his bowels. Jack had to wash down the fenders and ship's side every time, fuming.

"If ever I get a chance to give Hot Pants one little push overboard, he's for it," Jack would say, quite strong words for such a mild-tempered, high type fella.

"Hot Pants" was a natural epithet for Captain Lind. He always stood with both hands in his pockets, stooped over, rubbing vigorously, either playing pocket pool or just scratching himself. We wondered if he still had one hand busy in his pocket while he was at the steering wheel.

The *Ryou II* boasted an unstable, flat-bottomed six-foot dinghy, *Leviathan*. I slid it over the side every day or so, trolling for salmon, without success. Then one day I hooked something much too big for the *Leviathan* and hauled it back to *Ryou II*. I had a seven foot shark. Jack shot it, and hauled it aboard. Bennie asked if anyone liked shark steaks. We didn't know, and didn't want to find out.

Smitty's milk run kept reducing our load, and we were empty the second week in October, when we got a message: "Proceed to position Vancouver."

Thus, after an exciting trip, we arrived in Vancouver, twelve hundred cases added to my score on the *Ruth B*—total now eighty-seven hundred. It was October sixteenth. I was glad to learn we weren't paying off. The upper storeys of Tri State College were coming above the horizon. And there was still more good news, from Captain Ford.

"You'll be out for six months next time, down south. Bennie is going on another boat, so you'll have George Butts for cook."

Down south, wherever that was, sounded far better than the second winter off Cape Beale that I'd been resigned to. George Butts was almost as good news.

Charlie had a small but important list of engine room work essential for a long trip—new batteries, new battery charger, new bilge pump, new high pressure fuel pump plungers, and a new shaft bearing, or a re-babbited bearing.

Leviathan's shark off Cape Beale, August 1932. *MV Ryou II*, Bennie (sitting on the rail), Jack Wolf (left) and Charlie Smith.

We couldn't get the new fuel pump plungers—a special order would take weeks to deliver, or something—so the old worn plunger, pumping as high as thirty-five hundred pounds, kept on spitting out packing about as fast as we could replace it.

While we were waiting for the engine room work to be finished, Jack, George and I slept aboard. When the shipyard mechanic had the shaft bearing out for re-babbiting, Jack and I cleaned the hold. Right aft either side of the rudder post, between the after fuel tanks, narrow passages led to a space behind the tanks. It held about a hundred cases, and we had to stow there to get twelve hundred cases below decks.

Jack crawled in first with a flashlight.

"Well, well, what do you know," he said when I was part way in. "Look at this, Sparky."

"This" was two shapeless, oil-soaked sacks, Coon Hollow or Old Colonel, we couldn't tell which, that hadn't made it onto Smitty's last load.

"We sink these tonight," Jack said, "and in the meantime, they go under the coal in the dory. And I don't think we need tell anyone, especially Hot Pants, what we found."

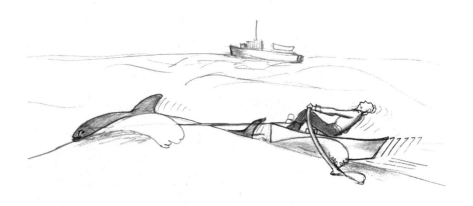

Leviathan catches a shark, sketch by Gallistel.

I went rowing in *Leviathan* that night.

The *Ryou II* left Vancouver on October twenty-fifth, as ordered. Hot Pants hadn't shown up by nine, so Jack took us over to North Vancouver to load oil, a full load of drums in the hold, and twenty more on deck, lashed to the bulwarks. Shortly after we returned to Benson's wharf, our peerless leader, rather the worse for strong drink, stumbled aboard, and looked in the galley door.

"Get under way, Jack," he said, "and you steer for a while. I don't feel too good."

"And I'm damn sure Hot Pants won't be steering too good, either," Jack said. "On this rainy misty night Bowen Island looks far safer than him steering us through the Gulf Islands. If he hollers, you can no doubt find some engine trouble adjustments we needed to stop for, Charlie?"

"No trouble, no trouble at all. A splendid idea," Charlie said.

We sailed as ordered, to Bowen Island, and had a quiet supper, tied alongside a fishboat. There was no hollering from the cabin, and we listened to our new radio, at rather low volume.

While we were on our way home on our last trip, Charlie, Bennie, Jack and I decided to buy a broadcast radio receiver, split four ways. Charlie put the batteries, along with my radio batteries, on his stores list. We had mounted the new set above the hatch over the engine room ladder, and it worked a treat. I ended up sole owner. Bennie never came back, and Charlie and Jack just forgot in the excitement of getting out to sea again.

George called us for breakfast after six. There was still no action from the cabin. George was about to bang on the forward galley wall when Jack stopped him.

"No emergency requires his presence," Jack said. "But we should move out. Sparky, you and I can steer two hours on and two hours off until supper-time if necessary, then we'll see."

There was mist and rain, but not much wind. While we were in quiet water, I rigged the transmitting aerial before darkness complicated a climb to the mast-head. Hot Pants appeared for supper, and took over the wheel at six, without a word.

By four in the morning watch, when we were well down the Strait of Juan de Fuca, the *Ryou II* began wallowing in the short seas. My stomach said no breakfast, thanks, but by lunch I was normal again.

The *Ryou II* ran south-southeast and southeast until November third, when we ran east and arrived at the *Lillehorn* at three, only sighting one ship, a coast guard cutter that picked us up at four in the morning on October thirty-first and followed us until two in the afternoon. We discharged oil that afternoon before supper, and tied astern for the night.

Some of my numbers, especially dates, are now exact, while other statements are still vague, particularly where we were, or were supposed to be, the two points not necessarily coinciding after Hot Pants took over as sole navigator. I had started a diary and kept it up daily, but on most of our days, nothing happened at all, and we were always out of sight of land.

Sparky in the *Leviathan,* 1932.

The next morning, November fourth, we loaded fifteen hundred and eleven cases—so my diary says anyway—and left, steering west, before supper. The *Ryou II* could only carry more than fourteen hundred cases when the two stern fuel tanks were empty. She carried twenty-six hundred gallons in six tanks, with six hundred plus in the two after tanks. Empty stern tanks relieved the hull of over two tons weight aft.

On November ninth we arrived on postion at six o'clock, having bucked a stiff northwester at half or three-quarter speed since the fourth. Jack said we were off San Francisco.

Thursday morning, the tenth, our No. 3 cylinder air-starting valve stuck. The cylinder head had to come off to clear it, a tiresome job in a small ship, even with the riding sail hoisted to reduce rolling. Friday and Saturday we were "cutterized". Then, on Sunday my transmitter tube failed, so I ordered a replacement spare. Three more days of bad weather brought us to Thursday, November seventeenth, on position in good weather in the morning.

San Francisco produced a lot of bad weather, not bad by Cape Beale's absolute standards, but frequent twenty or twenty-five knot northwesters that kicked up a small, steep sea, worse for a sixty-footer than the immense swell waves further north.

An American shore boat appeared after lunch, circled the *Ryou II* once, and pulled alongside, fifty feet away. Hot Pants recognized her skipper.

"He's okay, Jack, put the fenders over," he said. "Come alongside, Truscott you old rummy, and have a drink."

The speedboat tied along our starboard side. Hot Pants and his old buddy Truscott disappeared into our wheelhouse, with the small flat bottle of firewater from the galley. We hadn't received a release by radio as far as I knew, but maybe they had a different system down here. They were in the wheelhouse half an hour or more. Hot Pants had a slightly fuddled look on his face—more fuddled than usual that is—while his rummy buddy Truscott was smiling happily.

"Okay Jack, transfer two hundred and twenty-five off the deckload," Hot Pants said, throwing an empty brown bottle overboard.

Transferring alongside from a deckload is fast and easy; Truscott and his no-name speedboat were away in less than half an hour.

On the seven o'clock schedule we received a message from Vancouver, and Hot Pants gave me one to send. The next day, November eighteenth, we loaded two American shore boats in succession, in late afternoon, over two hundred cases each, leaving us with about eight hundred cases. We moved offshore thirty or forty miles and drifted.

We drifted from November eighteenth to December tenth. Quite ignored by all, until the tenth, when one of the larger size cutters picked us up and stayed close by, even after we traded a case of firewater for a crate of fresh fruit and vegetables. We received a message on the noon radio schedule, and met the *Ragna* on position December eleventh.

We took five hundred cases from her, by dory, in rough weather, finishing on the twelfth. After lashing down the small deckload, we moved off northwest, the big cutter staying with us

SS Brompton Manor, a supply ship from Europe that serviced the mother ships.

until dark, when it disappeared to the southeast.

The *Ruth B* met us after only a two-day run north, on December fifteenth. We could not be near Cape Beale, and our bad weather transfer hole, Port San Juan, after such a short run. Wherever we were, we transferred by dory in weather about as bad as dories can handle, taking two days to complete the thirteen hundred cases.

We left on December sixteenth, running southeast. The next day Charlie fell down the engine room hatch and broke some ribs.

25

THE *RYOU II* RAN SOUTH TO THE *LILLEHORN* SHORT HANDed. Hot Pants made George steer for him a couple of hours each morning during the run down, and also an hour or so after supper after the seven-thirty radio schedule. I was on call at any time for starting and stopping, as Charlie couldn't leave his bunk. I became used to sleeping on the engine room bench, sitting up, back against the lube oil day tank, feet based on the engine governor housing.

Several days before Charlie fell, my lower jaw swelled out on the left side, and pained me no end. I had visions of going ashore with Charlie, wiped out by a bad tooth before my dollar hoard would let me finish Tri State. Then a big pus pocket bulged out of the jaw. When I lanced it with a sail needle, all the pus drained out, and the pain disappeared overnight. Pus kept draining out, but appeared harmless, and I sure didn't want to go ashore unless it was absolutely necessary.

We pulled alongside the *Lillehorn* at eight the morning of December twenty-third and started loading right away, twelve hundred and ten cases, our loading interrupted for a few minutes around eleven to watch a cutter shooting at an American speedboat it had surprised. The speedboat wasn't in any danger—it was making three knots to the cutter's one, throwing a cloud of spray as good as any smokescreen. I slipped aboard the *Lillehorn* at lunch time to see Al Magee, her radio operator.

"*Zip* has a spare transmitting tube for you," he said. "And hey, what's the idea giving loads away to the bad guys?"

"Hot Pants met an old buddy, and did him a favour I guess," I said without thinking.

"Hot Pants! Hoo boy, that's great!" Al laughed. "Just wait until I tell Cap Vosper."

I was about to tell him it was a confidential nickname, for his ears only, but I didn't. Rum Row was a gloomy place, and a good laugh could make it a merrier Christmas. We left the *Lillehorn* that night.

Hot Pants came aboard about five, very sober and very glum, and took the galley bottle into the cabin with him. Cap Vosper didn't provide drink on the *Lillehorn*, but I think Hot Pants had a better reason to feel low. He didn't appear the next day, so Jack and I did four on and four off, and we got by with the engine on its best behaviour.

George had evidently visited the *Lillehorn* as well, for Christmas day he served us a more than respectable turkey dinner, with champagne breakage to finish off. Several cases of champagne were part of our load, and a couple of bottles became breakage, complete with corks. Breakage without corks is hard to explain.

Several times in the last few weeks I had heard Jack and Hot Pants arguing in the cabin, while we were stopped for radio and the noon sight. It seemed that Jack's position was frequently at variance with our skipper's. Hot Pants, after several arguments, refused to allow Jack to work up his sight, but simply took his sextant reading into the cabin. From then on, even Jack didn't know our noon position, or whether our actual position was the same as our ordered position. There was considerable doubt.

We stopped our run to the northwest December twenty-ninth, somewhere off San Francisco again, we guessed, and we received a message from Vancouver.

Each of the next two days we loaded a fast American shore boat, missed the third day in bad weather, and met the *Zip* Monday morning in calm weather. *Zip* was going in, after twelve months at sea. Charlie went north with her. She had a spare fifty-watt tube for me. We also transferred five hundred cases to the *Zip*, probably for the *Ruth B* up north.

Several days of bad weather took us to Wednesday, January eleventh, which broke clear and smooth. We received a signal on the eight-thirty radio schedule but no shore boat arrived. On the seven o'clock schedule we received a message for immediate answer. Hot Pants handed me the answers for Vancouver and our Jimmy came back with another, also for immediate answer.

Hot Pants called Jack into the cabin, and there was a subdued discussion in there for some time, and then another message for Vancouver, and Jack came into the galley.

Lillehorn from the masthead. Drums contain diesel oil.

"He couldn't navigate a rubber ducky in a bathtub," he said quietly. "We are a hundred miles away from position." Hot Pants rang for the engine, and we ran some fifteen hours, stopping just before noon on January twelfth.

Tapawinga arrived around three, and took our last three hundred cases. She was the real queen of the rum fleet, built by Menchions, sixty-five feet long, with three 860-horsepower Packard gasoline engines—that was a queen to rule the waves! She was built in 1932, working the rum fleet for a year and a half, until December 1933. Later, as a sports fishing boat out of San Diego, she burned at sea in 1935.

The five-masted schooner *Malahat* was called the queen of rum runners by writers who had never seen her or worked on her. She was a shabby old ship—the owners were as tight with

"Hot Pants" Lind, sketch by Gallistel.

paint as they were with sailors' pay. Crew members each received sixty-seven dollars and fifty cents a month and in the end, had to seize the ship to get paid, a shabby kind of queen.

After loading *Tapawinga* we ran northwest.

"Don't stop for radio, Sparky, we are going to Vancouver for a new engineer," Hot Pants said. That sounded odd; we were supposedly out for six months, and could easily get a replacement engineer out through Ensenada, and get a temporary replacement meanwhile from the *Lillehorn*.

I hadn't told anyone, but I had found that by reducing engine speed just a little and putting the short wave receiver on a cloth pad to reduce vibration even further, I could hold a radio schedule with *Ryou II* under way. I listened in on our regular schedules, and by the second day, both the *Lillehorn* and Vancouver were calling us persistently.

Every day I asked about stopping.

"Want to stop for radio check at noon, Cap?" I would ask, knowing well enough this wouldn't change his mind.

"No, no need to waste time, Sparky," was all he said.

By the fourth day, the *Lillehorn* and Vancouver were calling, both before and after their own traffic. On that day we stopped.

"Okay, we'll stop today," Hot Pants said. "We'll be up to Swiftsure late tomorrow, and the *Ruth B* might want us to take mail in."

We got a message all right, for immediate reply. When Hot Pants handed me the coded reply he said, "You should tell Vancouver your transmitter wasn't working."

"What do I tell them, it took me four or five days to fix? They sure will want to know."

Anyway, our Jimmy's first question had been, "Your sets okay?" and I had said yes. A message or so later Hot Pants came into the galley, unhappy.

"Run south-southeast when you start up, Jack, we are going back to the *Lillehorn*."

About the fifth night of our run back, we hit something. Hot Pants was at the wheel, the *Ryou II* plunging gently in a small following sea. I was half asleep in my usual position braced on the engine room bench.

Suddenly we bumped hard. The bow lifted a bit, then there was a tremendous crash forward and the bow leaped into the air, and came down a smashing blow on the water, and the engine stopped. I picked myself off the floor just as Jack and George looked in from the fo'c's'le, and Hot Pants looked down from the galley.

"What the hell happened?" Jack asked.

"I think we hit a whale," Hot Pants answered. "Sparky, check the bilges to see if we're making water. Have a look under the floorboards forward, Jack."

There was no water in the bilges, and no sign of the smallest leak forward.

"Well, let's go then, Start her up, Sparky," Hot Pants said. I barred the engine over, then found I couldn't pump fuel pressure—the pressure gauge just flickered up to a thousand pounds, then dropped back when I stopped pumping. I couldn't find any break in fuel lines, and finally figured that the check valve that should be on the discharge side of the pump to hold pressure for starting, must be stuck open.

There was nothing in the fuel lines that looked like it might be a check valve, but it was the only thing I could think of. So I banged everything around the fuel pumps a couple of hard blows with a spanner, tried the fuel pump, banged again and presto— fuel pressure.

We continued south for seven days, reaching the *Lillehorn* just before dark on January twenty-third.

On the twenty-fourth, we loaded twelve hundred cases, but then tied astern of the mother ship for the night. Jack didn't know why. The next morning we left right after breakfast, ran northwest for five days against a strong head-wind and were on position forty miles off Eureka, California, in good weather, January thirtieth. Jack was working out his own sights again.

We got a release on the morning schedule the next day, but no shore boat. Early on February first, in a rising northwest wind, a big fishboat pulled up—all names covered as usual— hollered our name, and Hot Pants waved him alongside.

"Weather's gonna blow up," the fishboat skipper said, "but we got everything arranged ashore for tonight. We want seven hundred, like in the release, and will load it all this trip if the wind will hold off a while."

There were three men on the fishboat, and we transported faster than we had ever done before, in a rising wind and sea. At first, the two ships were comfortable enough together, with tire fenders on each, but later the short, steep seas of those wretched Frisco northwesters rolled the ships so that the pipe rails around the wheelhouse roof were knocked off, then the *Ryou II* took a hard pitch, and smashed the port window of the fishboat cabin.

Footing was treacherous, the ships at times several feet apart, but we kept on throwing cases across, and a good few landed on the fishboat deck in a crunch of glass. A dark liquid dripped out when the sack was lifted. By now, we were slowing down the transfer, trying to stay on our feet.

"We'll run slow before the wind," Hot Pants hollered over to the fishboat skipper, who waved back.

Under way before the wind, the two boats rode much steadier. One of the fishboat men replaced Hot Pants, and we kept hard at it. The fishboat seemed to have the only count, and after

An American shoreboat with a heavy load on deck. Spring 1933.

a while hollered, "Two hundred more."

By then the *Ryou II* was taking water over the stern and we closed off part of the hatch. There was enough cold water coming aboard to soak everyone, with heavy spray blown forward off every sea swell in addition to the water sluicing around on deck.

With the last case, the fishboat skipper jumped across and went into the cabin for a minute or so, signing a receipt I suppose, and they pulled away. George took off for the galley—it was long past lunch—while Jack and I battened down and hoisted the gaff headed riding sail before we stopped. Hove to, we rode well.

"Well," Jack said while we ate lunch, "I hope there is a good market in Eureka for broken glass."

On February second, a cutter picked us up, but didn't stay long. With our sail we were quite steady but the cutter rolled her rails under. No shore boat could load in that weather.

We got a release for the last of our load. On Friday, February third, we transferred our last five hundred cases to a large American speedboat in good weather, and ran southeast back to the *Lillehorn*, after the fastest trip to date, twelve hundred cases in two loads. Eureka appeared very well organized. The total since October was now forty-four hundred and twenty-one cases, including two hundred or so to the wrong shore boat.

Monday, February sixth was my birthday—I was twenty-one years old.

Hot Pants was acting as though he had joined a temperance union, inspired no doubt by one or two discussions with Cap Vosper. We arrived at the *Lillehorn* February eighth and found *Zip* and *Ragna*, both subchaser types, 200-horsepower diesel and two 450-horsepower Liberty gas engines, already tied astern. They could make eighteen knots, faster than any but the speediest coast guard cutters.

We pulled alongside the mother ship and our cold sober captain climbed aboard. He returned almost immediately.

"Tie astern tonight," he said. "Tomorrow we drag for a lost anchor."

26

T HE *LILLEHORN* WAS REGRETTING THE LOSS OF AN EXPEN-
sive anchor, her anchor chain having parted in a short hard
northwester about a week before. The next morning, February
ninth, we pulled alongside and took aboard a grapnel, a hundred
fathoms or so of half-inch steel cable and Captain Vosper.

He was a well-mannered, soft-spoken man dressed in an ordinary grey suit that needed pressing, and a soft brown hat. We
dragged the grapnel around all morning without result. The
Mexican coast at Punta Santa Isidro, a minute point off which
the *Lillehorn* was anchored, is featureless, two or three other
points noted on the chart also owing their notation to an imagi-
native draughtsman. No one knew where the anchor had been
lost. I was stuck in the engine room the whole time, so never saw
anything, not that I missed much on this normal lazy Rum Row
day. Late in the afternoon, we returned Cap Vosper and his gear
to the mother ship, and tied astern off the *Ragna* for the night.

We pulled alongside again next morning, and Jack and I
started to remove the hatch covers.

"We're not loading," Hot Pants told Jack. After we battened down again, I slipped aboard the *Lillehorn* to see Al
Magee, her radio operator, who did talk, sometimes.

"What's going on?" I asked him.

"Just a supply schooner from Tahiti having trouble with
headwinds, a sick crew and an intermittent radio. *Zip* left yesterday, and you are leaving this afternoon. Here are some spare
tubes for the schooner. She's *Aratapu*, call sign OAZS. Happy
cruising—she's over a thousand miles out."

I got back aboard just ahead of Hot Pants. He rang for the
engine right away and we headed off southwest. The *Ryou II* ran
steadily, from the dark blue North Pacific water into warmer light
blue water, with the following northeast trade winds blowing a
gentle eight or ten knots from dead astern. On the third morning we had flying fish for breakfast, freshly dead on deck after

having flown into the cabin or galley wall during the night.

And they really do fly, flapping their large fins rapidly like wings, for fifty or sixty yards, then soaring for a few yards more before plunging abruptly into the sea. Another clever design, those wings/fins, quite usable in both water and air. I think they flew for fun; I never saw anything chasing them or breaking water just as the fish became airborne. George's fried flying fish was welcome; we had been at sea three and a half months, and fresh food was a distant memory.

We bathed every day—Jack, George and I that is—in a waterfall shower bath from a bucket of warm seawater. On the fourth day out Hot Pants stopped at two for a radio schedule with OAZS. We had no call sign for the *Ryou II*, so I invented one—V5AB. We exchanged coded messages. Next day we were in radio contact again, and pulled up to the old schooner a day later, February fifteenth.

She was an old two-master, sails almost black with age, the foresail with a large number of new sailcloth panels sewn in the center. *Zip* was close by, transferring by dory, in cloudy weather

Aratapu of Callao, Peru with supplies from Tahiti, 1,200 miles southwest of Santo Tomas, Mexico, 1933.

with frequent squalls. We put our dory overside, and started transferring between squalls. These squalls were a surprise, they just poured icy rain far colder than the ocean. Our sacked firewater bottles, protected in little corrugated cardboard boxes, soaked up water like sponges, and soon became shapeless masses of pulp, harder to stow and heavier to handle.

On a rough guess of fifty cases to the ton, each case weighed about forty pounds, dry—but wet cases were noticeably heavier. We didn't transfer in the squalls, not so much because of the cold rain, but because visibility dropped to a hundred feet or so. Thursday the sixteenth was worse—we transferred one dory load—fifty cases. Friday was better. *Zip* completed her load—eighteen hundred cases, maybe more.

Jack had been doing all the dory work, in other words, practically all of the work, as Cap kept me on the boat in case he needed the engine. On Friday night I showed Jack how to start the engine. On Saturday we took most of our load, Jack and I spelling off in the dory. The schooner had one boat over, so after *Zip* left our transfer rate about doubled.

Just by chance it was my spell on the last dory trip, with a squall heading our way. I pulled against *Aratapu*'s lee side—she made so much leeway the dory held close alongside even with slack lines. When her sailors stopped handing down cases, the load looked like more than fifty, but no trouble for the dory. The squall hit us just as I was trying to push away clear of *Aratapu*. She was blown sideways and backwards while still hove to, and I slid slowly forward until the dory dragged close under the bow.

The old ship rose on a swell, and I saw the bobstay chain coming straight down with great inevitability and force. I grabbed the painter, and jumped into the water ahead of the ship. When I surfaced the dory was clear but low in the water. I pulled myself back aboard, did a quick job of bailing, and sat in the heavy cold rain. Neither the *Ryou II* nor *Aratapu* were in sight, not surprising as I could see less than a hundred feet.

After twenty minutes of pouring water, the squall passed, and both ships appeared close by. I was good and cold. The sea felt a good twenty degrees warmer but I stayed in the rain, afraid of whatever nasties might lurk in the ocean depths. We hadn't seen any sharks, but you don't see many people at a dinner table either when there is no food in sight.

I passed the soaking wet cases up to Jack. Judging from the deckload, we were carrying about fifteen hundred cases. We lashed down, hauled the dory aboard and changed into dry clothes and had supper before starting off.

We left after dark, March nineteenth, for our thousand-mile run back to Rum Row, bucking the northeast trades most of the way. The re-supply ships from Tahiti were often schooners. The Tahiti/Rum Row run with its difficult currents and winds was a nightmare for vessels like the *Aratapu*, with small auxiliary power.

The *Ryou II* plugged along comfortably enough. For a long time I had been curious about one thing. On all my radio schedules, I could only hear Vancouver and the *Lillehorn*—all the other ships must be on different times, maybe even different fre-

quencies. After I padded my receiver against vibration, and could listen in with the *Ryou II* under way, I often tried to pick up other rum runner signals, particularly frequently now that I was alone below decks all afternoon with no witnesses.

On Wednesday, February twenty-second, I had tuned in to well below our frequency of 6975 kilocycles, down to around 6800 kilocycles, and surprise, I heard a signal. Even more surprising, the operator was transmitting in plain English.

The weak, rather unstable signal came in: "*Kagome* calling *Malahat*—*Kagome* calling *Malahat*," then, "*Kagome* calling *Old Maid*," several times over.

If it was really *Kagome*, something was quite wrong.

When neither *Malahat* nor *Old Maid* answered, I swung my transmitter to 6800 kilocycles and called "RG calling *Kagome*, RG calling *Kagome*. Call me."

The poor guy heard me, and was so excited I could hardly read his sending.

Opposite and right, transferring sacked cases from *Aratapu* to *Ryou II*. At right Jack Wolf in the dory facing aft.

"KG, KG from *Kagome*. What ship? Can you call *Malahat*? We are just out."

"No name—need ID first—can't call *Malahat*. Can call other ship seven tonight. If you are a friend of Bruce, give your last name."

Bruce Arundel, head of the Sprott-Shaw Wireless School. If the unknown sender knew Bruce he was beyond doubt friendly.

"I am friend of Bruce—name Gilmour."

Well, well, well—good old Art Gilmour, a classmate. *Kagome* had stumbled into something for sure.

"Okay, will call you this frequency seven tonight. Will try to set up contact *Malahat* for you."

I wondered what *Kagome* was just out of, maybe just out of luck.

That evening at seven I transmitted; first, a bit early, calling *Lillehorn* ending, "Important—have contact with JO."

That got Al's attention all right, so I gave him *Kagome*'s frequency to give *Malahat* and called *Kagome* back on 6800 kilocycles after Al signed off.

"Listen out for *Malahat* now. Call me eleven-thirty tonight

Ryou II with a 200 case deckload, covered and lashed down for heavy weather.

if no contact."

Kagome didn't call me back. That was the first and last strange signal I ever heard. For Art Gilmour, just luck.

When we arrived alongside the *Lillehorn* on the twenty-third, I made a quick trip aboard to see Al Magee.

"What happened to *Kagome*?" I asked.

"Nothing much. She was caught somehow, then released. Must have thrown all her codes and sets overboard. Art did pretty well with his makeshift setup."

Charlie Smith came back aboard from the *Lillehorn*, not looking too good. We left the *Lillehorn* before lunch the same day, ran northwest generally, at half speed against a stiff headwind for two days, and stopped at noon on Saturday, the twenty-fifth, obviously a long way from San Francisco.

"Now where are we?" I asked Jack after the noon sight.

"Forty miles west of China Point. San Clemente Island. Same latitude as San Diego."

The sea and sky were dull grey and hazy in a flat calm, no noise at all, with the engine stopped. No noise that is, except a great deal of foul English language from the galley. With the load of fifteen hundred cases transferred from *Aratapu*, we had also transferred about fifteen million cockroaches, if you could believe George.

Fifteen million or fifteen hundred, no matter, they settled happily into that fine warm galley, and never showed in the unheated fo'c's'le or in our bunks.

27

THE *RYOU II* RECEIVED A RELEASE THAT SATURDAY NIGHT and a "fireboat" pulled near us in the late afternoon of the twenty-sixth, Sunday.

"Fireboat" probably started off as a new name for a shore boat, "Firewater boat," later shortened to fireboat. Fireboats are manned by firemen and our new dark grey no-name no-number fireboat carried a pair we came to know quite well. That is, we knew their names, Clyde and Walt.

The stocky dark chap, Clyde, ran the show.

"Okay to pull alongside?" he hollered over to Hot Pants, who waved him okay. Walt was a husky blond six-footer, a friendly looking type with a couple of bruises on his face. Clyde and Hot Pants conferred in the cabin for quite a while—the release and ID numbers didn't jibe. When they came out, Clyde was saying, "Sure you can't give me a load, Cap?"

"No way at all Clyde. Sorry, but I did that about a month ago, and they raised hell with me—I'll be on the beach for sure, if I do it again."

In the last few years of rum running, release ID was by radio signal. The matching halves of dollar bills system, if it had ever been used very much, had been discarded long before. Earlier on, cash money was a substitute for ID—there was no credit system on Rum Row, that is, almost none.

Our two firemen pulled away, friendly as could be but empty. They were back on the twenty-eighth with good numbers, and a crate of fresh vegetables for us. They took two hundred and fifty cases a load, some five tons dry. The delivery system took a second load March second, a third on March third, and a fourth on March fifth, Sunday.

"You guys want us to bring out fresh stuff each trip?" Clyde asked Hot Pants after the second trip. "We can charge it against the ship, no trouble at all."

"No thanks," Hot Pants said, after a few moments' hesitation. "We get all our stuff from the *Lillehorn*."

So we did, but the fresh stuff was usually only some small Mexican pineapples, as tough and tasty as turnips.

"Say, wait a minute," Jack said quietly to Clyde and Walt after Hot Pants went forward, looking at me and George. "How are we fixed for credit? Like you bring out fresh stuff next trip, we could make a barter deal, private like. What say?"

"Sure, why not, Clyde?" Walt spoke up. "We waste our money anyway, so a few dollars lost if these guys can't pay, so what. You got a deal."

"Okay, fair enough for next trip," Clyde said as they pulled away.

"Whole damn country is busted," Clyde said when they arrived on the fifth. "Roosevelt closed all the banks yesterday."

The closure didn't affect deliveries, as the boys took a fifth load on Sunday, leaving us with about two hundred and fifty cases, quite a few with breakage. Jack and I fixed breakage Tuesday, and loaded Clyde and Walt on Wednesday.

Each trip the boys brought out a crate of fruit, milk, eggs and vegetables.

"Compliments of the management," Clyde said when Hot Pants questioned him. Management, hell, it was Jack and me. Each trip, after Clyde went into the *Ryou II* cabin, maybe signing a receipt, Jack and I would lift a case from the breakage pile set aside for repair, slide it across to Walt, straight barter after the first crate on credit was settled in cash, all the cash we had. I extended our want list to radio parts. High type fellas, Clyde and Walt, right easy to deal with, influenced no doubt by the 500 percent markup on every exchange.

Poor old Charlie was sick most of this time, not moving

Kagome, the best known Canadian shoreboat, 68 feet long, three 450-hp Liberty gas engines.

from his bunk.

On Friday the tenth of March, we were back tied astern of the *Lillehorn*. On Saturday we heard on our galley radio of a big earthquake in southern California.

We loaded twelve or thirteen hundred cases anyway, and were back on the San Clemente position late Sunday the twelfth, in good weather. We sat from the twelfth to the eighteenth without a release, then transferred the whole cargo to Clyde and Walt, five loads in six days and we had enough fresh fruit, vegetables, eggs and milk to start a grocery store. Breakage was a bit high though.

We were tied alongside the *Lillehorn* before supper on Saturday, March twenty-fifth, five months of our six-month trip behind us. Charlie was still sick.

Al Magee called down to me from the *Lillehorn*'s deck.

When I went aboard he said, "The *Ruth B*, your old love, is tied astern. New kid aboard can't get the radio going. Have a look, eh?"

On Sunday I put *Leviathan* in the water and rowed to the *Ruth B*—Cap Harwood and Nick Gjengsto were master and

Yurinohana, 72 feet long, one 80-hp diesel, two 450-hp Liberty gas engines, built in Vancouver, 1929.

mate. I checked the radio sets on the noon schedule. Nothing wrong, but the new operator, fresh out of Sprott-Shaw, had never operated for real before, not even an amateur station, and he apparently thought all signals were as loud and clear as the ones in code practice.

He had also lived comfortably at home all his life, and the black hole the *Ruth B* called fo'c's'le was as far from any home life as you can ever get. I had him listen while Vancouver worked the *Lillehorn*, then had him call Vancouver. After he had called back and forth a couple of times he was home free, and became quite cheerful, for one condemned to the *Ruth B*. I never did know his name, as everybody called him Sparky.

In the afternoon, I played cards with Cap Harwood and Nick until supper, while a stiff northwester blew up unnoticed.

"Don't chance it," Cap Harwood said when I put the *Leviathan* overside. "Stay for supper and overnight."

After watching the dinghy bounce around in the seas rolling alongside, I agreed.

We loaded from the *Lillehorn* on the twenty-eighth, twelve hundred and some cases. An American coast guard cutter fol-

An unidentified schooner possibly just sightseeing on Rum Row.

lowed the *Ryou II* and stuck with us until March eleventh, quite effectively putting us out of business though it was only a twelve knot cutter. While we had the cutter, we were still of some use to the other rum runners, as they knew where one cutter was, one less to make trouble in their area.

On April sixth, *Ragna* came up to us and the cutter and we transferred our load to her, over the next few days, slowly, in poor weather, the cutter watching the whole time. Charlie was getting worse. On the eleventh *Ragna* took the last few cases, and pulled away to the northwest. The cutter followed the *Ryou II* back to the *Lillehorn*, not interested in *Ragna*, whose two Liberty engines moved her along at eighteen knots.

Not our best trip. Charlie was still bad, and on the twelfth, Wednesday, we ran up to Santo Tomas, where the Mexican fisherman had an old Buick, and put him ashore, accompanied by a man from the *Lillehorn*. Charlie was in really bad shape now, and he never returned to us.

After we rowed Charlie ashore, we dropped a mile down the coast and anchored close in to a short sandy beach. A small stream of good sweet water ran across the beach into the sea from a lagoon. From the *Lillehorn* we had loaded a deck full of empty oil drums, a light-weight gasoline pump, and three deckhands.

Jack and I and one deckhand rowed ashore to get fresh water. We took a long line to haul in the empty drums launched from the *Ryou II*, and haul back the full ones. This was our first time ashore in five months, and nobody worked very hard. We took a long lunch hour and had a swim in the lagoon after we had filled the last drum. We returned to the mother ship in time for supper, then transferred the pump and deckhands back to the *Lillehorn* and tied astern for the night, our load of fresh water still on deck and on the hatch.

The next morning, April thirteenth, we pulled alongside the *Lillehorn* to unload. Hot Pants went aboard and had not returned by the time we finished unloading. I climbed aboard to ask Al Magee a question. Five months at sea, and weeks of running short-handed had more than used up my interest in a seafaring life, rum runner style, and I had nearly enough money for Tri State, enough to get through somehow.

"How do you get off these ships?" I asked Al. "Do you resign, or desert, or what?"

"Sailors don't resign," Al said. "And I don't recommend desertion on a barren coast. Even if you survived without money, you could spend time in jail, and lose out on pay. Sounds like you haven't heard the news. We're all finished—Roosevelt has ended prohibition. Every rum runner will be on the beach before Christmas."

On the *Ryou II* we listened only to radio music or comedy shows, we never received newspapers, and we lived entirely unaware of what was going on in the States or anywhere else. We were accordingly startled to learn that we were all headed for early unemployment, as far as rum running was concerned.

Aboard the *Ryou II,* left to right Fergie, George Butts, Harry "Hot Pants" Lind. A typical working day on an offshore rum-runner: nothing to do and all day to do it in.

Well, it was good while it lasted, and for me, it had lasted almost long enough. The six months' pay this trip, added to my horde in the bank, was two years plus at Tri State. Whether the plus was long enough, I didn't know, and didn't really care. Two years of assured future in school was so much more than I had ever had before it seemed like forever. If there was a shortfall, I would know it a long way ahead, at least a year, time enough to do something about it.

"So tough it out, old buddy," Al said. "You will be released from this slavery before you know it. Anyway, you are getting promoted to chief engineer, and we are giving you a second engineer, one of our oilers." I forgot to ask him if the promotion included chief engineer's pay.

We sure could use a replacement for Charlie. I wasn't quite as enthused about being chief engineer, for which job I had no more qualifications than a deckhand. Charlie had never shown me how to do anything except repack the high pressure fuel pumps. His only instructions were to call him when anything

High jinks during our shore leave at Santo Tomas, Mexico with the crew from the *Lillehorn*.

went wrong, which was good enough when he was around.

"Fergie" Ferguson came aboard next morning when we pulled alongside the *Lillehorn* to load, as we thought. Fergie was about my age, a pleasant young Irishman who looked easy enough to get along with. In a small boat with a small crew, living and working together for months on end, being easy to get along with was a much appreciated trait in a shipmate.

Instead of loading firewater, we loaded people, mostly high-priced help, for rest and recreation in Santo Tomas. Santo Tomas was four shacks and a Buick; nothing was too good for a rum runner. Ensenada, another twenty miles up the coast, was out of bounds. The Mexican authorities were not at all friendly to uninvited visitors without papers or passports.

We had aboard Cap Vosper, the chief engineer, and Al Magee from the *Lillehorn*; Captain Jack Wright and Alfie somebody from *Zip*; Captain Joe Keegan and somebody from *Ragna*; Hot Pants and me, and two or three others I didn't know. Jack rowed us ashore at the waterhole beach, and we all walked the

Rest and recreation at Santo Tomas, Mexico, "four shacks and a Buick" just south of Ensenada, spring 1933. Third from left, Jack from the *Lillehorn*; at right George from the *Lillehorn* and Alfie from the *Zip*.

wheel-rutted sandy track through the sagebrush to the shacks. As a recreation center, Santo Tomas, with its shacks and Mexicans, soon exhausted our interest. After taking a few pictures, we all walked back to the waterhole for a swim and some sunbathing.

After this orgy of relaxation we had a late lunch on the *Ryou II* while returning to the mother ship. A wild, wild day.

On Sunday, April sixteenth, we loaded about fourteen hundred cases, judging from the deckload, and were back on the San Clemente position on Monday. During these last few weeks my diary was less than comprehensive, and there are entries I have never been able to translate.

For example, on Friday the fourteenth, our day at Santo Tomas, I noted that historic event, and also made an entry "buy dog" which maybe meant something then, but is meaningless now. The *Ryou II* sure never had a dog, or even entertained so ridiculous an idea.

MV Ryou II, anchored at the waterhole, Santo Tomas, Mexico, Jack Wolf on the boom. Spring 1933.

28

W E RECEIVED A RELEASE ON THE EIGHTEENTH, AND OUR reliable fireboat, complete with firemen Clyde and Walt, appeared on the twenty-first and loaded. We told Fergie about our firewater barter arrangement, to head off any inappropriate remarks about the fresh milk, fruit and vegetables we all enjoyed.

The fireboat cockpit had a sloping after end, and a long rope coiled against it that had small loops every few feet.

"What's that line for?" I asked Walt while Clyde was in the *Ryou II*'s cabin.

"That's an emergency dump line. We put a case in each one of those loops, and tie a sea anchor on the end. If we drop the sea anchor over when we're going fast, the whole load snakes out over the stern in no time. It's just to get unloaded quick if we have engine trouble at the wrong time, like somebody chasing us. We don't have engine trouble, only one cutter around here can outrun us, that damn nuisance *CG 827*. We don't loop the cases here—it takes time. We don't like to stick around you guys—you show up a long way off."

By April thirtieth, I was about caught up on sleep, and dived back into the mysteries of my elementary algebra and elementary physics books, which hadn't had any attention for a long time.

That elementary physics was the real stuff—the book said a two-pole electric motor, with only two commutator segments, would actually run, given a little push to start. So I made one out of a three-quarter inch steel nut and bolt after a good many hours hacksawing and filing, wound the field poles and armature, and what do you know, it buzzed away like it had been designed by Thomas Edison himself.

Then I made a keying relay for my transmitter, sawing a U-shaped magnet from a link of steel chain, and it wouldn't work at all. I tried it on one coil finally, and *clickety-clickety-click*—I had the two coils connected in opposition—I still have the motor and relay, my only rum running souvenirs, aside from a few pictures.

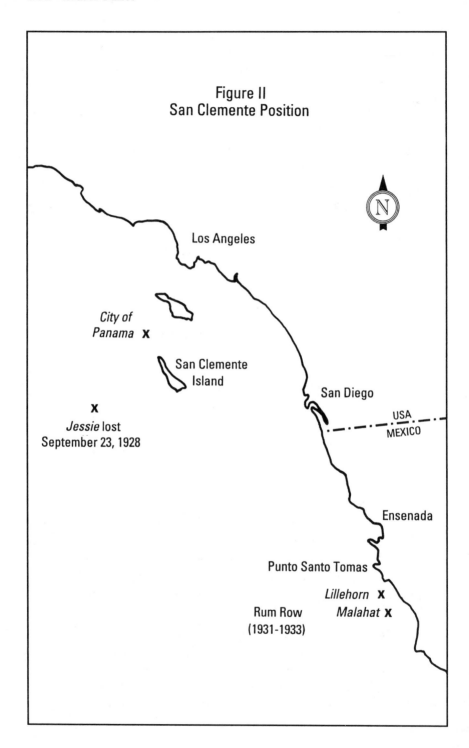

Figure II
San Clemente Position

A gale blew the full time from May first to May tenth. On May eleventh we got a release and the next day our boys took a load, and again on the sixteenth and seventeenth, and after more bad weather the last load on the twenty-third.

We arrived back at the *Lillehorn* the next day, seven months out of Vancouver. Things apparently were slow, as the *Ryou II* was the eighth boat tailing out astern of the *Lillehorn* that night—*Shuchona* (just built and on her first trip, which was also her last); *Tapawinga*; *Hickey* (ex-*Ocelot* with Fred Heathcote aboard; *Ruth B*; *Zip*; *Ryou II*; *Yukatrivol*; and one I didn't write down.

On May twenty-sixth we went to Santo Tomas again for fresh water. There was enough surf on the beach to swamp our dory with three captains, Cap Vosper, Joe Keegan and Hot Pants at the oars. We didn't get much fun out of the accident—ship captains are rather touchy about lapses in seamanship.

"The *Lillehorn*'s mate will buy my receiver now," I told

Hickey (ex-Ocelot), 110 feet long, built in San Francisco in 1917 for the US Navy. One 150-hp Cooper Bessemer diesel and two 400-hp Garwood 12-cylinder gas engines.

Jack. "But I told him you were first in line. Do you want to buy it?"

"Well no, not especially," Jack said. "Not now, when the whole fleet is headed for the beach. I don't want to have my money tied up either. Then again, I'd sure miss the radio programs."

"I'll chip in a bit if I have to," George Butts said. "But why not ask Clyde and Walt if the barter system is good for anything but groceries?"

I knew it was so I agreed to hold the sale, as our turnaround time on the San Clemente position was so short we would know in a week.

On May twenty-eighth we pulled alongside the *Lillehorn*, the first of the eight little duckies to load, and were back on position off San Clemente the next day, with a release.

The San Clemente position had changed from the original

The first San Clemente position assigned *Ryou II* was used by the US navy day and night. The *Ryou II* promptly relocated. The schooner *Jessie* was run down at night and sunk in this area in August 1928.

forty miles west of China Point, to I never knew where exactly. It was closer to shore, but still a long way outside the twelve-mile limit. A couple of times battleships had firing practice right close to us in daylight, lots of noise but no risk.

Then one night something huge and fast went speeding by maybe a quarter mile away, no sweat for that one, but later the same night another big fast one went by so close we took a terrific pounding from her wash.

Jack, George and Fergie all came up into the galley more than a bit alarmed. We had turned our lights on by then.

"That was too damn close," Hot Pants said. "It was just around here that Slattery and Keegan were run down in the *Jessie* and sunk several years ago. Start her up, Sparky, we'll move away now, and request a new position clear of the navy on the midnight schedule."

We moved and didn't have any more navy trouble.

Our happy-go-lucky firemen pulled alongside late the next afternoon, May thirtieth, and loaded their usual two hundred and fifty cases of firewater. They didn't bother much with the European brand-name stuff down here in California—who knows, maybe the customers hadn't been educated to such a level of appreciation.

"Yes indeed," Walt said when Jack brought up the subject of a second-hand battery radio. "The barter system has no limits. We'll get you a radio next trip." Considering the boys' profit margin, the unlimited barter offer was easy to understand.

That night we received not one, but two releases. Hot Pants poked his head in the galley door a short while after I handed him the messages.

"Jack, Jack, come and see where they want us to go," he said, all excited. "It's right on the beach, we'll be towed in for sure."

They went into the cabin, and were in there quite a while, talking away like a debating team. We turned the radio volume away down, but couldn't make out a word.

"It's a mite closer in than usual," Jack said when he came back later. "Right in the Santa Barbara Channel, fifteen miles from San Clemente to the southeast, fifteen miles from Santa Barbara Island to the northwest, and fifteen miles southwest of Santa Catalina Island. Contact at daylight tomorrow morning. He's decided he won't refuse to go in so close."

We all thought this over for a few moments. "Fifteen miles, eh," George said. "Somebody better pay goddamn good attention to somebody's navigating. Even ten miles error here and we could be removed to downtown Long Beach, guests of the city."

The position was only thirty-five miles northwest of the San Clemente position, which, in the flat grey sea/grey sky conditions we couldn't be sure we were near anyway. After dark, we weren't much worse off.

At midnight we started up, Jack at the wheel, Hot Pants and I lookouts port and starboard, Fergie lookout aft, and ran until the earliest light showed in the east. Twenty minutes after I went in for breakfast Hot Pants shouted from the foredeck.

"Shore boat coming, shore boat coming!"

George and I left the galley for a look. A low fast boat throwing a great white spray from her bow, was heading straight for us. It circled us once, then stopped, a hundred yards off. It was that damn nuisance, the *CG 827.*

"They're signalling the shore for a tug to tow us in," Hot Pants said scratching away furiously at his crotch. "The code book is ready to throw over. Sparky, you put the call sign sheet in the bilge, and disconnect the radios."

I disconnected the radios and stuck them in a food locker.

"Hot Pants better go easy on that scratching, or he'll be talking soprano before he knows it," George said, a bit loud. George didn't always show proper respect for the captain of the ship.

"Another ship, a big one," Fergie called from on top of the wheelhouse.

A small dot on the horizon showed under a cloud of black smoke, also coming straight for us.

"That's the tug to tow us in for sure," Jack said just to bug Hot Pants. "What are we going to tell them when they put a line on board, Cap?"

"No problem at all," George said. "Just tell them to go away. We're only helping Sparky here work his way through college."

The blob of smoke came up to us in no time, and turned out to be three ships, a three-hundred-foot passenger ship, the *City of Panama*, another coast guard cutter, and a third boat, a tugboat, that was just sightseeing. The *Panama* stopped near us, and a cargo door opened on her port side, a few feet above the water-line.

"Pull alongside under the door," a great loudhailer voice boomed down from her bridge. We moved alongside and took the bow and stern lines. From a stage rigged outside the cargo door a ship's officer dropped down to the *Ryou II* and went into our cabin with Hot Pants.

"Okay, get the hatch off," Hot Pants said when the officer climbed back aboard *Panama*. "They're taking three hundred cases, Old Colonel and Coon Hollow, half each. And get to it— we want to get the hell back to San Clemente."

We worked at more than our usual easy pace, not so much

US Coast Guard cutter *CG 827* (ex US rum runner *Diatome*), summer 1933.

because of Hot Pants' orders, but for the benefit of our audiences. The upper deck of the *Panama* was lined with men and women, all fairly young, half of them with cameras snapping away at us. The two cutters came in close and took pictures, and the sightseeing boat did the same. The *Panama* steamed slowly ahead all the while, making a couple of knots.

Even Hot Pants relaxed a bit, with a convenient assist from the small brown bottle that had reappeared in the holder over the galley sink. What struck me most was how clean all the passengers looked and how carefully dressed they were. After so many months bathing in a bucket of water on the afterdeck, and washing our clothes the same way, we were more than grubby and untidy. I was the grubbiest, I think, with engine room oil and dirt on top of ordinary body dirt.

When the red-haired sailor on the landing stage had our last case, the officer came aboard again for a minute in the cabin with Hot Pants. After their business was completed, we quickly dropped the *Panama*'s lines and were on our leisurely way back to the San Clemente position. We moved sluggishly—months of these southern waters had given our hull an outstanding crop of goose barnacles and weed—the barnacles were approaching six inches long, and were growing by the week. Both cutters stayed with the *Panama*.

Late in the afternoon, we were back at San Clemente. Walt and Clyde were there, munching away happily on the barter system's crate of produce. We told them about the *City of Panama* and *CG 827*.

"The *Panama* is an offshore gambling ship," Clyde said. "And *CG 827* is one of the fastest cutters around. She's the old rum runner *Diatome* they caught a year or so back. We got a radio for you too. Let's get loading."

The fireboat had her two hundred and fifty cases by dark. We slid over the usual breakage case for our groceries. Clyde brought out our new radio. It was something, about a yard long and the whole front panel crowded with five big dials and a lot of little ones. I looked inside—not factory-built, but a good job for an amateur.

"That's thirty dollars, Jack," Clyde said loud enough for Hot Pants to hear and Jack and Clyde fumbled money back and forth convincingly.

"And we were short one case last trip, Jack," Clyde said. "We need another, a good one."

We argued a bit—we thought our case was enough for both groceries and the radio. But Clyde and Walt had all the leverage, and finally we slid across another case of "*Ryou*'s Best Breakage—Guaranteed Not More Than Two Broken Bottles Per Case."

That night we stood three-hour watches to catch up on sleep, loaded our firemen again the next day, missed a day, and transferred the last two hundred cases to them on June third, and were back on Rum Row, tied to the *Zip* astern of *Lillehorn* twenty-four hours later.

Ryou's total to date—thirteen thousand, three hundred cases, give or take a couple hundred.

29

JUST BEFORE SUPPER THAT NIGHT A SMALL DORY ROWED BY Harry Slattery dropped down the line of boats trailing behind the *Lillehorn*.

"Come on up for supper, Sparky," he called to me. "Some people you know are eating with us, and playing poker."

The *Shuchona* was another fish packer, sixty-five feet long, but with all crew berthed in the deckhouse, which left room below in the fo'c's'le for a galley and a comparatively large living space.

My diary says, "Good party on *Shuchona*." It wasn't really a party, more a last supper, a fraternal gathering, a wake and a going-away party combined—the no partying/no visiting rule quite ignored. I didn't know all of the high type fellas there, but remember Jack Vosper and Al Magee from the *Lillehorn*, Jack Wright from *Zip*, Jack Harwood and Nick Gjengsto from the

Ruth B, Jack Wolf, and Hot Pants from *Ryou II*, Fred Heathe-cote from *Hickey*, and of the *Shuchona*'s crew, Harry Slattery and Smoky Hoodspith.

After supper, when the guests had crowded in, Jack Harwood rose to his feet and rapped a coffee mug on the table.

"We are gathered here this evening, brothers in spirits, we Brethren of the Row, high type fellas all, to mark the end of a way of life, which for some has lasted these many years—we shall first nominate a Great Elder Brother from our long service brothers, maybe a bit ahead of time but we are unlikely to have another chance. Brother Vosper, Sir, your seniority in the service, please, and first ship?" "January, 1924, *Lirio de Agua*," Vosper said.

"The *Water Lily*—a most suitable name for rum runner— Brother Slattery?"

"January, 1924, same ship."

"Brother Wright?"

A Columbian schooner from Tahiti bringing supplies to Rum Row, 1933.

"November, 1926—*Kuzakuzmt*, the alphabet ship."

"Brother Lind?"

"*Gunhild II*, April, 1923. But Brother Keegan had her the trip before me in November, 1922."

"Brother Joe Keegan, here in spirit only but still on active service, is therefore nominated to Great Elder Brother for his long dedicated service in American drought relief work, from November 1922, to sometime soon in 1933. As runner-up, Brother Lind is asked to accept this award for second place, a whole case of Coon Hollow Bourbon, with one hundred percent breakage." Cap Harwood handed Hot Pants a case of Coon Hollow, with a great rattle of broken glass, to much applause.

"In our kiddies corner," Cap went on, "an honourable mention goes jointly to those two refugees from the kindergarten, Small Brother Hoodspith and Small Brother Miles, who, after years of loyal and spirited service, are now almost old enough to vote." Applause.

"Our last award goes to Brother Slattery, the Honourable Surviving Brother. One night while drifting off San Diego in the schooner *Jessie*, he hit something big and sunk with the loss of all cargo. Later off San Francisco, he burned the *Fleetwood*, again with the loss of all cargo. Good job there weren't many like him around, or we would have run out of ships years ago." Lengthy applause.

"And now for the toasts," Cap Harwood went on. "And we are not going to drink them with just any old firewater filched from a previous cargo—Brother Vosper knows we never, never, never broach cargo—we will drink with a distillation suitable for men of distinction, we Brethren of the Row. Especially we wish to introduce our kindergarten to one of the finer things in life, Apricot Brandy, my contribution to this final meeting of the Brethren—Smoky, the glasses please."

Smoky set out half a dozen chipped coffee mugs.

"Our catering service is not the best—you will have to toast in turn, not the usual all at once—and sippers only, no bottoms up. I don't have enough brandy for gulpers, let alone bottoms up. We toast ourselves, Brethren of the Row, *Lillehorn* Chapter, and also our absent Brethren of the *Malahat* Chapter, high type fellas all, and also the unknown organizers of this international drought relief project, who through their initiative, spirit and enterprise, have kept us in funds these many years; and others from thirst.

"Rum running is finished—we are all on our last trip but will do our duty to the end, buoyed up by those fat paycheques and the thought that we shall soon be fondly embraced by our loved ones, the cuddly kittens at Celestine's, who surely love us for ourselves alone."

Cries of, "Yeah, love those cuddly kittens."

"And finally," Cap Harwood went on, "we must never forget the Brethren's motto 'Don't never tell nothin' to nobody nohow.' We shall close this notable occasion as usual by singing our very own song. I shall lead in song—is the band in tune, the chorus in voice?"

There were loud cries of, "Yeah, yeah, tune the chorus, love those kittens," while a guitar strummed in the background.

"Our song is, as you know, John Thomas's 'Farewell to Celestine'."

We ask that you, John Thomas, our joy, our pride,
Our single delight in time of great need,
Please find strength for another Miss Deed,
Just once more 'fore we sail on salty tide.

First chorus please—

Oh my darling, oh my darling, oh my darling Thomas mine,
You are limp and down forever, dreadful sorrow, Celestine.
We thank you John, for joy on many a night,
But John, we need you again for our pleasure.
To comfort, to charm our beloved, our treasure,
Our Celestine, with hours of true delight.

The second chorus please—

Oh my darling, oh my darling, oh my darling Thomas mine,
Stand firm and serve your master, faithful soldier, Thomas mine.

Last verse—

You wake, you rise, you come up strong,

You feel the touch of loving, soft white hand,
Of the lovely Celestine, and rise upon command,
To please your master for all the night long.
Last chorus please—
Oh my darling, oh my darling, oh my darling Thomas mine,
You are limp and down forever, treasured rapture, Thomas
   mine.

So what if rum running was occasionally boring, with a party like that every ten years or so? And that apricot brandy was a noble libation, something to rejoice your tonsils, not at all like that feeble fizzy stuff, champagne, that Jack dug out for last Christmas.

Much has been written about the mythical millionaires created by rum running and the fabulous (according to Charlie Hudson) sums spent on building fast boats, buying engines, fuel, supplies, and paying crews. No mention has yet been made of the more certain indirect benefits accruing to Celestine and her kittens. Money in the hands of most rum runners had a short retention time, rather large chunks going immediately into the acquisition of high-priced works of time-sharing art.

On June fourth we ran down to the *Malahat*, now riding

Algie, 105 feet long, from the east coast.

high in the water, took three of her crew aboard, and spent the day transferring from the *Marechal Foch*, just up from Tahiti, to the *Mogul*, a large old ore carrier taking over from the *Malahat*.

We wondered—to ourselves, not to others—why such a large supply ship was bringing more stock, with rum running so close to the end. A brain good enough to organize rum running on the whole west coast must surely know it was all over.

Two days of bad weather held us tied astern of the *Lillehorn*, then another day transferring. Two more days of bad weather brought us to Sunday June eleventh, when we did more transferring, alternating with the *Zip* alongside the *Foch*.

The *Marechal Foch*, a beautiful three-masted schooner, had a large brass plate on the quarterdeck cabin wall, proclaiming her

Marechal Foch, a supply schooner from Tahiti, 1933. Formerly Zane Grey's yacht *Fisherman.*

distinguished past as the fishing yacht of Zane Grey, who had spent a fortune catching huge fish around Tahiti not long before.

Monday was loading day, some from *Marechal Foch*, some from *Mogul* and some from *Malahat*, about thirteen hundred cases in all. Then we were back off San Clemente, Friday, June sixteenth, with a release in the late afternoon, and transferred a load the same day.

On Saturday, Clyde and Walt arrived again, but we had no release and couldn't transfer. Sunday was rough, Monday we gave them a second load, then were off position for three days, two with a cutter in company, and one drifting in thick fog.

Friday, June twenty-third, dawned clear, with a stiff northwest breeze raising small waves. We ran back to position after the noon sight, and lay rolling easily in the small waves. On position and expecting a fireboat, we didn't use the riding sail as it was far too visible. Jack and I were lookouts aft, Hot Pants forward. He suddenly shouted, "Boat! Boat!" pointing southeast.

We jumped up and ran forward, to the higher foredeck. A low profile boat was heading straight upwind towards us at high speed, throwing sheets of spray from every sea.

"Something wrong there," Jack said. "Clyde and Walt would never run like that, throwing spray you can see for miles."

He ran into the wheelhouse for the glasses.

"*CG 827*, sure as hell," he said.

"Start up, Sparky," Hot Pants said. "Jack, run west to get away from position."

CG 827 slowed down half a mile to leeward, nearly invisible when she stopped throwing spray.

I was just coming out on deck again when Fergie hollered, "Boat to windward, another fast boat."

"What bloody luck, now we got trouble," Jack grumbled. "Clyde and Walt, sure as hell."

Our happy-go-lucky firemen kept coming downwind towards the *Ryou II*, the cutter keeping pace with us, directly to leeward.

"They won't see the cutter downwind," Hot Pants said. "We gotta warn them before they get too close. Run in circles,

Jack. Sparky, you and Fergie hoist the flag and the sail."

Fergie and I never had time to raise the sail. Our first circle told both boats that things were wrong. *CG 827* knew a few seconds before Clyde and Walt—we assumed it was our happy pair—who reversed course in a flash and roared off into the wind, a great plume of spray behind them, fleeing from the only cutter on the California coast which was faster than they were.

As *CG 827* flashed by us, a man stood up half out of a wheelhouse hatch, with an automatic rifle. In minutes both boats disappeared, to the intermittent *rat-tat-tat-tat* of the automatic, the sound still coming downwind some time after we had the ocean to ourselves. (See the whole story in *Appendix II.*)

"Well damn," Jack said, "some good luck, some bad. If *CG 827* showed up ten minutes later, with Clyde and Walt tied alongside, finish for them. I hope they make it."

"Run off west by south, Jack," Hot Pants said.

We ran offshore until the seven o'clock radio schedule, when we exchanged messages with Vancouver, none of us at all cheerful. Hot Pants disappeared into his cabin with the galley bottle of firewater. I stayed on watch, in theory, but dozed in the galley, lights on, with the radio turned down low. At midnight I called Fergie and turned in.

On the eight-thirty morning schedule we received orders to transfer our remaining load to *Zip*. We transferred the next day, and arrived back at the *Lillehorn* on Monday, June twenty-sixth, eight months of what was to have been a six-month trip out of Vancouver.

On Tuesday morning we had just left the *Lillehorn* to load off *Malahat* when the engine changed from a regular *puff-puff-puff* to *sput-sput-sput* and stopped dead. White smoke blew out the exhaust when she *sput-sputted*. I climbed down into the engine room, and found Fergie barring the engine into position to start. He pumped fuel pressure up to two thousand pounds, and tried a start. No go at all, nor at the next try either.

We were standing there by the engine controls, just looking at each other, when a boat bumped alongside and a clean-shaven, well-dressed guy dropped down the engine room ladder.

"From the smoke you made, you got water in your fuel lines, Fergie," he said. "Where's your day tank?"

Day tank, what day tank? Charlie never told me about any day tank. The officer found it boarded in under the workbench, and when he opened the drain valve, a lot of water and brown sludge ran into the bilge. He closed the valve, and worked a hand pump to refill it with diesel oil.

"Now we'll look at your fuel screens," he said. Damn Charlie anyway, he never told me about any fuel screens either. They were stuck away under the bench too, full of more brown sludge and water.

"Now we clear your fuel lines and fuel nozzles," our visitor said, very busy undoing pipes, pumping until clean fuel spilled out, and tightening up again, until finally everything was clear including the nozzles.

"Okay, try her now, Fergie," he said after he had replaced the last fuel nozzle.

Away it went, just like it had never seen water. "Thanks

US Coast Guard cutter *Tamaroa*.

Blondy," Fergie said as the man left. "That was Blondy, the second engineer on the *Lillehorn*," he added for my benefit.

This delay made it noon before we arrived at the *Malahat*, where we loaded a few hundred cases of firewater, then moved over to the *Mogul* for fresh water, diesel oil, coal, stores, and more firewater. We moved back up to the *Lillehorn* for the night, then pulled alongside next morning, June 28th, for the last few hundred cases. With two hundred cases on deck, we had loaded fourteen hundred in all.

"Last load for sure," Jack said hopefully as we battened down.

I took Al Magee all the odds and ends of radio stuff I had accumulated, as I had agreed when he bought my short wave receiver. After supper we pulled away on a westerly course.

A stiff northwester cut us down to half speed for a couple of days. The third day was calm, with thin intermittent fog. Just before noon, a small ship showed dead ahead, drifting, a dark grey ship with three deck cabins. Half an hour later we pulled alongside the *Algie*, an east coast boat one hundred and five feet long. With about twice the beam of a subchaser, and only a diesel engine, she was almost as slow as the *Ryou II*. Two of the three "deckhouses" were cases of firewater piled high on foredeck and afterdeck, covered with tarpaulins and lashed down.

Hot Pants and *Algie*'s skipper, Joe Keegan, talked a few minutes and we pulled away northwest again until July third, when we stopped and hoisted our riding sail, and drifted. Two hours later a big cutter came up. We moved off position twenty miles, and drifted again; the cutter in company, for a couple of days, with our lights on at night. When we blacked out, the cutter just switched on her searchlight.

Late the second night, just before midnight, I was in the galley, my back to the sink, reading something interesting in my Ontario physics book, when all of a sudden a freak wave struck the *Ryou II*, smashed in all the port side windows, and poured a torrent of water into the galley. I was thrown face down on the galley table with water pouring over me.

By the time I had got my wind back, the flood had drained

out the open galley door and down the engine room hatchway. The *Ryou II* was rocking gently on small seas. Through the open windows a light breeze blew wisps of steam from the galley stove. I called Jack and we rigged the canvas blackout screen over the port windows, and cleaned broken glass from the table and galley floor.

The next morning we found one plank on the dory's port side split from stem to stern, something requiring more force than just the crest of a breaking wave coming aboard.

30

MY BACK WAS SORE FOR A COUPLE OF DAYS FROM THE BLOW I took, but there was no serious damage to either me or the dory. The worst news was the semi-gloom in the galley, but we all felt we were going home after this last trip anyway.

Sometime in that week I found a wet, exhausted pigeon huddled up on the winch behind the mast. I brought it into the galley, where George wrapped it in a dish towel before putting it close to the stove to warm up. When it showed signs of revival he fed it milk, pancake crumbs, and cockroaches. A couple of days later we took it outside and put it on the hatch where the pigeon flexed and stretched for a few minutes then took off. We were then about sixty miles from land, off San Francisco.

We had a release when the *Yukatrivol* arrived on Sunday, July ninth, but the numbers didn't match. They were sorted out by the next morning when we transferred three hundred cases of firewater, and filled her diesel tanks from our deckload of drums. The *Yukatrivol*, a sixty-two footer, was a brand new Canadian shore boat with a fast planing hull, a 200-horsepower diesel and the usual pair of 450-horsepower Liberty gasoline engines. She had the distinction of being the last boat built especially for rum running, and her first voyage was also her last, from mid-April 1933 to late 1933.

The next day we were supposed to transfer to *Shuchona* but

we couldn't find her. We received a long message the next morning then did a lot of running around and found her about noon. Somebody's navigation was wrong—maybe again? We transferred five hundred cases to her that afternoon, and were back on our former position next morning, according to Jack.

We transferred a couple of hundred cases to an American shore boat Friday, July fourteenth. Next day the *Algie* showed up, with a cutter, then another cutter arrived, then in the afternoon we transferred the last of our load to the *Yukatrivol*, in rough weather off San Francisco with everybody else floating around watching. That was the big reason, other than money, for Canadian shore boats—they could load right under the eye of the coast guard and with their superior speed, could lose the cutters any time. Mostly the cutters never attempted to follow, but presumably signalled the departure to officials on shore. The cutters were *Cygan* and *Shawnee*.

Then damned if we didn't run off southeast, not going home at all.

The third or fourth day on our run south, I came out of the galley after a lunch of bully beef and green beans—we were nearly out of food, as our living standard had fallen drastically with

Audrey B in spring 1933 with the hold full to its 2,500 case capacity and two large deckloads. 100 feet long, she came to the west coast after seizure on the east coast in 1930.

the loss of our barter system—and found Jack leaning out over the side looking at our water-line.

"Those goose barnacles look too deep, Sparky," he said. "How long since you pumped out?"

"We pump the end of every watch. Keep an eye on the pump discharge while I get Fergie to pump the hold."

The pump spewed out a little water, then foam, then nothing.

"Looks dry, all right," Jack said. "But something's queer—give me a hand with the hatch covers."

And what do you know, we had wall-to-wall dunnage, sacking and oil covering the surface of two feet of water sloshing back and forth in the hold.

"Well nothing for it, we clean the hold and unplug the bilge intake screen. No need to tell Hot Pants that we forgot to clean the hold last load. We don't need to stop—I know where the intake is, and can keep my hands clear of the propeller shaft. Come dive with me—I need you to hold the dunnage off while I feel around for the screen. We can clean the hold easier when we get the water down."

We stripped off to shorts and lowered ourselves slowly through the floating crap.

It was easy enough, just messy. Jack brought up two big handfuls of lint and chips, and said, "Okay Fergie, I think the intake is clear enough to pump." And so it was, the pump discharge running a steady stream as the water level fell slowly.

The shaft gland leaked quite a stream of water, but Fergie decided not to touch it until we arrived at the *Lillehorn* where there must surely be someone who knew more about repacking stern glands than we did—and had some packing, if that was what was needed.

We tied astern of the *Lillehorn* on Wednesday, July nineteenth—for the last time? Please, the last time; I wanted to start Tri State College in September.

An engineer from the *Lillehorn* repacked our stern gland, and also did a job on our intermediate shaft bearing, which had been vibrating and rattling noisily after its two or three days in salt water.

On the twenty-second we ran up towards Santo Tomas for a swim in the lagoon. There was too much surf to land on the beach, so we anchored behind the kelp beds off the shacks and landed there, leaving George Butts on the *Ryou*. Hot Pants stayed at the shacks, while Jack, Fergie and I walked to the lagoon, washed and swam in the warm fresh water.

When we arrived back at the shacks, Hot Pants was gone. "He go Ensenada in car," the Mexican woman said.

"We could get lucky," Jack said. "Maybe he won't come back."

But Hot Pants returned late the next afternoon with the Mexican lobster fisherman, cold sober, but not in good shape. His face looked like it had just been extruded from a hamburger machine, he had a quite incredible black eye, and his clothes looked as though he had been dragged from Ensenada behind the Buick, not ridden in it.

He didn't seem quite aware of his surroundings, and he kept muttering to himself over and over, "Thrown out of a Mexican cat house, damn me."

After a bit of this, he shut himself in his cabin, and didn't appear for supper.

We bought lobsters from the Mexican and gave him the brown bottle from the galley as thanks for carrying Hot Pants.

"This will keep him off the firewater, until we load again," Jack said as he handed the bottle over.

That was all the excitement for this stay at the *Lillehorn*, which lasted until July twenty-sixth, when we loaded twelve hundred cases and fifteen drums of diesel fuel from the *Lillehorn* and *Mogul*, leaving the big ships before supper. The *Malahat* was already on her way to Vancouver, the end of a long and well publicized rum running career.

The next day my ulcerated tooth started aching for the first time since I had lanced the pus pocket months ago, but it gradually subsided over the next two days while I kept applying hot pads to my lower jaw.

On July thirty-first, after a run of five hundred and ninety miles, mostly against a strong northwester, we arrived on position somewhere off San Francisco and received a release.

On August first, we loaded an American shore boat with two hundred cases, then moved about fifty miles to a new position, where the cutter *Cahokia* promptly picked us up, and stayed with us until the ninth, after we had transferred some three hundred cases and diesel oil to *Yukatrivol* on the eighth.

August tenth was the day we had been thinking about for the last four months—we received orders to transfer the remaining seven hundred cases to *Shuchona* and return to Vancouver. Rum running was all over for the *Ryou II*.

Or almost all over: on August tenth we arrived on position in a stiff northwester that lasted through to the twelfth, followed by two days of good weather, then two days of fog on the fourteenth and fifteenth. We were close to *Shuchona*—Smoky and I had a schedule every two hours while the *Ryou* blew her whistle and ran in bigger and bigger circles looking for an accidental contact, a remote probability with fog limiting visibility to a hun-

The waterhole at Santo Tomas, with the fresh water stream (at lower left) from a spring a half mile inland, 1933.

dred yards or so.

Wednesday, August sixteenth, was *Shuchona* day. The fog lifted, and there she was, a couple of miles away. Probably the best word to describe our transfer was "expeditiously." I went aboard *Shuchona* for a farewell to Smoky Hoodspith and Harry Slattery, then we headed away to the northwest at our best speed. Our goose barnacles now covered our hull to a depth of eight inches or so—I measured some in the shipyard—and our best speed was a modest six knots.

The *Ryou II* arrived in Vancouver, Wednesday, August twenty-third, 1933 after three hundred and four days at sea, a long time, but still short of the *Zip*'s record of three hundred and sixty-six days. Only three other boats besides *Zip* had trips longer than ours—*Hickey, Ragna* and *Tapawinga.*

The *Ryou*'s total haul was now, by my reckoning, some fif-

MV Ryou II homeward bound after ten months at sea, August 1933. Left to right: Fergie, George Butts, Sparky.

teen thousand two hundred cases—my records included some estimates. Anyway, fifteen thousand is a pretty good figure.

For the ten months I was paid fifteen hundred dollars. Ten
cents a case, my share of its estimated, totally unverified value of
two hundred American dollars.

Rum running lasted only a few months more. *Kagome* re-
turned home in September. *Lillehorn* came back in November.
The *Tapawinga, Principio/Tooya* and *Chief Skugaid* arrived in
December.

The last five small boats, *Shuchona, Algie, Audrey B, Hickey*
and *Zip*, all returned in January, 1934, with *Shuchona* the last
one by a clear two weeks.

Mogul, a sort of holding tank without any distribution
boats, returned June, 1934.

Ryou II paid off at the office on Hamilton Street the next
day, August twenty-fourth. Everybody was in really clean clothes,
and with complexions several shades lighter than they had been
for months. How splendid to be clean again!

Nobody exchanged addresses, or promised to write. So I
took leave of Jack, Fergie, and George, three really high type fellas who made a long tedious trip quite tolerable.

And maybe, Charlie Smith—from him I learned at least one
useful thing—if ever you have anyone working under you, teach
him all he can absorb about the job. He will be most appreciative
and may even give you the ultimate accolade, "Best boss I ever
had."

The countdown to Tri State was necessarily short—have my bad
tooth pulled, write the College I was coming, buy some school
clothes, a twenty-one jewel railroad watch I didn't need, an over-
coat I didn't need, and a bus ticket to Chicago, one way. The
ticket man said Chicago would know where Angola, Indiana was.
He couldn't find it in the schedule.

I started higher learning even before I arrived at the college.
I learned some economics. When I traded my two thousand dollars school money at the bank for American money, I received a
bank draft for only eighteen hundred dollars, a notable reduction

in my safety margin. Anyway, not to worry, the crunch, if it came at all, was two years away at least.

Finally, in early September, with my shrunken but still quite fabulous earnings from rum running in a money belt around my waist, I did what many thousands of young Canadians had done before me, I headed south across the border. It seemed rather appropriate that I was going to school in the States, for it was American money, paid out initially for costly imported necessities, and now being recycled, that was making Tri State possible.

Chief Skugaid, 77 feet long, one of the old timers, loaded. In for the duration, she started rum-running in 1922 and her last trip was November 1933.

III

Appendices

Appendix I

A Short History of West Coast Rum Running

The Fabulous Years of Rum Running 1922–1923

In the first two years of Canadian rum running on the Pacific Coast, rum running was simple, presumably profitable, and quite trouble free. Ships loaded the merchandise in Vancouver or New Westminster, hovered off the California coast for a few weeks while unloading to American shore boats, and when empty came home, the crews laughing all the way to the bank or more likely to Celestine's, as rum running sailors weren't big on banks.

The Years of Disaster 1924–1925

The second two years were mostly trouble for the Canadian entrepreneurs. A major portion of the losses was due to error, carelessness or overconfidence on the part of the rum runner ship captains involved, of which the U.S. Coast Guard was happy to take advantage.

Quadra was seized, *Pescawha* was seized, *Speedway* burned (an accident) and *Westcoast* was seized. In the case of *Pescawha*, almost all blame for the seizure and loss of ship and cargo must be assigned to the ship's captain, Captain Robert Pamphlett. On February 3, 1925, visibility was good off the Washington coast, just north of the Columbia River mouth, a heavy southwesterly swell was running, but the wind was then only Beaufort Force 4, around fifteen knots, also southwest.

Around noon of February 3, *Pescawha* picked up a small lifeboat with nine men in it, crew of the U.S. steam schooner *Caoba* who had abandoned their (presumably) sinking ship two or three days before, after sending distress signals. Captain Pamphlett may not have known of this before he picked up the *Caoba's* crew at noon.

When interrogated February 4, 1925 aboard the cutter *Algonquin* in Astoria, Oregon, Captain Pamphlett claimed that he had picked up the *Caoba's* boat shortly before noon February

3, 1925, some eighteen miles west-southwest (magnetic) from Gray's Harbour entrance gas buoy.

Captain Alfred Sandnig, mate of the steam schooner *Caoba* stated February 4, "While we were in our small boat we could not see land, but as soon as we got on board the *Pescawha* we could see land clearly. I know it was the Willapa Bay entrance, as I have been sailing out of Willapa Bay and Gray's Harbour for over six years...."

The *Pescawha* was about six miles off the Washington Coast at noon February 3, when Captain Pamphlett definitely learned of the distress call from and abandonment of *Caoba* two days before.

Distress calls and ship abandonments always generate sea searches by the coast guard and coastal rescue services, but Captain Pamphlett made no move to take his ship further offshore outside the one hour steaming limit, the governing distance in force in this incident.

Thus four hours later at 4:05 p.m., when *Pescawha* was sighted by the cutter *Algonquin,* the Canadian ship was still only six and a half miles off the coast of Washington, and was seized.

The rum runners thus lost their ship and 1075 cases of liquor, mostly quality brands of scotch. This loss was easily avoidable, if, in the four hours available to him, Captain Pamphlett had only used one of them to take his ship further offshore. The *Pescawha* made something over eight knots under power alone and with the fifteen knot southwesterly blowing, could have approached ten knots under power and sail on a west-northwest course offshore. Those four hours between noon and 4:05 p.m. on February 3, 1925, were a most inappropriate time for Captain Pamphlett to do nothing. All this data came from the *Algonquin*'s log dated February 6, 1925, "Seizure of Canadian Schooner *Pescawha* by *Algonquin*."

A similar misjudgement on the part of Captain Lilly in December, 1932, led to the seizure of *Kagome* off San Francisco, though *Kagome* for some unknown reason was subsequently released.

The seizure of *Quadra* off San Francisco can also be blamed on error, carelessness, or overconfidence on the part of her skipper, Captain George Ford, as the rum runner was proven to be within the twelve mile limit when seen loading a small American fishboat, *C-55*, also seized with 55 cases of liquor aboard.

The *Quadra*'s loss was 12,000 cases, and the ship.

Little detail is available on *Westcoast*, which was reported seized in San Diego, May 12, 1924, and confiscated in Ensenada, Mexico, September 15, 1925. Both events were probably caused by unpaid bills, as no liquor law violations appeared involved.

These seizures and the burning of the *Speedway* so reduced the number of offshore rum ships delivering refreshments to the American shore boats that the coast guard cutters had little trouble limiting the activities of the few remaining ships. No American shore boat could load from a Canadian ship no matter how far it was outside the Mexican three mile or the U.S. twelve mile limit, while an American cutter was standing by the Canadian ship. Even though a fast shore boat could easily outrun most U.S. cutters, it was a sure capture if it attempted to load, if it was American.

The Coast Guard Years 1926–1929

In these years the U.S. Coast Guard clearly had the upper hand, although it was only involved in one of the major losses suffered by the rum runners, the seizure of *Federalship*. Losses were:

1927 *Kiltuish*—87-foot fish packer—wrecked
  Federalship—222-foot steamer—seized but released
1928 *Jessie*—two-masted schooner, run over at night by fast vessel running without lights.
  Captain Joe Keegan and Charlie Smith in the crew.
  All cargo lost, crew saved.
1929 *Noble*—76-foot schooner wrecked January 14, 1929 on Escalante Reef, Vancouver Island.
  Captain W. Kerr. Four lives lost.
  Noble was formerly *Lady Mine*—built 1889 in Port Ludlow, Washington—*Ououkinsh*—56-foot two-masted schooner—burned September. Captain Joe Keegan and shipmates Harry Slattery and Slim "Hot Pants" Lind.

The 222-foot *Federalship* (ex *Gertrude,* later *La Golodrina*) with Captain S.S. Stone in command, was seized over two hundred miles off the California coast by the U.S. Coast Guard on a technicality. *Federalship* was registered in Panama, and under Panamanian Law 54, enacted December 11, 1926, a Panamanian merchant ship lost that nationality if it was devoted to smuggling. The U.S. Coast Guard called her a "pirate" ship.

Some 12,500 cases of scotch whiskey were found on board when she was seized, so there was no doubt about the ship's illegal activity. The ship was towed to San Francisco, and the cargo was removed to the U.S. appraiser's stores for safekeeping.

The U.S. Federal Court disagreed with the seizure and ruled the release of the vessel and cargo and ordered the Coast Guard to tow the ship to the point of seizure.

But the entire cargo of 12,500 cases, weighing about two hundred and fifty tons, had mysteriously vanished.

Considering the closely controlled organizations handling the San Francisco part of Pacific Coast rum running, and the sheer size of the cargo, there can be hardly any doubt that the original consignees got their hands on the lot. And the Coast Guard, in addition to losing the seized ship, had the further mortification of realizing that they had, in towing *Federalship* to San Francisco, provided free, totally safe landing services to the rum runners.

The seizure of *Federalship* in 1927, although not the primary cause of the rum runners' poor showing in the early coast guard years, spurred the rum ships' owners to either replace their master minds, or to send them into a "retreat" to come up with new plans to get the operation out of the doldrums.

The Rum Runner's Years 1920–1933

The graph below summarizes the increased activity resulting from the ultimatum issued by the owners to their managers.

The growth was spectacular, with nearly a threefold increase in ships at sea, and more than a fourfold increase in a more important number, ship months spent at sea. These figures escalate drastically from 1929 to 1932, and are still well up in 1933, the second highest year.

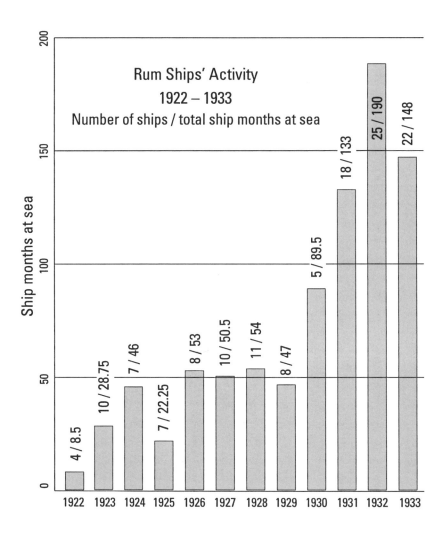

Rum Ships' Activity
1922 – 1933
Number of ships / total ship months at sea

What changed?

The whole system changed. The simple "load-in-Vancouver, unload-at-sea, return-to-Vancouver" system used up to 1929 with such modest results, was abandoned completely. Large ships with large crews need lots of food and water, and can be incapacitated for long periods by one slow old cutter in company.

However, large ships were necessary, as liquor is heavy, bulky and fragile, and in view of its value once ashore, requires secure storage. So the large mother ships, which filled the long-term storage requirements perfectly once the food and water problem was solved, came to anchor on Rum Row, off the Mexican Coast at Punta San Isidro (called Santo Tomas by the rum runners).

The Santo Tomas anchorage is some thirty miles down the coast from Ensenada, a convenient shipping point for supplies, and five miles off the "water hole" at Santo Tomas. The water-hole was a lagoon of sweet fresh water just back of a small beach

A celebration in native dress aboard the *Lillehorn,* crossing the equator en route to Tahiti. Fergie is on the far left.

on the usually rocky desert west coast of Mexico. The location was ideal from the business point of view, and not important from the crew's point of view, as they weren't allowed shore leave anyway. Mexican authorities more or less ignored Rum Row, but they were rather short with Canadian sailors without passports or entry papers showing up unannounced in Ensenada, demanding instant love.

One apparent effect of the *Federalship* fiasco was increased U.S. pressure on Canada to hinder rum running by passing a law requiring that all Canadian ships cleared for a foreign port loaded with liquor, actually go to the named port and discharge its cargo.

A ship could no longer clear from Vancouver and go to Rum Row to unload, and return to Vancouver empty. Consequently, a trans-shipment port was needed, with suitable warehouse facilities and broad-minded port authorities who wouldn't care whether any given cargo actually arrived at its declared destination or not.

Mexico and Central America lacked suitable ports, and Panama was considered to be too much under U.S. influence. Finally Papeete, Tahiti, was selected as the ideal port, to the great delight of the few Canadians who sailed there.

Captain S.S. Stone, in the steamship *La Golondrina*, apparently initiated the Papeete operation. The ship cleared Vancouver on June 27, 1927 for San Jose, Guatemala, then showed up in Papeete, no doubt with the Vancouver cargo still in her hold, but with ship's papers in good order covering a cargo from San Jose to Papeete. Later, ships went straight from Vancouver to Papeete. Maybe *La Golondrina* was just a trial run, before "arrangements" were firmed up in Tahiti.

Food supply to the mother ships, and to the long-time-at-sea distributors as well, for they were provisioned from the mother ships, was very probably maintained by the M.S. *Gryme*, owned by George W. Beermaher, 322 W. F. Street, San Diego, California. The *Gryme*, 110 tons gross, registry No. 120855, Victoria, B.C. Canada, under Captain Carl All, sailed out of Ensenada, Mexico, clearing, on January 27, 1929 as follows:

Ensenada, B.C., Mexico to any port or ports on the Pacific Coast or Coast of Mexico. Final discharge port of Ensenada, B.C. Mexico. Terms of service not to exceed twenty-four months. The master reserves to himself the right to dismiss all or any member of the crew on giving them 24 hours notice, and it is also agreed that if any member of the crew wishes to leave before the expiration of this agreement, that he shall give the master 24 hours notice of his intention to leave the ship.

Captain All was paid $175 U.S. per month, about one third of the going rate for Canadian rum skippers on the offshore boats. Captain All was skipper of the *City of San Diego* on her first trip in 1922, April 17 to May 25, but "failed to join" her second trip, and served as mate on the third and fourth trips, at $400 Canadian per month.

The Canadian merchandise was brought initially by the mother ship voyaging to Tahiti, doing a little creative paperwork, and sailing back up to Rum Row to carry on with its real business. Stocks were maintained in the mother ships by sailing schooners, from the small two-masted *Aratapu* (Peruvian) to the big three-masted *Marechal Foch* (Tahitian) and several others.

Ships clearing from Europe with additional merchandise were not affected by the Canadian law so came directly to Rum Row—the *Brompton Manor* and the *Nedereide*, to name a couple.

Small distributor boats, like the *Ryou II*, with an absolute maxiumum capacity of 1400 cases, carried on up the coast. The afterdeck started to go under water at 1500 cases, even with the two stern fuel tanks empty, and she became a trifle unstable with a 300-case deckload weighing six tons.

The U.S. Coast Guard cutter problem was overcome by increasing the ratio of distributors to cutters; one cutter could only deactivate one distributor. Then, to limit the effectiveness of this one cutter, fast Canadian shore boats were built, which could load from any Canadian ship anywhere outside the twelve mile limit at any time, regardless of the U.S. cutters.

Kagome was the first of these, 68 feet long, propelled by three 450-horsepower Liberty gas engines, and others followed:

Taiheiyo, 90 feet long, *Skeezix*, *Yurinohana*, *Amigo*, *Tapawinga*, *Adanesne*, *Colnet*, and last of all *Yukatrivol*, in the spring of 1933.

All ships large and small, even the Tahitian schooners, were linked by a short wave radio telegraph network operating around 6,950 kilocycles, just below the amateur radio forty meter band of 7000 to 7300 kilocycles. This also helped the coast guard, though it wasn't planned that way of course. The coast guard cutters installed short wave radio direction finders and could pinpoint rum runners, with their four daily radio schedules, quite quickly and accurately, whether they were new arrivals or old friends just relocating. The direction-finding operators were soon able to identify the rum runner transmissions, as each ship had a different signal quality and each operator a different style of sending—a different "fist" in amateur radio jargon.

But with so many more rum runners at sea, especially the fast Canadian shore boats, knowing where any given rum running ship was did not really help the coast guard very much.

There was very little observable coast guard reaction to the increased rum running activity that peaked in 1932. One reason was that the coast guard officials didn't seem to realize that it was happening. They were slow to give up the comforting thought that Canadian rum running was reduced to practically nothing after the seizure of *Federalship* in 1927. Also, by 1932, when the cutter patrol reports were beginning to disturb this comfortable illusion, it was rather widely accepted that the Volstead Act would soon be repealed, thus ending all rum running without effort or expenditure on the part of the coast guard.

But possibly a more important reason for the lack of coast guard activity was the very deep and long recession the United States was in from 1931 onwards. This received almost total government attention, as the social and economic damage of the Great Depression far exceeded the social impact made by Canadian liquor flooding into California, Washington and Oregon.

Appendix II

Clyde and Walt vs. *CG 827*

Clyde and Walt didn't make it.

Item 9 of the *CG 257's* cruise report, June 15-25, 1933, reads as follows:

9. 23 June: 1020, weighed anchor and stood out of Pyramid Cove on course 123 Psc. 1128, hove to. 1148, *CG 827* alongside. I went aboard the *CG 827* and proceeded to the vicinity of the *Ryou II's* contact position. The CG 257 returned to Pyramid Cove. 1425, sighted the *Ryou II*, drifting; *CG 827* hove to and drifted, at a distance of about three miles, for over an hour. It was evident that the *Ryou II* did not sight us during this time. Because of the danger of sea water getting into the exhaust manifolds due to an increasing sea, got underway at 1530 and headed for the *Ryou II*.

1545, *Ryou II* sighted the *CG 827* and got underway on course south magnetic. 1610, sighted speedboat approaching from northward. We pulled in front of the *Ryou II* so the speedboat would not see us until close aboard. 1610, *Ryou II* hoisted Canadian flag and speedboat immediately turned and headed northwest into a heavy sea. The *CG 827* gave chase. At this time the speedboat was less that half a mile from the *Ryou II*. 1613, speedboat changed course to northeast. 1615, fired three warning shots with service rifle, followed by two shots at the speedboat. 1625, overhauled the *A-1772* (*Agilis*) and took her into custody for failure to stop. Proceeded to Pyramid Cove with *A-1772* and rejoined the *CG 257* on arrival there.

Clyde and Walt had not received any cargo from the *Ryou II* when captured, so would likely face only a "failure to stop" charge.

Appendix III

Seizure of *Kagome*, December 31, 1932

The cruise report for the Coast Guard cutter *Morris* from December 26 to December 31 details the seizure. As per paragraph 5, the *Kagome* was fourteen and a half miles southwest of Cobrillo Point, only twelve nautical miles from land, in broad daylight. The captain was A.G. Lilly, the radio operator was Arthur Gilmour.

3. December 28. Patrolling area as before. 1:15 p.m., proceeded toward Fort Bragg Buoy to intercept *Kagome*, attempting to land cargo in Noyo River as per Commander, Patrol Force orders. Encountered strong Northwest wind and rough sea.
4. December 29. 12:40 a.m., arrived at Fort Bragg Buoy. *Shawnee* near buoy. Scouted in vicinity of buoy for *Kagome*. Vesssel being kept dark. No suspicious craft sighted. 8:25 a.m., proceeded to area in compliance with Commander, Patrol Force orders. 1:16 p.m., proceeded toward Russian Gulch at maximum speed to scout for *Kagome*, as per Commander, Patrol Force orders. 2:44 p.m., orders were changed to proceed to position 40 degrees Southwest magnetic of Bodega Head to intercept *Ryou II.* Changed course to comply with said orders. 5:30 p.m., sighted *Shoshone*. Fired three flare-signals for recognition. *Shoshone* proceeded toward this vessel and ordered *Morris* to run for Fort Bragg Buoy. *Morris* immediately set course for Fort Bragg Buoy and proceeded at full speed. 8:40 p.m., arrived at buoy and began scouting for *Kagome*. Vessel being kept dark throughout. No small craft were sighted.
5. December 30. Scouting as before in vicinity of Fort Bragg Buoy, 7:10 a.m., proceeded toward position 30 degrees Southwest magnetic off Point Cabrillo in search of *Zip*, as per Commander, Patrol Force orders. 8:30 a.m., sighted *Kagome*, which was found to be fourteen and a half miles Southwest of Cabrillo lighthouse. Communicated with Commander, Patrol Force and received orders to remain with *Kagome* until *Shoshone*'s arrival. *Shoshone* arrived at 10:25 a.m., and advised Officer-in-charge that *Shoshone* would run to land and verify place of seizure. About

1:00 p.m., received orders from Commander, Patrol Force to prohibit *Kagome* from transmitting by radio. *Morris* placed six armed men in charge of Chief boatswain's mate Marion J. Stokes on board *Kagome* with instructions to carry out these orders. The orders were carried out. 1:25 p.m., *Shoshone* returned and Officer-in-charge *Morris* went on board *Shoshone* and conferred with Commanding Officer regarding seizure. 6:55 p.m., *Shoshone* got underway with *Kagome* in tow, *Morris* following close astern as per orders of the Commanding Officer of the *Shoshone*.
6. December 31. *Morris* following *Shoshone* and *Kagome* to San Francisco. 12:30 p.m., arrived off Pier #26, San Francisco, California.

The following is correspondence from the Treasury Department, United States Coast Guard, Oakland California, 4 January, 1933 to Commander, Section Base 11 Correspondence File of the Vessel *Morris*, 1932, National Archives, Washington, D.C., U.S.A.

1. Forwarded. Paragraph 5 of basic report omits the notation that a boarding party from the *Morris* in charge of Chief Boatswain's Mate Stokes boarded the *Kagome* at 10:40 a.m., 30 December, 1932. The master of the *Kagome* was unable to produce a manifest or other required papers. The boarding party left the *Kagome* at 2:45 p.m., and the *Morris* ordered the *Kagome* to remain stopped. The *Kagome* ignored the order and proceeded. The above information was embodied in *Morris* letters of 4 January, 1933 (821).

Captain A.G. Lilly, in charge of the *Kagome* at the time of its seizure, was a longtime rum running skipper, starting in 1922 on the *City of San Diego*.

It is not obvious why the *Kagome*, loaded, was only twelve nautical miles from land in broad daylight on December 30, 1931—a major error in navigation? Possible in poor weather, but under poor conditions a prudent rum runner moves offshore. Overconfident? No cutters reported in that area—maybe but unlikely. Skipper drunk? Not likely either. Arthur Gilmour, the radio operator, would have known, but I could not locate him in 1975 when I started putting all this together. So it remains a puzzle.

Appendix IV

Jack Adams:
Improbable Rum Running Experiences

As I have mentioned several times before, rum runners never talked. One exception was Jack Adams, whom I interviewed twice in 1976. This is what he told me (you can believe as much of this as you want to):

The *Chakawana* was an old sealer with a canoe stern, later owned by Turner in North Vancouver. She was slow, making only eight knots with a three-cylinder gas engine. Archie McGillis bought her from the RCMP in the early 1920s. Supplies were obtained from Jack Campbell's store.

The captain was William Steen, who got in his bunk in Vancouver, and stayed there all the time. "Slim" Lind was in the

Jack Adams, engineer,
after a winter sealing trip.

crew. Our first trip was to Halfmoon Bay, California. We had a smooth sea, an Indian guided us through the breakers in Halfmoon Bay, and we were back in Vancouver in ten days.

On our second trip the weather was bad. We had a load of five hundred cases plus five ninety-gallon barrels of bourbon which we landed in Bodega Bay. We also had bad weather going down on the third trip. Harry Rolf, the engineer, fell in the engine clutch while stepping over to visit the head. The mate and cook fainted; but I was half drunk, and Rolf was knocked out, so I put on a tourniquet and cut off his leg above the knee. Later Rolf was taken ashore to hospital.

On the return trip we were blown offshore, almost to Hawaii, by a gale. We had no power, as our fuel was almost gone. Then we ran out of fresh water and made a small evaporator. We

Borealis, an old sealing schooner.

burned all the wood we could strip out inside the ship: bunks, table, shelves, everything. It took us thirty-one days to return to Vancouver.

I was engineer on another schooner, the *Borealis*, skippered by "Whiskers" Thompson. We went to Eureka, California, where the ship was seized by the U.S. marshal, who sealed all the hatches. We cut our lines and sailed away at two a.m. and went down to Pescadero, where we had the name of the ship changed to *Odeon*.

I made four or five trips on the *Trucilla* and the *Etta Mac*, both long thin sub-chasers. We landed 2000 cases per trip at a wharf in Halfmoon Bay. The shore buyer was a hotel owner, Patroni.

Then the big ships started operating off the coast. Jack Nichols had the *Prince Albert*. I went to California and ran a shore boat to the beach. $1000 per night on a fast boat (it had two 400-horsepower Fiat engines), holding four hundred cases. The landing places had numbers, No. 3 was Halfmoon, No. 9 Vallejo inside the Golden Gate—I can't remember Pescadero. By then I had a bar pilot's licence for the Columbia and Gray's Harbour, Washington. Had three years of this.

Gus Johnson offered me the first job. Our worst loss happened one night in really bad weather. I left the *Albert* early—there were five other boats to load. Everyone else stayed for drinks. Too many drinks I guess, as all five were wrecked in Halfmoon Bay, boats and bodies washed up on shore.

Jack Nichols, on the *Prince Albert*, accidentally hooked onto the Pacific Cable when he anchored away off San Francisco. He hauled up the anchor and cut the cable.

Joe Ferris' shore gang was our opposition. We were bushwhacked one night, but got ashore, stole a car, then ditched it and grabbed a bus for Seattle. I bribed an oiler on a CPR boat to let me take his place to get to Canada—we suspected someone might be watching at the border. That ended my U.S. shore work.

The *City of San Diego* was another small schooner with two 40-horsepower Frisco Standard Gas engines. It was an old, dried out ship, and leaked badly. On the way out we had to put in at Becher Bay, on the southern tip of Vancouver Island, for repairs. Eventually our position was one hundred miles offshore, fifty miles south of the Farallones. We lost thirty days due to bad weather. One day when we were all on the fo'c's'le the engine room blew up, and we started to sink slowly. We sent up two rockets and Cap Vosper showed up with the *Kuyakuzmt* (ex *Dolores*, ex *Moonlight Maid*) and took our load before we sunk.

The *Ardenza*, a Belgian ship, sat off San Francisco for seven months, trying to sell twenty or thirty thousand cases of Black Label. It was finally bought by the police, and the whole cargo was off-loaded in one night with the ship anchored eight miles off the beach. The police paid two million dollars in counterfeit money.

"Whiskers" Thompson and Stuart Stone (in bosun's chair) about 1925.

Appendix V

Clarence Greenan:
The Rum Running Life

The following is a taped interview with Clarence Greenan, May 9, 1977, by unknown interviewer. The tapes were given to me by *Raincoast Chronicles* in 1977, when I first talked to Harbour Publishing about this book.

I was born in 1904, and left the *Malahat* in 1924 after almost five years on her, so I was quite young when this all happened.

At the end of the war, during the big flu epidemic, I drove an ambulance for Kearneys, I think, carrying bodies both to hospitals and to the funeral parlour. All the schools were closed, and were being used for hospitals. A lot of people died in that epidemic.

As a safeguard against the flu, we carried a bottle of whiskey in the ambulance, and took a nip every once in a while, but never too much when we were driving.

After driving ambulance, I went into car driving for the rum runners. Big Pierce-Arrow and Chandler cars would load up at the warehouse on Hamilton Street, in the 1000 block, then cross the border by back roads in Langley and Sumas to transfer to American cars in Mount Vernon. Not much risk, but not much pay either, for eight months to a year.

Around 1920 I went out on the *Malahat*, under Captain Murray, as donkey man and shore boat runner. The *Malahat* carried 84,000 cases below decks and loaded in Vancouver in those early days. Outside Cape Flattery we transferred our first 10,000 cases to *Kiltuish*, a slow boat, which ran north to Prince Rupert and Alaska.

The *Malahat* ran south to San Francisco, and transferred to various types of boats there, for the hundred mile run to shore. One ninety-footer, the *Comet*, had two high speed diesels and one 450-horsepower Liberty gas engine. She ran empty out of

Vancouver. An American speedboat called the *Skedaddle* had two 400-horsepower straight eight Dusenburg gas engines. They claimed she could do sixty-five knots—maybe she could, on a smooth river, but not at sea.

The *Malahat* loaded many small fishboats, thirty to thirty-five feet long, mostly gill netters. The rum running fishermen had two boats, and carried on with the second if the first one was caught. The authorities used to auction off seized small boats they had no use for, and the fishermen had an understanding that only the former owner would bid on his boat, which let him buy it back at his own price. These fishermen would bring out empty one-gallon earthenware demijohns, which the *Malahat* filled from ninety-gallon casks of bourbon she carried on deck.

In addition to my donkey work, I also ran a fast shore boat (can't remember the name), once or twice a week, inshore all the way up to Sacramento, to a private dock on the river. We gassed up after unloading, around five hundred gallons per trip. We would leave the *Malahat* just before dark, and be back alongside after daylight. It was a long trip in the dark.

One time we transferred fifty thousand cases from a ship called the *Norburg*, by lifeboat. Took us nearly two weeks in the small boats. The *Norburg* was some kind of independent, and couldn't sell all her cargo before a fixed charter date when she had to load another cargo in Vancouver. Once or twice I ate on the *Norburg*—terrible food and not much of it; we ate ten times better on the *Malahat*, all you wanted, and young fellows wanted plenty.

We had one fire scare on the *Malahat*—some smoke rising from the hold. When we dug down towards the fire—it was not much of a fire, just some smouldering sacks and straw—we found the hot spot in the Chinese wine, which was in earthenware jugs. After this the crew always thought Chinese wine would start a fire by spontaneous combustion if one of the jugs broke, but I think somebody just dropped a cigarette butt when we were loading or sacking cargo.

All cases were then shipped in wooden boxes which are real hard to handle in small boats, slippery wood and sharp corners needed two hands all the time.

We saved the broken boxes to burn under the boiler we used for condensing fresh water—we washed clothes in salt water, but there was always enough fresh water for a bath once in a while.

In 1924 when I stopped rum running, I had a real big stake for those days—about twenty thousand dollars—my monthly pay on the *Malahat* was over two hundred dollars a month, plus a trip bonus of two months' pay. Most of it, though, I got for driving the fast shore boat. I sure wish I could remember its name—I was paid four hundred and fifty dollars a trip, and would sometimes make two trips a week.

I took a two year holiday, and spent the whole lot. My father had died, family matters kept me ashore, and I never went back to rum running.

Transferring firewater by lifeboat.

Appendix VI

"His Britannic Majesty agrees..."

*"One Hour Steaming Distance," or
how lawyers can make a ship go much farther
in one hour than sailors can.*

Canadian rum runners were generally familiar with the federal law requiring Canadian vessels loaded with liquor and cleared for a foreign port to actually discharge the liquor at the named foreign port. Fortunately for them, if the foreign port took no interest in where the liquor was actually unloaded, there was often no problem in "re-loading" the cargo and sailing somewhere on the high seas to transfer. This law was paid little heed after the rum ships began to use Tahiti as their base, in 1927.

The skippers were equally aware that a liquor-laden foreign ship must stay outside the U.S. twelve mile limit (nautical miles; one knot = 6080 feet, 1.85 km) or beyond a distance the ship could steam in one hour, whichever was greater. They, as sailors, realized that a ship's speed in knots through the water was really a variable, affected by the weather, the condition of the ship's bottom, clean or foul, the efficiency of the engine, the weight of the cargo carried, and that the speed named, meant speed over the ocean bottom, so any ocean currents also had an effect.

Marine lawyers were of course also aware of these factors affecting speed, so to close any defense loopholes on this question, the coast guard in some cases made speed trials at or near the time of a capture, with the actual cargo on board the seized vessel. For instance, this was done when *Pescawha* was seized in 1925.

The "one hour steaming" distance for a single ship was thus equal to or less than the maximum speed of the fully-loaded hull in good condition, as all of the variables, except loads lighter than capacity, tended to shorten the distance. We didn't know of anything else that could increase it except a a following wind or current, but their effects would be slight.

On the *Ryou II* and *Ruth B*, both eight knot ships, we were sure we were safe when we were outside the twelve mile limit. As a high school dropout I knew that ignorance was not bliss, but for rum runners it brought a certain peace of mind. We knew when we were safe, and never even suspected that legal magic could change an eight-knot ship to a thirty-knot ship in the definition of one hour steaming off the U.S. coast. This explains why rum runners stayed 50 miles or more off the U.S. coast, but only fifteen miles off the Canadian coast at Cape Beale.

Nosy questions were never welcomed on rum runners so I never asked why the difference. Someone—probably someone on land—certainly knew what we didn't, that the treaty of May 22, 1924 between the United States and Great Britain differentiated in the definitions of "one hour steaming" between one ship operating entirely alone and two ships—or more—operating together.

The relevant provisions of this treaty were cited in Judge D. J. Partridge's confirmation, on appeal, of the legal conviction of Captain George Ford and crew of the *Quadra*, seized off San Francisco in the fall of 1924, judgement given January 5, 1925, in District Court for the Northern District of California:

Any American vessel, or American citizen engaging in this traffic, is of course, liable to seizure and arrest. So, great organizations have arisen who conduct this illicit business in foreign ships, manned by foreign officers and crews. They approach our shores as nearly as they dare, lie to, and transfer their cargoes to small swift boats. In recognition of this situation, the United States and Great Britain, on May 22, 1924, entered into a Treaty, the pertinent provisions of which are as follows:

1. His Britannic Majesty agrees that he will raise no objection to the boarding of private vessels under the British Flag outside the limits of territorial waters by the authorities of the United States, its territories or possessions in order that enquiries may be addressed to those on board and an examination be made of the ship's papers for the purpose of ascertaining whether the vessel or those on board are endeavoring to import or have imported alcoholic beverages into the United States, its territories or possessions in violation of the laws there in force. When such enquiries and ex-

aminations show a reasonable ground for suspicion, a search of the vessel may be instituted.

2. If there is reasonable cause for belief that the vessel has committed or is committing or attempting to commit an offense against the laws of the United States, its territories or possessions prohibiting the importation of alcoholic beverages the vessel may be seized and taken into a port of the United States, its territories or possessions for adjudication in accordance with such laws.

3. The rights conferred by this article shall not be exercised at a greater distance from the coast of the United States, its territories or possessions than can be traversed in one hour by the vessel suspected of endeavoring to commit the offense. In cases, however, in which the liquor is intended to be conveyed to the United States, its territories or possessions by a vessel other than the one boarded and searched, it shall be the speed of such other vessel and not the speed of the vessel boarded which shall determine the distance from the coast at which the right under this article can be exercised.

That treaty specified in section 3 that when more than one ship was importing illegal liquor along the coast of the United States, if "one hour steaming" was the steaming distance of the faster ship, it would be applied to both ships, regardless of the slower ship's real speed.

Thus for purposes of legal seizure, the *Ryou II*'s "one hour steaming" speed could jump from a lowly eight knots to thirty knots if she was working with a thirty-knot shore boat.

It is probably just as well Captain Harry (Hot Pants) Lind didn't know this when the *Ryou II* approached the twelve mile limit in transferring several hundred cases to the gambling ship *City of Panama* in 1933, or he would have been a great deal more worried than he was, or if this was not possible at least just as worried, for a better reason.

And if his loyal crew had known, he would have had several assistant worriers. Ignorance was indeed peace of mind.

Appendix VII
Coast Guard Radio Direction Finding

We believed the Coast Guard found us so easily by using radio direction finders on our radio transmissions. They did indeed, as the radio bearing log from *CG 257*'s cruise from June 15 to June 25, 1933 illustrates. Pyramid Cove is on the southeast end of San Clemente Island, some forty miles from *Ryou II*'s position, more or less.

Radio Bearings
for Patrol June 15 to June 25, 1933

Station Vessel	True Bearing	Position taken from	Remarks
Taiheiyo	129	Anacapa Passage	Doubtful due to disturbance
Ryou II	140	4 miles east of Santa Barbara Is.	Very good
Yurinohana	138	Pyramid Cove	Very good
Ryou II	177	Pyramid Cove	Very good
Mogul	132	Pyramid Cove	Very good
Yurinohana	132	Pyramid Cove	Very good
Ryou II	171	Pyramid Cove	Very good
Taiheiyo	203	Pyramid Cove	Very good
Ryou II	170	Pyramid Cove	Very good
Ryou II	172	Pyramid Cove	Very good
Yurinohana	130	Pyramid Cove	Very good
Ryou II	153	32;35N 116;12W	Very good
Taiheiyo	155	Pyramid Cove	Very good
Ryou II	170	Pyramid Cove	Very good
Taiheiyo	151	Pyramid Cove	Very good

Station Vessel	True Bearing	Position taken from	Remarks
(DE) Shore Station San Pedro, Cal.	349	Base 17	Very good
Ryou II	176	33;19N 118;17W	Very good
(SL) Vancouver	337	Pyramid Cove	Very good
Yurinohana	123	Pyramid Cove	Very good
Ryou II	194	32;40N 118;12W	Very good
Yurinohana	139	Pyramid Cove	Doubtful broad min.
(GN) Shore Station	2	Pyramid Cove	Very good
Taiheiyo	135	Pyramid Cove	Doubtful broad min.
Ryou II	164	Pyramid Cove	Very good
Ryou II	168	Pyramid Cove	Very good

SIGNED: H. J. Doebler

From Correspondence file 601-*CG 257*, National Archives, Washington, D.C.

Appendix VIII

Canadian Rum Running Ships
1922–1933

Strictly speaking, not all of these ships were Canadian; not all of them were rum runners. But they each played a part in the lively trade that I describe in *Slow Boat on Rum Row*.

ADANESNE   Length 47.4 ft.   Built 1932,
(shore boat)   beam 12.2 ft.   Bidwell Boat Works,
Reg. No. 157234   Coal Harbour, Vancouver
Engines: One 6-cylinder 125-HP diesel, Two 450-HP Liberty gas.
First owner: Arctic Traders Ltd., 1206 Homer St., Vancouver.
Wrecked December 16, 1932.

ALGIE   No data, but similar to *Audrey B.*
(fish packer East Coast type)   *Photo page 215.*

AMIGO   Length 55.4 ft.   Built 1931,
(shore boat)   beam 12 ft.   Bidwell Boat Works,
Reg. No. 157223   Coal Harbour, Vancouver
Engines: One 6-cylinder 150-HP Atlas Imperial Diesel,
         Two 450-HP Liberty gas engines.
First owner: Triangle Freighters, 921–470 Rogers Building, Vancouver.
Re-named *Carry Bell*, May 26, 1934.

ARATAPU (two-masted schooner)
Registered Callao, Peru
Employed as a re-supply ship carrying liquor from warehouses in Tahiti to the mother ships on Rum Row. During 1933 carried 5,000 cases. *Photos pages 188 and 256.*

ARWYCO (mother ship large steam freighter)
No Canadian registry. Used as relief mother ship.

AUDREY B   Length 109 ft.   Built 1928,
(fish packer   beam 20 ft.   James S. Gardner,
East Coast type)   Liverpool, Nova Scotia
Reg. No. 154793
Engines: Two 6-cylinder 180-HP Fairbanks Morse diesels.
Owner: Yarmouth Shipping Co, Yarmouth, Nova Scotia. *Photo page 222.*

BAMFIELD   No data available
(fish packer)
Reg. No. 141197
Owner: Captain A.W. Abbott, 1528 Foul Bay Road, Victoria.
Sunk by CPR Steamer *Princess Joan,* June 6, 1930, while leaving Victoria harbour on first rum running trip. No lives lost.

BOREALIS   Built 1880
(two-masted schooner former sealer)
Reg. No. 97159   *Photo page 244.*

CANUCK   Length 62 ft.   Built 1922,
(fish packer)   beam 18 ft.   Harbour Boat Builders
Reg. No. 155234
Owner: William Charles Splan, 1155 Pacific St., Vancouver.
Made only one rum running trip, 60 days long, Oct.–Dec. 1930.

CAOBA
(steam schooner)
American registry
Sunk in heavy weather off Astoria, Oregon in early Feb. 1925. Cargo unknown, but was suspected of working with Canadian rum runner *Pescawha,* which picked up *Caoba*'s nine man crew. See also *Appendix I.*

The two-masted schooner
Aratapu was a re-supply ship
carrying liquor from Tahiti to
the mother ships on Rum Row.

CHAKAWANA   Length 62 ft.   Built 1910
(two-masted schooner)
Reg. No. 130441
Engine: One 3-cylinder gas engine.
Owner: Archibald McGillis.
May have been a former sealer. Believed to have been seized in Mexico
in early years of rum running, while operating out of Ensenada.

CHARLES EDWARD   Length 72 ft.   Built 1918,
(two-masted schooner)   beam 17 ft.   Wedgeport,
Reg. No. 138743   Nova Scotia
Engine: One 4-cylinder 32-HP diesel.
Owner: General Navigation Co. of Canada,
        1048 Hamilton St., Vancouver.
Operated out of Belize, British Honduras, East Coast.

CHASINA   258 tons
(steam yacht)
Photo and full history in Greene's *Personality Ships of British Columbia.*

CHIEF SKUGAID   Length 77 ft.
(fish packer)   beam 18 ft.
Reg. No. 133736   derrick rigged
Engine: One 100-HP diesel.
        Union Gas Engine Co., Oakland, California.
Owner: General Navigation Co., 1048 Hamilton St., Vancouver, 1929.
Served longest term of any rum runner, March 1923 to December
1933. *Photo page 228.*

CITY OF SAN DIEGO   Length 67.5 ft.   Built 1881,
(two-masted schooner)   beam 20.5 ft.   San Francisco
Reg. No. 100645
Engines: Two 3-cylinder 80-HP Standard gas engines.
Owner: Northern Freighters Ltd., 627 Vancouver Block, Vancouver.
Became the first Canadian rum running ship on April 15, 1922.

COAL HARBOUR   Length 127 ft.   Built 1881,
(three-masted schooner)   beam 32.8 ft.   Hall Brothers, Port
Reg. No. 150569   Blakely, Washington
Engines: Two 55-HP Imperial Gas Engine Co., San Francisco.
Owner: Canadian Mexican Shipping Co., Archibald McGillis,
        1747 37th Ave., Vancouver; July 23, 1923.

Ex *Gunhild II.* Seized early in 1925, its story appears in Willoughby's *Rum War at Sea,* and Greene's *Personality Ships.* Crew seized: Captain C.H. Hudson, Mate E.F.C. Best, Chief Engineer R.J. Bell.

COLNET   Length 54 ft.   Built 1932,
(shore boat)   beam 13.2 ft.   Bidwell Boat Works,
Reg. No. 157238   Coal Harbour, Vancouver
Engine: One 80-HP Atlas Imperial diesel, One 450-HP Liberty gas.
Owner: General Navigation Co. of Canada,
        1048 Hamilton St., Vancouver.
Captain C.H. Hudson. Made only two rum running trips a total of ten months at sea.

COROZAL   Length 72 ft.   Built 1929,
(fish packer)   beam 15 ft.   Harbour Boat Builders,
Reg. No. 156609   Vancouver
Engine: One 300-HP 6-cylinder diesel.
Owner: General Navigation Co. of Canada,
        1048 Hamilton St., Vancouver, 1929.
Captain Malcolm K. Savage.
Operated on East Coast out of Belize, British Honduras.

ETTAMAC   Length 105.3 ft.   Built 1918,
(sub-chaser)   beam 14.6 ft.   U.S. Navy,
Reg. No. 1150649   Puget Sound
Engines: Three 450-HP Liberty gas.
Owner: George W. Morgan, 1050 Hamilton St., Vancouver.

FEDERALSHIP   Length 222 ft.   Built 1884,
(steamship)   beam 31 ft.   G. Howaldt,
Reg. No. 153023   Kiel, Germany
Engine: 2-cylinder steam.
Owner: Edward Thompson MacLennan,
        416 W. Pender St., Vancouver.
Ex *Gertrude,* later *La Golondrina.* Captain: S.S. Stone. Seized at sea early 1927 by U.S. Coast Guard, later released. Cargo was 12,500 cases. (See also *Appendix I,* Willoughby and Greene.)

FISHER LASSIE I   Length 61 ft.   Built 1929,
(fish packer)   beam 18 ft.   John Stebbland,
Reg. No. 155233   New Westminster
Engine: One 180-HP 4-cylinder diesel Union Gas Engine Company.

Owner: Robert Swanson, Exporter, 1845 E. Pender St., Vancouver.
First trip Oct. 18, 1930, Captain J. McCulloch. Seized by customs
about Jan. 20, 1932. Released on board. *Photo below.*

GERTRUDE and
LA GOLONDRINA (*Federalship* under other names)
Reg. No. 153023
German freelance, but couldn't sell cargo at sea. Ended up in Vancou-
ver, where local interests bought the cargo.

GRYME   110 tons gross,
(motor ship)   75 tons net.
Reg. No. 130855
Engine: 160-HP diesel.
Owner: George W. Beermaher, 322 W.F. Street,
        San Diego, California, 1929–1931.
Captain: Carl All (see *City of San Diego*). Supply ship to rum row oper-
ating out of Ensenada, Mexico. Was in legitimate trade; did no rum
running.

GUNHILD II   Length 127 ft.   Built 1881,
(three-masted schooner) beam 32 ft.   Port Blakely,
Reg. No. 150569   Washington
Engines: Two 55-HP Imperial Gas Engine Co., San Francisco.
Owner: Archibald McGillis.
Captain George Murray, 2nd Mate G. Keegan. Made two rum running

Fisher Lassie with
her hold full and
deck loaded, until
the waterline and
deckline were the
same. 1931.

trips, November 1922 to June 1923, before becoming the famous *Coal Harbour.*

HAYSPORT II   64.5 ft.   Built 1906,
(schooner?)   beam 17.6 ft.   Seattle, Washington
Reg. No. 134127   40 tons gross
Owner: Henry L. Higgins.
Made only one three-month rum running trip, during 1923.

HEDWIG   Built Batavia,
(motor ship)   Dutch East Indies
Captain L.H. Eppina. Made one rum running trip starting May 30, 1930 for nine months, no date of return to port.

HICKEY   Length 110 ft.
(sub-chaser)   beam 15 ft.
Reg. No. 157448
Engines: Two Garwood 12-cylinder gas engines, 400-HP,
         One Cooper Bessimer 6-cylinder 150-HP diesel.
Owner: General Navigation Co. of Canada,
         1048 Hamilton St., Vancouver.
Ex *Ocelot. Photos pages 205 and 263.*

HURRY HOME
(sub-chaser)
Reg. No. 156633
Engines: One 120-HP Cummins diesel, Two 450-HP Liberty gas engines, fitted with smoke-making apparatus per U.S.C.G. report.
Owner: Atlantic & Pacific Navigation Co., 1206 Homer St., Vancouver.

HURRY ON   Length 174 ft.
(mother ship)
Reg. No. 148914
Captain G.B. Murray, Mate J.A. Wright.
Made two trips only 1927, total time at sea nine months.

IRONBARK   Length 50 ft.   Built 1917,
(motor boat)   beam 10.6 ft.   U.S. Navy, New York
Reg. No. 150978
Engine: One 200-HP 3-cylinder gas.
Owner: Archibald McGillis, 1701 Georgia St. West, Vancouver.
There were two *Ironbarks.* One was never cleared for deep sea trips. If indeed used in rum running, it was in the Vancouver–Victoria–Seattle

runs. Clarence Greenan (see *Appendix V*) says he ran a 35 foot *Ironbark* while rum running between Vancouver and the Gulf Islands. This smaller *Ironbark* had a 220-HP 6-cylinder Standard Motors gas engine removed from *Trucilla* when she was converted for use as a tugboat with two diesels replacing the Standard gas engines. Greenan's *Ironbark* went 35-40 knots with a 26" x 26" propeller on the 220-HP Standard gas engine.

JESSIE
(two-masted schooner)
Reg. No. 111787
Owner: Arctic Fur Traders, 1008 Credit Foncier Bldg., Vancouver.
Captain Joe Keegan, Mate Harry Slattery, Eng. C.E. Smith.
Sailed Sept. 1, 1928. Run down and sunk by unknown vessel 100 miles west of San Diego at night, Sept. 23, per note H. Slattery, January 8, 1929: "The motor schooner *Jessie* of Vancouver, B.C. was lost with the loss of all ship's papers about 100 miles west of San Diego, Cal. on the 23rd of September 1928, in collision with an unknown vessel. This statement is made by me for Captain J. Keegan, Master of the *Jessie* who hasn't yet returned to Vancouver."
—H. Slattery, Mate Sch. *Jessie*, 3726 West 34th Ave., Vancouver.

KAGOME   Length 68 ft.   Built 1929,
(shore boat)   beam 13 ft.   Harbour Boat Builders
Reg. No. 155120
Engines: Three 450-HP Liberty gas engines.
Owner: Charles Henry Hudson and later General Navigation Co. of
          British Columbia, 1048 Hamilton St.
Seized December 1932, released early 1933. *Photo page 195.*
Later known as *Salt Mist* in Greene's *Personality Ships.*

KANAWAKA   Length 76 ft.   Built 1930,
(fish packer)   beam 18 ft.   Cumberland Shipyards,
Reg. No. 156733   Wallace, Nova Scotia
Engine: One 275-HP diesel, 8-cylinder Cooper Bessimer.
Owner: Union Navigation Co., Crame's Wharf, North Front St.,
          Belize, British Honduras, Reg. No. 11/1931.
Operated out of Belize.

KILTUISH   Length 87.6 ft.   Built 1920,
(fish packer)   beam 20.4 ft.   Pacific Construction Co.
Reg. No. 141722 (or 141732?)
Engine: One 150-HP 3-cylinder Fairbanks Morse semi-diesel.
Owner: Consolidated Exporters, 1050 Hamilton St., Vancouver, 1924.
Wrecked 1927 but believed salvaged and returned to fishpacking.

KITNAYAKWA   Length 45.8 ft.
(shore boat)
Reg. No. 154833
Engines: Two 450-HP Liberty gas engines.
Owner: Johnny Schnarr.
Worked Gulf of Georgia and Puget Sound area. *Photo page 266.*

KOUCHIDBOUZUACC   Built Lunenberg,
(fish packer)?   Nova Scotia, C. Iverson
Reg. No. 185126
Ship sunk (course unknown) Sept. 11, 1931, lat. 37 degrees 20 minutes north, long. 124 degrees 15 minutes west, about 100 miles just
south of San Francisco, 100 miles offshore, possibly on its first and only
trip.

KUYAKUZMT   Length 168 ft.   Built 1893,
(steam yacht)   beam 33 ft   Philadelphia, PA
Reg. No. 138073   clipper bow
Engine: One 690-HP Triple Expansion steam engine.
Ex *Stadacona* later *Moonlight Maid.* Story in Greene's *Personality Ships.*

LILLEHORN   Length 207 ft.   Built 1922, Rennie,
(motor ship)   beam 33 ft.   Ritchie and Newport?
Reg. No. 147527   Essex, UK
Engines: Two 750-HP Bolinder diesels.
Owner: Atlantic Pacific Navigation Co.,
        302 Pacific Building, Vancouver, 1927.
Long-time mother ship. *Photo page 134.*

MABEL DELL   Length 80 ft.   Built 1913,
(two-masted schooner) beam 20 ft.   Wallace Shipyards,
Reg. No. 133942   Vancouver
Engine: One 220-HP gas engine.
Owner: Joseph William Hobbs, 510 West Hastings St., Vancouver, 1925.
No identified rum running trips. Sold to U.S.A. May 27, 1927.

MALAHAT   Length 245.7 ft.   Built 1917,
(five-masted schooner)   beam 43.8 ft.   Cameron Genoa Mills
Reg. No. 134655   Shipbuilders, Victoria
Engines: Two 160-HP Bolinder diesels.
Owners: Archibald McGillis, 1701 Georgia St. West, Vancouver, 1923;
       General Navigation Co., 1048 Hamilton St., Vancouver, 1929.
Capacity 84,000 cases in the hold plus approximately 16,000 on deck
when the *Ryuo II* loaded from her, summer 1933. Well-known, long-
service mother ship. Story in Greene's *Personality Ships*. *Photo page 133.*

MARECHAL FOCH
(three-masted schooner)
Reg. Tahiti
Employed as a re-supply ship from Tahiti warehouses to mother ships
on Rum Row. Reported capacity 15,000 cases Formerly Zane Grey's
yacht *Fisherman* when the author was fishing in Tahitian waters; See
Zane Grey, *Tales of Tahitian Waters*, Harper Press, New York, 1931.
Photo page 216.

MARIE BARNARD
(two-masted auxiliary schooner U.S. smuggler?)
Cleared from Astoria, Oregon for Shanghai, China, January 23, 1919.
Joe Kelgan, 2nd officer left in hospital at Astoria, Oregon, wages of
$107.00 left with British vice-consul.

Hickey, ex
Ocelot, from
the pilot
house
looking aft,
all out on
all three
engines.

MOGUL
(mother ship)
A large ore carrier plying the route from Britannia Beach to a smelter near Tacoma, Washington. Last mother ship to return to Vancouver, June 1934.

NOBLE	Length 76 ft.	Built circa 1880,
(two-masted schooner)	beam 21 ft.	Hall Brothers,
Reg. No. 126951		Port Ludlow, Washington

Engines: Two 100-HP Hall Scott gas engines.
Owner: Richard Barnet Wright Pirie,
　　　407 Metropolitan Bldg., Vancouver, July 1927.
Ex *Lady Mine*. Sailed Oct. 20, 1927, under Captain W. Kerr, and wrecked on Escalante Reef, Vancouver Island, January 14, 1928. Four of its five crewmen were lost in the heavy gale.

NORBURG
(large steamer)
European registry
One of early, freelance mother ships from Europe. Because the *Norburg* failed to sell her cargo to Americans, she sold it to Canadians; 50,000 cases were transferred via small boat to the *Malahat* at sea during three painstaking weeks in 1924. See also *Appendix V*.

OCELOT
Reg. No. 157448
Re-named when she became a rum runner; see *Hickey* for details.

OLD MAID NO. II	Length 104 ft.	Built 1882,
(two-masted schooner)	beam 29.8 ft.	Dickie Brothers,
Reg. No. 153013		San Francisco

Engine: One 150-HP Atlas Imperial diesel.
Owner: Coast Shipping Co., 921–470 Granville St., Vancouver, 1931;
　　　C.H. Hudson, Manager, 1048 Hamilton St., Vancouver.
Rum running 1931 to 1933 with Captain R. Sinclair, George Tutt, wireless operator, and Ronald Stone who, at age sixteen, was the third generation of Stones in rum running. Ex *Maid of Orleans*, later *Joan G* owned by Gibson Bros., who replaced her 150-HP Atlas with the two Bolinder diesels removed from the *Malahat* after the hull was condemned and installed them in the *Joan G*, using her for towing on the B.C. coast. Story in Greene's *Personality Ships*.

OUITACHOUAN   Length 56 ft.   Built 1910,
(two-masted schooner) beam 16 ft.   Kohs(?) Nelson,
Reg. No. 150741   Seattle, Washington
Engine: One 3-cylinder 65-HP Union gas engine.
Owner: General Navigation Co., 1048 Hamilton St., Vancouver, 1929.
Registry changed to Belize, British Honduras, July 11, 1932. Wrecked
Nov. 10, 1938.

OUOUKINSH   Length 56 ft.   Built 1912,
(two-masted schooner) beam 17 ft.   Ballard Marine Ways,
Reg. No. 151113 (or 151112)   Seattle, Washington
Engine: One 50-HP Standard gas engine.
Owner: Atlantic Pacific Navigation Co.,
       807 Metropolitan Bldg., Vancouver, August 1928.
Ship burned at sea Sept. 19, 1929. Crew members Captain Joe Keegan,
H. Slattery, H. Lind.

PACINACO I   Length 70 ft.   Built 1908, re-built 1927,
(two-masted schooner) beam 12 ft.   Ericksen Boat Works,
Reg. No. 131034   North Vancouver
Engine: One 70-HP diesel.
Owner: Pacific Navigation Co., 834 W. Pender St., Vancouver, 1931.
Ex *Chasam II*, Ex *Doncella*. Captain D.J. MacDonald, Mate Jack Wolf,
Oct. 22–Nov. 18, 1930.

PACINACO II
(schooner?)
Reg. No. 154567
Owner: Pacific Navigation Co., 834 W. Pender St., Vancouver, 1930.
Burned at sea? Sept. 15, 1931.

PESCAWHA   Length 90 ft.   Built 1906,
(two-masted schooner) beam 23 ft.   Robie McLeod,
Reg. No. 122022   Liverpool, Nova Scotia
Engine: One 3-cylinder 100-HP Union Gas Engine Co.
Owner: Western Freighters Ltd., 1923.
Seized February 3, 1925 by U.S. Coast Guard cutter *Algonquin*, 6.6
miles off the coast of Washington with 1075 cases of liquor and the res-
cued nine man crew of the U.S. steam schooner *Caoba* on board.
There is no logical explanation why the *Pescawha,* which could make
more than eight knots an hour under engine alone, was only 6.6 miles
off the Washington coast on a clear day. See also *Appendix I.*

PLEASURE   Length 60 ft.   Built 1928,
(fast yacht)   beam 11 ft.   Harbour Boat Builders,
Reg. No. 154939   Vancouver
Engines: Two 580-HP Sterling gas engines.
Owners: Vested Estates Ltd., 1206 Homer St., Vancouver, 1928; Henry
       Frederick Reifel, 2170 West Marine Drive, Vancouver, 1933.
Rumoured rum runner in Puget Sound/Gulf of Georgia area, but no
evidence in any records of deep sea operations.

PRINCE ALBERT   Length 232 ft.   Built 1892,
(steamship)   beam 30 ft.(?)   Hull, England
Reg. No. 99584
Engine: One 3-cylinder steam engine.
Owners: Pan American Shipping Co., 1206 Homer St., Vancouver,
       1928; Atlantic and Pacific Navigation Co., 1930.
Photos pages 142 and 169.

PRINCIPIO   Length 190 ft.   Built 1910,
(motor ship)   beam 24 ft.   Flensburg, Germany
Reg. No. 151192
Engines: Two 6-cylinder 550 BHP Vulcan Werke diesels.
Owner: Canadian Mexican Shipping Co.,
       331 Dunsmuir St., Vancouver, 1925.
Later *Tooya*. Captain Pat MacManus, Mate Harry Slattery, Sept. 1–Nov.
29, 1930. *Photo page 122.*

Kitnayakwa, a
Canadian shoreboat,
45 feet long, two 450-hp
Liberty gas engines,
summer 1932.

PROSPERATIVE   Length 71 ft.   Built 1891,
(two-masted schooner)?   beam 20 ft.   Benicia, California
Reg. No. 141198
Engine: One 220-HP 6-cylinder diesel.
Rumoured as a rum runner, but no evidence found.

QUADRA   Length 175 ft.
(steamship)   683 tons
British registry
Engine: British Twin Screw Steam.
Sailed from Vancouver, Sept. 24, 1924, seized by Cutter *Shawnee* with 12,000 cases of liquor off San Francisco later that year—a sensational seizure. See *Rum War at Sea* and *Personality Ships*.

RAGNA   Length 94.5 ft.   Built 1917,
(sub-chaser)   beam 16 ft.   Mare Island Navy Yard
Reg. No. 156612
Engines: One 200-HP diesel, One 450-HP Liberty gas engine.
Owners: Foreign and Pacific Navigation Co., 1206 Homer St., Van-
     couver, Jan. 1930; Atlantic and Pacific Navigation Co., 1206
     Homer St., Vancouver, Dec. 1930.
Ex *Ramona* of Mexican registry. Wrecked Ruby Rock near Egg Island, July 26, 1962. *Photo page 131.*

RAY ROBERTS   Length 53 ft.   Built 1925,
(fish packer)   beam 14 ft.   W.R. Menchions Shipyard,
Reg. No. 152806   derrick rigged   Coal Harbour, Vancouver
Engine: One 65-HP gas engine.
Owner: General Navigation Co., 1048 Hamilton St., Vancouver, 1929.
There was also a *Roy Roberts* Reg. No. 155254, built 1929; not a rum runner.

REVUOCNAV   Length 55.3 ft.   Built Nov. 1932,
(shore boat)   beam 11.4 ft.   Bidwell Boat Works,
Reg. No. 158285   Coal Harbour, Vancouver
Engines: Two 860-HP Packard gas engines.
Step hydroplane design, with engine exhausts under water through the step, for quiet running.
Owner: Johnny Schnarr.

RUTH B   Length 61.6 ft.   Built 1919,
(fish packer)   beam 14.8 ft.   Pacific Mills
Reg. No. 141551
Engine: One 100-HP Fairbanks-Morse diesel.
Owner: Goose Island Fisheries, Frank Eccles,
        837 West Hastings St., Vancouver, 1926.
Burned Bella Coola, B.C. Sept. 8, 1966. *Photos pages 92, 104, 105.*

RYOU II   Length 60 ft.   Built 1929,
(fish packer)   beam 17 ft.   Bidwell Boat Works,
Reg. No. 155247   Coal Harbour, Vancouver
Engine: One 3-cylinder 100-HP Atlas Imperial diesel.
Owners: Henry Reifel, 1451 Angus Drive, Vancouver, 1929; Atlantic
        and Pacific Navigation Co., 1206 Homer St., Vancouver, 1932
Photos pages 165, 173, 192, 199, 202.

SHUCHONA III   Length 57 ft.   Built 1926,
(fish packer)   beam 15 ft.   Vancouver Shipyards,
Reg. No. 153040   derrick rigged   Coal Harbour
Engine: One 65-HP diesel.
Owner: Northwest Navigation Co., 678 Howe St., Vancouver, 1933.

SKEEZIX   Length 56 ft.   Built 1930,
(shore boat)   beam 12 ft.   Vancouver Shipyards,
Reg. No. 156889   Coal Harbour
Engines: One 4-cylinder 150-HP Atlas Imperial,
         Two 450-HP Liberty gas engines.
Owner: Pacific and Foreign Navigation Co.,
        1206 Homer St., Vancouver, 1930.
Became private yacht *Fleetwood,* owned in 1976 by Robert James Turn-
bull of Edmonton, Alberta. *Photo page 148.*

SPEEDWAY   Length 155 ft.   Built 1917
(three-masted schooner)   beam 35 ft.
Reg. No. 138449
Engines: Two 330-HP gas engines.
Owner: John Murray Bowman, 1218 Howe St., Vancouver, 1924.
Captain R. Sinclair, second mate Harry Slattery, age 21. Burned at sea
Jan. 29, 1925—ship and cargo lost, all crew saved.

STADACONA
(steam yacht)
Reg. No. 138073   See *Kuyakuzmt.*

TAIHEIYO	Length 90 ft.	Built 1929,
(sub-chaser)	beam 14 ft.	Harbour Boat Builders,
Reg. No. 156591		Vancouver

Engines: One 6-cylinder 250-HP Atlas diesel, Two 450-HP Liberty gas
engines. Liberties were later removed when she became a fish
packer with two 200-HP diesels.
Owners: Harry Milner, 4430 Welwyn St., Vancouver, 1929; South Sea
Traders Ltd., 706–626 West Pender St., Vancouver, 1932.

TAPAWINGA	Length 54 ft.	Built 1932,
(shore boat)	beam 13.5 ft.	W.R. Menchion's Shipyard,
Reg. No. 157236		Coal Harbour, Vancouver

Engines: Three 860-HP Packard gas engines, Murphy Marine Engine
Co., Melrose Ave., Los Angeles, California.
Owner: South Sea Traders Ltd., 706–626 West Pender St.,
Vancouver, Manager C.H. Hudson.
Burned at sea, May 4, 1935 while sport fishing in California.

TEMISCONDA	Length 60 ft.	Built 1930,
(fish packer)	beam 13 ft.	Meteghan Shipbuilding Co.,
Reg. No. 156835		Meteghan, Nova Scotia

Engines: One 6-cylinder 100-HP diesel Standard Motor Const. Co.,
Jersey City.
Made only one Pacific Coast rum running trip, Nov. 1932 to March
1933. Captain J.D.A. Wood, radio operator "Smoky" Hoodspith.

TOOYA	Length 190 ft.
Reg. No. 151192	beam 24 ft.
Ex *Principio.*	

TRUCILLA	Length 94.5 ft.	Built 1918,
(sub-chaser)	beam 14.6 ft.	U.S. Navy Yard,
Reg. No. 150650		Puget Sound

Engines: Three 220-HP 6-cylinder Standard Motors, Const. Co.,
Jersey City.
Owner: Coal Harbour Wharf and Trading Co., 1701 W. Georgia St.,
Vancouver.
An early rum runner, returned to legitimate trade by August 1924.

WESTCOAST   Length 55 ft.   Built 1913,
(two-masted schooner)   Captain W. Hursleg,
Reg. No. 150747   Suquamish, Washington
Engine: One 3-cylinder 50-HP gas engine,
        Garham Engine Co., Oakland, California.
Owner: Red Star Navigation Co.,
        202–739 West Hastings St., Vancouver, 1924.
Short rum running career, no details except seized in San Diego May
12, 1924 and confiscated in Ensenada, Mexico Sept. 15, 1925.

YUKATRIVOL   Built 1933,
(shore boat)   Union Boat Works,
Reg. No. 158291   Coal Harbour, Vancouver
Engines: Three 450-HP Liberty gas engines, A.J. Murph, L.A.
Owner: Arctic Traders Ltd., 1206 Homer St., Vancouver, 1933.
Captain C.R. Brewster. Last rum runner built. Made only one trip,
April 21, 1933.

YURINOHANA   Length 71.9 ft.   Built 1929,
(shore boat)   beam 12 ft.   Harbour Boat Builders,
Reg. No. 155274   Coal Harbour, Vancouver
Engine: One 200-HP Atlas Imperial diesel,
        Two 450-HP Liberty gas engines.
Owner: John Henry McKee, Belmont Hotel, Vancouver, 1929.
Photo page 196.

ZIP   Length 109 ft.   Built 1918,
(sub-chaser)   beam 14.9 ft.   Navy Yard,
Reg. No. 156898   Bremerton, Washington
Engines: One 200-HP Atlas Imperial diesel,
        Two 450-HP Liberty gas engines.
Owner: Atlantic and Pacific Navigation Co.,
        1206 Homer St., Vancouver, 1930.
Sunk November 1936.

Printed in Canada